DAVID MILLAR

David Millar was a professional cyclist for eighteen years, and was the first Briton to wear the leader's jerseys in the Tour de France, Vuelta a España and Giro d'Italia. He is now part of the ITV cycling commentary team and a key spokesman on anti-doping. His first book, *Racing Through the Dark*, was a bestseller and was shortlisted for the William Hill Sports Book of the Year award.

ALSO BY DAVID MILLAR

Racing Through the Dark

DAVID MILLAR
THE RACER

THE INSIDE STORY OF LIFE ON THE ROAD

YELLOW JERSEY PRESS
LONDON

Published by Yellow Jersey Press 2016
6 8 10 9 7

Penguin
Random House
UK

Published by Yellow Jersey Press in 2016
(First published in Great Britain in 2015 by Yellow Jersey Press)
Random House, 20 Vauxhall Bridge Road, London SW1V 2SA

Addresses for companies within The Random House Group Limited can be
found at: www.randomhouse.co.uk/offices.htm

The Random House Group Limited Reg. No. 954009

A CIP catalogue record for this book is available from the British Library

ISBN 9780224100083

The quotations from T. S. Eliot appear courtesy of the Estate of T. S. Eliot and
Faber and Faber

Printed and bound in Great Britain by Clays Ltd, St Ives plc

The Random House Group Limited supports the Forest Stewardship Council®
(FSC®), the leading international forest-certification organisation. Our
books carrying the FSC label are printed on FSC®-certified paper. FSC is the
only forest-certification scheme supported by the leading environmental
organisations, including Greenpeace. Our paper procurement policy can be
found at www.randomhouse.co.uk/environment

MIX
Paper from
responsible sources
FSC® C018179

To all my boys – I raced to impress you,
I raced to beat you, I raced for you; that is, until
my two favourite boys came on the scene: Archibald
Ignasi and Harvey Nicolau, you never knew,
this book is for you.

Contents

We are not now that strength which in old days
Moved earth and heaven, that which we are, we are;
One equal temper of heroic hearts,
Made weak by time and fate, but strong in will
To strive, to seek, to find, and not to yield.

'Ulysses', Lord Alfred Tennyson

Nobody grows old merely by living a number of years. We grow old
by deserting our ideals. Years may wrinkle the skin, but to give up
enthusiasm wrinkles the soul.

'Youth', Samuel Ullman

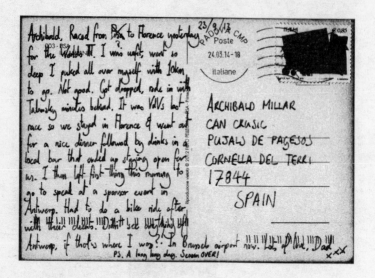

The Racer

There's something very strange about a last race with your friends. I don't know if there's an ideal scenario. Vomiting all over yourself and being dropped certainly doesn't sound like it would be the one, yet maybe it is. It's fairly representative of what most of it has been like.

Christian Vande Velde, Dave Zabriskie and I had raced together over a period of fourteen years, which, in the grand scheme of things, is not so much, yet for us it has been a lifetime. That day, 22 September 2013, was the last time. We got our heads kicked in, yet we managed to enjoy ourselves, because without saying it I think we all knew we were going to miss each other – that they'd been golden days we were lucky to have lived through.

All three of us came into the sport at a bad time, when doping was rife and ethics were something that we knew of yet rarely saw put into practice along the shadowy roads of professional cycling. We came, we didn't quite conquer, we doped, we sort of conquered, we crashed and burned, and some of us got back up and tried to fix the mess we'd made. It was a common narrative although the actions and consequences were different for each of us, and, sadly, there is enough collateral damage to haunt the sport for many years to come.

We know a lot about that time now. I've written about it, and so have many others. I want to write something else, a book that years from now my children can read and see what it was like, what their dad actually did all those years ago, the racer he was. But not only that, I want my friends from this generation to have something that will remind us of who we were. There was more to it than doping. We lived on the road because we loved to race.

Welcome to the Suck

I fucking hate January. It's always a bastard of a month because there's no soft tapping it back into the routine, it's all systems go from the off. November and December is the time for the pedestrian, steady build-up; but it mustn't be forgotten that all that controlled plodding along is in preparation for having all cylinders firing ready to go now. And right now, at the beginning of 2014, I feel like shit.

Christmas and New Year and then my birthday on 4 January is the worst trifecta possible for staying in shape. I can count on one hand the amount of times I have traversed those ten days without taking two or more steps back as regards my physical condition, and those few times necessitated me disappearing into a hermit-like, full-lockdown state, hiding myself from the world.

I had hoped this year would be better; it was the last one I had to get through, after all. Alas no: we ended up having the whole family over and then friends for New Year. It was [ ] ay for my normal human beingness, yet not exactly ideal for the weakened pro cyclist within me. I managed to keep riding through

3

being the person I am – eager to please and duty bound – I tend to be persuaded to do things I wouldn't have considered before the 'discussion'.

This year, being my last, has allowed me to be more steadfast in my desires for the upcoming season. I have five principal goals: Paris–Roubaix, Tour de France, Commonwealth Games, Vuelta a España and the World Championships. That means April, July, August and September at my peak. In the past I have tended to phase my start up: 1 November – Phase One – I stop spoiling myself with food, drink, socialising and travelling, and begin riding again, start doing some weight training, get back into the routine – the basics, really. The second part of this winter programme, Phase Two, begins on 1 December; this is when a precise training schedule is put into place. Hopefully by that point I will have achieved a level of fitness that enables me to start training properly, rather than mincing around the Catalan roads stopping at cafés complaining about how much my legs hurt from the weight training that, almost without fail, I will have start[ ] far too ambitiously. January is Phase Three: no margin [ ] excuses forbidden, action only. Train. Eat. Sleep. [ ] Sleep train eat, train eat sleep. That's how [ ] Three to be anyway; it gives me co[ ] Phase Two knowing that Ph[ ] comfort.

As soon [ ] season break w[ ] year; as professi[ ] summer holiday i[ ] is November and I[ ] normal civilisation is [ ] with neuroses about wh[ ] and overindulge through[ ] which leads to deep self-ha[ ] in comparison. We're all over[ ] the whole period, which I have to admit I was impressed with.

Unfortunately I lost any sense of routine in the process. I'd used up so much willpower trying to keep myself in check that, come January, when I really needed it, I was spent. This was not good.

I think this is the same for everybody – it doesn't matter if you're a professional athlete or a New Year's resolution gym bunny – the moment the routine is broken it's a bit of a battle to get it going again. In many ways I feel I bear a striking resemblance to all the people who decide to quit their bad habits and go on a fitness binge then find themselves a month in, letting themselves slip. They wake up one day and realise the fitness binge is over . . . except I have to keep it going.

The irony of ironies is that this year the team have actually done what I'd been begging them to do for years: that is to postpone the *de rigueur* January training camp until February. So whereas normally I'd have been all over the opportunity to control my training at home, this year I was left thinking, 'NO, NO, NO. Why NOW? I can't do this on my own any more.'

The Racing Calendar

We always set ourselves goals. After so many yea[rs] granted – it becomes a routine or, more [...]

The first and most import[ant ...] winter training. In 'the old day[s ...] January, before gradually bec[...] it became sometime in Dece[...] By the end of the 1990s it [...] nium, 1 November. Nowade[...]

The date we choose [...] our racing programme. If we [...] from a discussion with the tea[m ...] [...] in the discussion [...] August getting [...]

Biarritz in [...]

The only thing that gives our life some sense of order is the racing calendar; this is what we consider our constant. It's a bit like a world map. If you look at one in New York then the United States is the middle point; if you look at one in London then the UK is the middle point. The map is always the same, it is simply altered to fit the eye of the beholder. That's what a calendar is like for a professional cyclist. We know it's the same calendar that everybody else sees, only ours has been moved slightly to the left. The centre of our universe is 1 November; it's where we can reset everything and begin anew. If it's been a good year you have the responsibility to repeat or improve; if it's been a bad year then it's a chance to be better. Everything seems possible on 1 November.

All my life is affected by this phenomenon. If, in conversation, my family or friends refer to a year in the past I have first to think of what that season was like. I'll have a vague initial emotionally-based reaction of it having been a good or bad season, then I'll try to remember why that was, the races and results from that year, then the reasons and the feelings. Then I try to figure out what moments I shared with family and friends – that's always hardest to remember.

1999 – A mixed year.

Initial reaction – Good then bad.

Races – Étoile de Bességes 4th, Vuelta Valenciana 4th, Chiasso 3rd in snow, bad Tirreno (as usual), Critérium International 2nd by two hundredths of a second to Jens Voigt . . . No other clear memories of races.

Reasons – Great winter training, regretfully grew a goatee, pinging for the start of the season, believe that maybe the doping has relented after '98 Festina affair, then realise my te[am ...] doping and nobody cares, get depressed. Trainin[g ...] tains during Tour de France, where I get[...] roof and break my heel. Rest of the [...]

Family and friends – H[...]

sort of conquered, we crashed and burned, and some of us got back up and tried to fix the mess we'd made. It was a common narrative although the actions and consequences were different for each of us, and, sadly, there is enough collateral damage to haunt the sport for many years to come.

We know a lot about that time now. I've written about it, and so have many others. I want to write something else, a book that years from now my children can read and see what it was like, what their dad actually did all those years ago, the racer he was. But not only that, I want my friends from this generation to have something that will remind us of who we were. There was more to it than doping. We lived on the road because we loved to race.

Welcome to the Suck

I fucking hate January. It's always a bastard of a month because there's no soft tapping it back into the routine, it's all systems go from the off. November and December is the time for the pedestrian, steady build-up; but it mustn't be forgotten that all that controlled plodding along is in preparation for having all cylinders firing ready to go now. And right now, at the beginning of 2014, I feel like shit.

Christmas and New Year and then my birthday on 4 January is the worst trifecta possible for staying in shape. I can count on one hand the amount of times I have traversed those ten days without taking two or more steps back as regards my physical condition, and those few times necessitated me disappearing into a hermit-like, full-lockdown state, hiding myself from the world.

I had hoped this year would be better; it was the last one I had to get through, after all. Alas no: we ended up having the whole family over and then friends for New Year. It was lovely for my normal human beingness, yet not exactly ideal for the weakened pro cyclist within me. I managed to keep riding through the whole period, which I have to admit I was impressed with. Unfortunately I lost any sense of routine in the process. I'd used up so much willpower trying to keep myself in check that, come January, when I really needed it, I was spent. This was not good.

I think this is the same for everybody – it doesn't matter if you're a professional athlete or a New Year's resolution gym bunny – the moment the routine is broken it's a bit of a battle to get it going again. In many ways I feel I bear a striking resemblance to all the people who decide to quit their bad habits and go on a fitness binge then find themselves a month in, letting themselves slip. They wake up one day and realise the fitness binge is over . . . except I have to keep it going.

The irony of ironies is that this year the team have actually done what I'd been begging them to do for years: that is to postpone the *de rigueur* January training camp until February. So whereas normally I'd have been all over the opportunity to control my training at home, this year I was left thinking, 'NO, NO, NO. Why NOW? I can't do this on my own any more.'

The Racing Calendar

We always set ourselves goals. After so many years we take this for granted – it becomes a routine or, more precisely, a pattern.

The first and most important is the date we begin our winter training. In 'the old days' (i.e. pre-1990) it was sometime in January, before gradually becoming 1 January. In the early 1990s it became sometime in December, then before long, 1 December. By the end of the 1990s it was November; into the new millennium, 1 November. Nowadays some guys don't even stop.

The date we choose to start this process is dependent on our racing programme. If we're in a privileged position this results from a discussion with the team management rather than an order. I have fallen in the discussion group for many years, although being the person I am – eager to please and duty bound – I tend to be persuaded to do things I wouldn't have considered before the 'discussion'.

This year, being my last, has allowed me to be more stead-fast in my desires for the upcoming season. I have five principal goals: Paris–Roubaix, Tour de France, Commonwealth Games, Vuelta a España and the World Championships. That means April, July, August and September at my peak. In the past I have tended to phase my start up: 1 November – Phase One – I stop spoiling myself with food, drink, socialising and travelling, and begin riding again, start doing some weight training, get back into the routine – the basics, really. The second part of this winter programme, Phase Two, begins on 1 December; this is when a precise training schedule is put into place. Hopefully by that point I will have achieved a level of fitness that enables me to start training properly, rather than mincing around the Catalan roads stopping at cafés complaining about how much my legs hurt from the weight training that, almost without fail, I will have started far too ambitiously. January is Phase Three: no margin for error, excuses forbidden, action only. Train. Eat. Sleep. Eat, train, sleep. Sleep train eat, train eat sleep. That's how I always expect Phase Three to be anyway; it gives me comfort during Phase One and Phase Two knowing that Phase Three exists. Perhaps too much comfort.

As soon as we get back on our bikes after our end-of-season break we already consider ourselves to be in the next year; as professional cyclists we have our own calendar. Our summer holiday is October. Our back-to-work-January-feeling is November and December. The only time we sync up with normal civilisation is Christmas, and even then we're riddled with neuroses about what we eat and drink – or go the other way and overindulge through a lack of self-control and desire to fit in, which leads to deep self-hating guilt – being neurotic is a picnic in comparison. We're all over the place.

The only thing that gives our life some sense of order is the racing calendar; this is what we consider our constant. It's a bit like a world map. If you look at one in London then the UK is the middle point; if you look at one in New York then the United States is the middle point. The map is always the same, it is simply altered to fit the eye of the beholder. That's what a calendar is like for a professional cyclist. We know it's the same calendar that everybody else sees, only ours has been moved slightly to the left. The centre of our universe is 1 November, it's where we can reset everything and begin anew. If it's been a good year you have the responsibility to repeat or improve; if it's been a bad year then it's a chance to be better. Everything seems possible on 1 November.

All my life is affected by this phenomenon. If, in conversation, my family or friends refer to a year in the past I have first to think of what that season was like. I'll have a vague initial emotionally-based reaction of it having been a good or bad season, then I'll try to remember why that was, the races and results from that year, then the reasons and the feelings. Then I try to figure out what moments I shared with family and friends – that's always hardest to remember.

1999 – A mixed year.

Initial reaction – Good then bad.

Races – Étoile de Bessèges 4th, Vuelta Valenciana 4th, Chiasso 3rd in snow, bad Tirreno (as usual), Critérium International 2nd by two hundredths of a second to Jens Voigt . . . No other clear memories of races.

Reasons – Great winter training, regretfully grew a goatee, pinging for the start of the season, believe that maybe the doping has relented after '98 Festina affair, then realise my teammates are doping and nobody cares, get depressed. Training camp in mountains during Tour de France, where I get drunk and jump off a roof and break my heel. Rest of the year: no racing.

Family and friends – Hanging out with Stuart O'Grady in Biarritz in August getting drunk.

6

January

During the whole of my career the start of a new year has meant only one thing: training camp. My first was in Amélie-les-Bains in the Pyrenees with Cofidis. That was in another century, millennium even, definitely feels like a lifetime ago: 1997. I arrived there underprepared, having been in Hong Kong in December visiting for the first time since leaving school eighteen months previously. Needless to say this had not been conducive to my rapidly approaching baptism of fire into professional cycling, and was the principal reason I spent the first part of 1997 getting my head kicked in from every angle.

I spent those first few years as a professional always seeming to be travelling to northern France on my birthday, 4 January. As buzzkills go this ranks among the biggest – apart from one year when I got the French actress Laetitia Casta's autograph in Charles de Gaulle Airport; that ranks up there as one of the uncoolest things I've ever done. I justified it as being my birthday present to myself. Those were the days when pre-season fitness tests were obligatory and done in labs with guys in white coats. Our Cofidis testing was always done at the Amiens university hospital. It still makes me shiver to think about it.

When I was younger, the season didn't really begin properly till March with Paris–Nice and Tirreno–Adriatico (the two most important stage races of the early season), and so being out of shape in January wasn't such a big deal. There was still plenty of time to get it together and, being young, I didn't even require plenty of time to get it together – it would only take me a few weeks to gain respectable condition. It also helped that I was confident as hell back then and didn't see the point in rushing. I refused to race at the training camps, contrary to many of my teammates, who would test themselves and each other. I didn't really get that. I mean, it wasn't a race, so what was the point?

It's not like that any more. The first important race is the Australian Tour Down Under, held in January. It's a World

Tour event which means there are important ranking points up for grabs. This race has been around for most of my career, but only recently has it become a serious affair – when it first came on the calendar it was legendary for being a fun week of racing and partying. Now it's just racing, and even that doesn't look like much fun to me. Temperatures in the 40s, and a super-motivated, no-holds-barred peloton means crashes galore and no hiding from the suffering. To me it was unfathomable to imagine taking part in it back when it was for shits and giggles; now that it's serious it seems downright alien. January is not made for that sort of thing in my book: total bloody madness.

My feelings for January, now more than ever, show how old I am. I'm in a minority to have this attitude towards it. My teammate Dan Martin is a member of this exclusive club, but that's thanks to my brainwashing more than anything else. It works for Dan – nobody would say he's having a bummer of a career from building up slowly – but there is one big difference between Dan and me: he's in his prime; I, on the other hand, am not.

I used to count on the fact that I could get fit quickly. I relied on my body's ability to rapidly adapt to almost any work-load I put upon it. Of course, I'd get this wrong as much as I'd get it right, but even *in extremis* it wouldn't take me long to climb out of whatever overtraining hole I'd got myself into. Now everything takes longer.

With the training camp in February this year, I spend January in Girona – north of Barcelona, it's the place I've called home for quite a few years now – mainly biking with Dan and Tao Geoghegan Hart, a young London lad. Tao was in the same position I had been in nineteen years before, in 1996. An eighteen-year-old kid, a first-year senior straight out of juniors with dreams that still matched ambition. Anything is possible for Tao: it's that lovely point in a career where everything is in front of you and, although the mountain ahead looks colossal, there is no reason why the top can't be reached. He was refreshing to ride with. His enthusiasm was the perfect antithesis to my weariness: it reminded me of what I used to be like, it was a reminder I needed at this point in my career. Because we forget we were once young and full of dreams.

Tao is part of the new generation. He was born and bred in Hackney in east London, an area not known for developing cyclists, yet cycling is in his blood. He has grown up knowing only British success in the sport – he didn't have to rebel against the system as I had done at his age; the system has nurtured him and given him opportunities. For him it is normal that Team GB are one of the most powerful cycling nations in the world. That would have been a laughable thought just fifteen years ago.

Tao's knowledge of the sport is encyclopaedic. He studied English literature at school (and liked it!) and has a voracious reading habit which is easily satisfied by the ever-growing *oeuvre* of cycling literature. While we were training, every few days he'd be on to a new cycling book. I got the impression he wasn't just doing it out of curiosity or for amusement, but also because he wanted to learn as much as possible. Because, although GB is now a cycling powerhouse, it doesn't actually have any cultural history when it comes to road racing. I was the first pro that Tao had ever really spent any time with beyond his books. I was part of the continental culture – I could tell him first-person stories and share the lessons I had learnt. It was good for both of us.

By the end of the month even Dan and I were at our wits' end: the two guys who always complain about winter training camps were wishing we'd never opened our mouths. We were beginning to go slightly insane, we had made a terrible mistake thinking we could manage January on our own. We were counting down the days till we would leave for Mallorca for the first races, followed by the training camp. It was pitiful.

Fortunately, we both began to feel good on the bike. It's strange when this happens, and it generally comes like a bolt from the blue. It happened to me on 20 January, and it was wonderful and made everything seem OK again. Our form on the bike always dictates our mood. When we feel good physically we float along on a cloud off the bike – albeit a very slow cloud, as the faster we are on the bike the slower we are off it. This is all part of the energy conservation game that becomes built into us over time. As the old adage goes: 'Don't stand if you can sit, don't sit if you can lie down.'

Dan was the same. All of a sudden the two of us were back on top of it. Meanwhile, Tao's puppyish eagerness had not once diminished: he was into his third straight sickening month of it.

Bastard.

The relief of realising the training is actually starting to have an effect makes everything so much easier – for starters, I stop caring so much about the weather. This is a given when we're struggling in training. Weather becomes the number one preoccupation.

During a bad patch a few years previously my wife bought me what looked like a scientific meteorological measuring station, the type normally found deep in the Arctic. I had to anchor it down with lines and ground hooks, it stood taller than me and had a little windmill – it was a beauty. I managed to delay going out on my bike for another two hours that particular day, setting it up. It was the ultimate pro cyclist procrastination. But from then on I felt like I was in control of the weather. I felt like a god. Briefly, anyway; then I realised my wife had tricked me: no longer could I stand at the kitchen window and lie to myself about what was going on outside.

Towards the end of January everybody starts returning from their off-season visits home. Before long the seasonal group-rides start again. Once this routine begins it's easy enough to spot the guys who are having their own bad patches by their no-shows.

We all live within a fairly small radius of each other. I'm the furthest away, at fifteen kilometres from town, yet, depending on our mental state, we all see different conditions outside our windows. When things are good a quick glance outside is enough to know what clothes you'll need to wear. You won't even worry about what direction you're going to take once you leave the house, as no weather is going to affect what training has to be done. On the other hand, if you're in a bad mental state your morning could go something like this:

Struggle to get out of bed. Finally get out of bed. Skulk to the coffee machine and make an espresso, then stare out of the kitchen window only to see clouds. If you look long and hard enough you manage to spot at least one cloud that might produce rain. Go and sit down at the computer and google 'weather, Girona' then spend ten minutes going over different weather sites checking hour-by-hour reports looking for the one that is bad enough to justify giving the day's training some serious thought. Not once does it enter your mind to pick up the phone and send the 'Going biking?' message to anyone, because the worst-case scenario is that one of your potential training partners is in a sparky mood and super-excited about getting out. You don't need that right now.

Time to think about breakfast, but you're not committed, so don't really want to have a proper breakfast, as then you'll have to go training . . . so that gets put on hold for the time being. Another coffee and an even more searching look out of the window. This time evidence of wind can be spotted on a distant tree. Things are getting worse out there.

Next move is to start thinking of a potential training partner who you can trust to share this procrastination. In the old days Christian Vande Velde was a star candidate for this – NEVER Michael Barry, he'd always be up for anything; even if he was on a rest day he'd probably bin it and come out if he thought there was the chance of a good ride. Christian, on the other hand, is easily talked down. So I'd send a message saying: 'Seen the weather? Doesn't look so good.'

A few minutes later the phone would buzz, I'd get a reply: 'Yeah. I think it might rain, and the wind's picking up. We should wait.'

So we wait. Once we get past 10 a.m. we know we've missed any group-rides leaving Girona, so at least that means we won't get roped into a big ride we don't want to do. We are now masters of our fate. 'Masters' is a strong word; 'passive witnesses' would be a more accurate description.

Once we've passed the 10 a.m. watershed we only have two hours to get our shit together, because once past midday it becomes exponentially harder to get out of the house. In fact, if we're not out by midday then our whole outlook changes. Simply getting kitted up is an achievement; to make it outside and actually sit on our bike and start pedalling is a win of sorts. A post-midday two-hour ride is worth four or five hours of normal training regarding the self-satisfaction it generates. It doesn't actually have any training effect but it reboots us to start all over again the next day. The older we get the more regularly these days occur, and, although Tao might not believe it now, sometime in the distant future even he will have days like this.

I fucking hate January.

I am Light, I am Strong

In the meantime I have, of course, been doing weights – albeit not many of them, and they could barely be described as heavy. The fact I've had to take it easy – I banged my head on a wooden beam back in the autumn (long story) – has probably made for the most productive weight-training programme I've ever done. To date, every year, I've gone too deep in the first week of doing weights. I go in fresh, which I confuse with being strong, and lift too much too many times and leave myself barely able to walk the next few days and, worse than that, find myself saying out loud, 'Argh, my legs' every time I get up from a seated position, much to my wife's amusement.

I'm like a stupid rat that doesn't learn when electrocuted. Every year when I come back from the break I do the same, if not in the first session then the second, or third, or fourth, etc. There's always one day when I feel stronger than I actually am, and in the process rip my muscles to pieces. There are a few rules to adhere to when weight training. The one I recommend the most is: if it starts to feel like you're doing damage, you *are* doing damage. Stop immediately, or reduce the weight.

People always ask if I cross-train. The answer is no. There's not really anything else out there that works better for making a cyclist than simply riding a bike. The only thing we sometimes use are the weights. It's all high rep, leg specific: e.g. thirty squats – break for a minute – do that three times. Then jump on the home trainer for ten minutes to spin the legs out. Then back to the squat rack and repeat the 3 x 30 squats with a one-minute break between each set. Then back on the home trainer for ten minutes. Then the last 3 x 30 reps – so, in total, 270 squats. When we get stronger we add, with a similar workload, the leg press to this routine.

The idea of this is that it builds up more muscle strength than it does muscle weight. The neural pathways are made stronger. This is important, as weight is our greatest nemesis: we constantly walk a tightrope between wanting to be stronger yet needing to be lighter. The magic mantra is: I am light, I am strong.

The other benefit of this type of weight training is that, when done properly, it takes a little while to train the muscles to cope with the load and learn the technique to support it, so we're able to use it as a type of lactic-acid tolerance training. By doing such high reps we engage the only energy system that can support such high power output: the anaerobic system. This is just like doing a sprint: the anaerobic system is very powerful but can only be used *in extremis* as it burns bright and dies young; instead of smoke there is lactic acid, and lactic acid hurts. It hurts a lot.

The point of all the training we do is to force the body to adapt and tolerate higher workloads. We do this by constantly pushing our body to a level that is beyond what is comfortable, beyond what it is accustomed to. By doing this we stress the body, often by damaging it. When muscles hurt, post-exercise, the pain is caused by microscopic tears in the fibres. This is from damage incurred during the effort due to them not being strong enough to hold the contraction and therefore causing them to rip apart.

That's one of the reasons our muscles shake when we hold some-thing that we're not strong enough to manage; the shaking is a result of the muscle fibres releasing their grip against each other, or, on occasions, actually ripping.

It's then by resting and recuperating properly that the body recovers – the clever bit is that it will repair the fibre in a manner that makes it stronger and more likely to handle a similar work-load next time. This is also where the term 'muscle memory' comes from, although it's not the actual muscle, it's the neural pathways between the brain and the muscles that do the remembering.

When we learn a new sport we're pretty crap to begin with – our technique is terrible because we haven't yet learnt what the precise movements are and what muscles to engage, or when to fire them, or how to co-ordinate them. The more training we do, the better the technique becomes, which obviously leads to a more efficient use of muscles, because only the ones necessary are being fired and in co-ordination. Once those neural pathways have been learnt it's hard to lose them fully – hence why, even after a long break from a sport that you were once very good at, it's possible to start up again quite quickly. The body only has to strengthen the necessary muscles rather than hardwire neural pathways and waste time repairing the wrong muscles.

Almost all professional cyclists have a fluid pedalling style – even the worst of us has something different in their move-ment from a non-pro. That's simply thousands of kilometres and hours in the saddle training and racing; we have trained ourselves to be efficient, which resembles fluidity. It's the same with all sports. Often the greatest athletes have something effortless in their movements, which is as much about genetics as it is about training, because as much as I believe hard work is a common denominator when it comes to success I'm also aware, from expe-rience, that each one of the elite athletes I've ever known was born with a genetic advantage they've subsequently maximised through hard work. I think most elite international athletes will tell a similar story of simply being better at their sport than their peers when young – it's that natural ability that is then trained, and the ability to work hard that separates the initial genetic advantage, because on a global stage genetic freaks are competing against other genetic freaks. In a way the playing field is levelled once the pinnacle of any sport is reached. Marginal gains and losses are the only things that separate the best.

This goes beyond actual muscles but also to energy systems. The more we use each energy system the more efficient it becomes – from fat-burning, to aerobic, and finally to anaerobic, which is where lactic acid is produced.

The anaerobic system is the one we use the least in cycling, although probably still as much if not more so than any other sport out there. In one day of racing it's possible we do the equivalent of taking part in every single athletics track event, while also doing two marathons, back to back. Occasionally we do that for twenty days in a row. It's quite hard to train for that. We try though, hence starting the weight-training lactic tolerance stuff back in November – or, in the words of my old friend, Matt White, aka Whitey: 'Gotta keep ya body guessing, Dave.' Otherwise we spend three months never going into that zone, meaning it takes longer for the body to adapt to it once we do start racing again.

The weight training begins back in November. The great thing about starting so early is that it feels like you're actually doing something productive because, to begin with, going out for a bike ride isn't much fun. In the time we've had off between our last race of the season and getting back on the bike we will have gone from hero to zero. It doesn't take long for this to happen to a professional cyclist. I think a common misconception people have about us is that we're always killing it; that jumping on a bike is always effortless. This is not true. We lose our condition so quickly. We can go from being world beaters to seriously average creepers (relatively speaking, of course) in a matter of weeks. It's soul-destroying.

I was mentored briefly by Tony Rominger when I was a young professional. Tony had been one of the greatest cyclists of his generation, a multiple Grand Tour winner, no less. I went to stay with him in Monaco not long after his retirement. He picked me up from Nice airport and on the drive to Monaco I asked him how retirement was going.

'Ah, David, you know, it's OK. Ha! I can eat what I want!' He laughed a lot at this. Then he paused and thought. 'There are other things that are not so good. I see my friends in Monaco, they are retired tennis players, racing drivers, golfers. You know, that type of thing, normal here, it's Monaco, yes?!' Lots more laughter. 'I see something different with them to me. They never lose *completely* what they had. They always have a bit of "Za Magic", ya know?! For an exhibition match or something. Me? I'm fucked! Never again will I be good on a bike.' He sort of laughed and finished with, 'This is life, David. In professional cycling there are no gifts.'

That conversation always haunted me, because it is so true. Our magic is in our physical condition, the ability to be super-trained. When we stop training the magic goes; very quickly we are indistinguishable from any other person – we're not about to dazzle with a football that mistakenly got hit in our direction. Nor go and play an exhibition game of golf or tennis and show flashes of genius. Nor get behind the wheel of a car and show why once we were the best in the world. With us it's gone the moment we hang it up, and the sooner we realise that the better.

When we're professional we get glimpses of this ultimate fate. Only two or three weeks off can set us back enormously. Granted, we can get it back reasonably quickly. I've learnt a simple rule: it will take the same amount of time I've had off to recover the level I was at before I stopped. Two weeks off means two weeks to get it back. Of course, this recovery time must be uninterrupted quality training time – hard, often monotonous work to get back to our best. No matter what genetic gifts we're born with it always comes down to the training. After all, professional cycling is effectively an ultra-endurance sport – it doesn't matter what we've been blessed with at birth, it has to be trained a shit-load to be maximised.

So, back in November, say, the thought of doing a Grand Tour is to us as foreign as it is to a London commuter. I've had times when I've got back on the bike in November forgetting that I'm not the same person I was in September and found myself blown to pieces forty kilometres from my house, sitting on a curb outside a petrol station looking like a lost and starving garden gnome, stuffing my face with chocolate doughnuts and Coke, wondering how I'm going to get home. That has happened more than once.

Two months after the close of the season we are riddled with self-doubt, wondering how on earth we can even start another Giro d'Italia, Tour de France or Vuelta a España, let alone finish one. And forget about competing. Those are a strange few weeks, and not very enjoyable, so usually it's good to be in the gym pretending to be an athlete, although it has to be said we barely look like such to the regular gym bunnies, who see the skinny-fatguy standing there doing hundreds of reps with essentially no weight on the bar. It probably looks like we're on some rehabilitation programme.

Last autumn I realised I should get back in touch with my old coach, Adrie van Deimen, as I needed somebody to help me get back into the right head space. It used to be so easy for me to switch into a focused training period. It would be an extreme change, in that I would essentially isolate myself and go into hiding, which allowed me to switch my persona to what I needed it to be. I can't do this any more – it requires being fundamentally selfish, as you have to become totally self-obsessed. Everything in life has to fit around the training, diet and rest, and when I say everything I also mean everybody.

Being the father of two boys has changed that for me. I love spending time with them, and I want to help my wife when I'm at home. She's the one who spends the majority of the year looking after the two of them single-handedly while I'm off pursuing my passion. And although it's my job and I'm paid very well to do it, it's also what I love doing. I don't think it's fair that I then come home and carry on being totally self-obsessed. But, equally, I'm beginning to see that state of mind as a failing, too – disrespectful to my teammates, irresponsible in terms of my team responsibilities. All this is the primary reason I decided to make this my final season. I can still race – that's a given for me – it's the training that kills me now and if I can't train properly then I'm not getting the best out of myself, which is what I'm paid to do.

This aside, I also know I can do what is expected of me in my final year. I am a road captain now and that holds different responsibilities to a leader who is expected to bring in the big results. There are only a handful of people in the professional peloton who have raced more than me at the top level. I know myself well enough that when the big occasions arise I can be relied upon. I have proved this throughout my career, and trust my team to trust me on that. We've been through enough for us to have this mutual understanding.

Fundamentally, I've always been a driven, ambitious person. This is the biggest difference between being an old pro and a young pro – my job is now clearly defined and recognised, pragmatism has taken over from ambition. Am I falling into the trap of complacency? Have I become comfortable, dare I say, content? This is not a good place to be as a professional cyclist.

The Goals

So, racing head on. The goals for this year. Each one of these targets has a reasoning behind it. I'm standing strong on them (rather than opening myself up to the usual mind-bending I am so susceptible to when it comes to my calendar). They all have a personal value to me: in my final season I am determined to close as many doors as I can. Paris–Roubaix has been my nemesis throughout my career. This year I am determined to race it with full commitment and be done with it once and for all. Although this is a personal mission I am fully aware my role in the race will be that of loyal teammate – there are no delusions of grandeur here, simply a desire to remove its proverbial monkey from my back once and for all.

The Tour de France is my race, the one that got me into bike racing. If there was no Tour I'd never have fallen in love with the sport. My relationship with the Tour goes beyond the actual racing. I have become friends with the people who work on it – to the degree I no longer shake the hand of ex-director Jean-Marie Leblanc or current boss Christian Prudhomme but greet them with the very French familial kiss on the cheeks. We are friends, we share a history and mutual respect. I've always dreamt of my final time on the Champs-Elysées, my family and friends there to share my farewell to the race I loved so much. It will be one of the most important days of my career. And it seems almost fate that this, my last Tour, also starts in the UK, in Yorkshire no less, where my father has now relocated from the Hong Kong of my youth. It is the perfect scenario.

The Commonwealth Games in Glasgow is a gift like no other. For one of my last ever races to be in the city where most of my family are from, where I will be racing for only the second time in my career in a Scotland jersey, seems too good to be true. The fact it comes straight after the Tour de France, when it's a given I'll be at my strongest, makes the possibility of victory real-istic – if not, at least there's always the chance to honour the jersey of my home nation.

And then the Vuelta a España, which is my favourite race, in the purest sense, in that there aren't the emotional attach-ments that the Tour de France carries. The Vuelta is simply the race where I can be a bike racer without the stresses and expecta-tions or responsibilities of other Grand Tours. I can race for the sake of racing. It's always been that way for me; I can't imagine a better way to end my career with my team than to be allowed to race for fun.

And, finally, there are the Worlds – the completion of everything, finishing where I began among the people I've known the longest in the cycling world, the Great Britain national team. The fact the race is in Spain, my adopted home, makes it all the more special. I've always taken great pride in racing for Great Britain, and they've stood by me through thick and thin. They are the people among whom I feel most at home. It feels right that the last time I race as a professional will be in a GB jersey.

'Good winter?'

It feels so good to be back in a race. There's only so much training I can do before I get bored of it. I bought my first road bike as a fifteen-year-old in Hong Kong because I wanted to race it. I'd never thought about doing anything else with it. The reason I rode it outside of races was to train myself to go faster in the races. That's just the way it was.

As I've got older I've learnt that a bike ride is maybe one of the great ways to spend time with a friend, or friends, yet I treat that as something totally separate to my racer self. There are now two distinctly different cycling personalities that exist within me: the racer and the gentleman. The latter has come with maturity and *does not race*; the other is still, in essence, the fifteen-year-old boy who bought that first bike in Hong Kong – only with over a thousand professional races under his scarred and sun-damaged skin.

The first race of the season brings with it a new lease of life. We're back in our natural habitat, on the road with our teams, staying in mostly mediocre hotels, finding comfort in the routine. It's in total contrast to the last time the peloton was together in the final races of the previous year, when everybody was on their last legs, physically and mentally, wishing it all to stop so we could go home and curl up in a ball, away from the mediocre hotels. Now, the peloton is fresh and ready to go, everybody actually seems happy and motivated to be there. This is unusual behaviour, to say the least.

There are new sponsors, different colours and designs of kits, new riders on old teams, old riders on new teams. Everybody is chatty and curious. The conversation always goes something like this, with slight variations, in roughly a dozen different languages:

'Good winter?'

'Great. One of the best I've had.'

'Yeah, me too. You get good weather?'

'OK. Went on training camp in December, got the Ks in. Took it easy over Christmas, massive January.'

'Yeah, me too. What's your race programme?'

'This, Tirreno, Classics. Usual!'

'Yeah, me too.'

Two minutes later, bump into another rider you kind of know:

'Hey, man! How was the winter?'

'It was awesome, racked up the kilometres!'

'Yeah, me too. You get good weather?'

And so on . . .

This line of questioning isn't confined to the first race. Oh no: it can go on till April. We'll call it the Pro Cyclist Early Season Ice Breaker. As a rule of thumb the start of the season is over after Liège–Bastogne–Liège, the last of the spring Classics. So from the Tour de Romandie on it's best to stop asking about the winter and start asking how the start of the season has been. The thing is, this is a two-edged sword, because although you're showing willing by engaging and driving the conversation, you are also risking alienating the target by revealing your total indifference to their results. Because if you actually cared, even a little bit, you'd know exactly how their early season form had been. Often it's simply a desperate gamble in order to fill the silence, but, if handled wrongly, it is a silence neither of you will ever need to worry about filling again. For example:

'Hey, man, how's it going? You do the Classics?'

If you have to ask this question it means the pro you're talking to has had a shit start to the year, because if they'd had a good start to the year you'd have noticed their presence some-where. So if you ask this and they say, 'Yes, all of them,' you'll find yourself a little stumped. This is the worst possible answer you could have expected, only you didn't expect it, because you never really cared, and so didn't plan your moves that far ahead.

From my experience the best way to handle this situation (because it arises, there are enough quiet moments: signing on, standing on the start line, the ever-rarer relaxed time in the bunch when chat is possible, when you find yourself next to a fellow racer with whom you cross wheels enough to merit engaging with on human terms) is to be vague. Remove specifics, allow yourself wiggle room, ask more generic questions like, 'How you doing?' or 'This race/weather is amazing/sucks.' Or, a personal favourite, 'What's new?' That's the ultimate Open-ended Ice Breaker – you needn't know anything about what they've been up to.

A few to avoid include:

'Is this your first race this year?' It could be their fortieth race, in which case you're reminding them of how invisible their start to the year has been, which sets the wrong tone immediately.

'What races have you done so far?' Again, there's the risk that you've raced with them numerous times already and simply haven't noticed.

Then there's the ultimate faux pas, never to be used under any circumstances: 'Have you put on weight?' Every professional cyclist has a weight obsession – we have to, it's an integral part of the job. If somebody is looking fat, never, *ever*, remind them of this. Of course, it will be brought up behind their backs at every opportunity, yet there shouldn't be the slightest mention of it to their faces: that wouldn't be cool.

On the other hand if somebody is looking fit, i.e. skinny and ripped and tanned, then it's totally acceptable to bring this up – in fact, it is encouraged: 'Wow, you look super-fit. You going for this?' To which they'll reply, almost without fail, 'Thanks! Yeah, training's been going well. We'll see how it goes here, I feel good.' This laid-back attitude is a thinly veiled attempt to hide the fact they've been living like a monk for months in preparation for that very race and if they don't perform well they'll probably have a mild nervous breakdown before slipping, riddled with neuroses, into a hole of self-doubt which could take them weeks or months to recover from. The honest answer would have been, 'Ouf, thank you, I've been working so hard for months getting ready for this race. I'm going to be devastated if I don't go well.'

As we get older we learn to manage the pressure better. The weight of expectations, internal and external, is lightened. When we are younger everything is so important, because racing is the most important thing in our lives, we're too young to understand there is more. For many of us life has been a steadily ascending spiral of success and respect, we've yet to endure any significant failure, and, of course, if we don't know failure we can't fully appreciate success. For this reason we never fully take the time to soak up where we are or how we're doing. Everything we achieve is considered another step up the ladder towards greater heights.

If we are lucky (fundamentally, I think there is a lot of luck involved, there are too many variables that we cannot control to ever be arrogant enough to claim we are the sole architects of our success) we will have a career long enough to grow beyond that narrow mindset of youth. It is only time that can give us the opportunity to experience more and mature into a state of mind where we can appreciate that where we have come from is just as important as where we are going – and as we get older and live through more we begin to separate things: what was once all-encompassing can be but a footnote at another point in our lives, and vice versa.

This is the same in all walks of life, I'm sure. Except as racers we appreciate this more than most; our lives are lived at a higher rate – they have to be as we only have a finite amount of time in which to maximise the genetic gifts we've been lucky enough to discover. Ten years, I'd say, and that's roughly it for us. From eighteen to twenty-eight is when most of the ascending takes place, then we plateau for varying lengths of time, and then, in a relatively short period of time, maybe one to three years, we endure the endgame slide through mediocrity to has-been. It's quite an intense ride. I think most of us only come to terms with it years later.

I'm more fortunate than most in that I have had what feels like two careers played out in three acts: it began with the classic rise and fall, which led to two years banned from the sport, and culminated in a renaissance-like second chance. It's safe to say I have lived through dramatic failure, and it's for this reason that when given the opportunity to come back I seized it with the deep-down knowledge that I was lucky to have it and should respect and appreciate it for what it was: a second and last chance to do it all over again, the right way. So, contrary to many of my peers, I have had a slightly different sense of what it is we are doing. I know it's not real, and I know it will end, and this has helped me prepare myself for the inevitable farewell that all of us have to confront eventually.

The Suck (2)

The first race is a shock to the system. The initial excitement at being back on the road with the guys is quickly diminished when we find ourselves unable to unlock our eyes from the rear wheel in front of us, moving at what feels like warp speed. That's what it feels like: warp speed. Everything shrinks down to a small visual point of focus, and so everything in the periphery is out of focus and flashing past in abstraction. Let's not confuse this with the famous 'Zone' (or 'Flow' as it likes to be called these days) that athletes describe. This is 'the Suck'. I've seen guys so deeply in the Suck that they lose control of their bike and crash, and don't feel a thing except relief that it's stopped.

Every pro cyclist has had a moment in their career when they were so deep in the Suck that they wished a crash upon themselves. A puncture or mechanical isn't good enough because then you have to chase back on; a crash allows you to let go of the race. This is a fundamental problem we have: we don't give up, even if we puncture or our bike breaks, we have a spare bike and a mechanic in, or on, a motorised vehicle behind us ready to rescue the situation. I don't think anybody truly understands how different being rescued in that situation is from being saved from any other. Sometimes crashing feels like being saved.

Our first races are a harsh reminder of this. In the four months preceding, when riding during training, we have allowed ourselves to forget the suffering of racing because we are in control of the speed and exertion, ergo the suffering. Yes, we'll push ourselves, but there's only so far we can go, we become accustomed to managing our own efforts, which reminds us, importantly, that most of us aren't true masochists. We don't actually enjoy the suffering, it's simply a shitty by-product of doing what we love, i.e. racing.

It's our ability to manage the suffering that defines us. I've heard it said so many times about great bike racers: 'He won't stay down.' 'He knows how to suffer.' 'He'll get back on his bike.' 'He'll be back.' There is a theme. It's an ability to be rational when everything hurts, because that's what it comes down to: being able to rationalise with yourself that everything is fixable, not giving up and thinking everything is lost. Ultimately, it's an absence of self-pity when shit gets bad.

In these first races everything hurts. Probably the most common thing I'll hear myself and others say to each other during these first races is, 'Fuck. I forgot how hard it is.'

Fortunately, I'm on the Mallorca programme. This is like a gift of a first race compared to most others.

There's Mallorca, then there are three other common options to start the year:

Tour Down Under

As I've already said, Down Under is out of the question for me, although supposedly it's a great race and allows for some good training in the sun, away from the European winter – if you are so inclined to spend some time there before or after the race, which I would, but only if I wasn't racing in between. There are some places in the world that I simply can't imagine racing my bike. Australia is one of them.

Tour Mediterranean

This can be put under the generic banner of French early season. Nothing has changed in the twenty years I've been racing there. It can be summed up quite briefly:

1. Cold, probably windy.
2. Maybe a little low budget, certainly a bit shabby round the edges.
3. A strike. Could be farmers at the side of road, maybe riders in the road. Neither tend to have much effect.
4. Unique racing. It could go from the gun, equally might be neutralised for most of the day. No one ever really knows.
5. Inevitably the evening meal will comprise pasta that has been (over)cooked hours before and reheated with butter in a microwave, chicken – technique used to cook unknown – green beans (boiled), and apple tart (highlight) and natural yoghurt to finish. Oh, and bread, shitloads of bread.

Daniel Mangeas will be on the PA system at the start and finish – as he has been since the mid-1970s at what seems like every single race in France. This is the best bit.

Tour of Qatar

Qatar is carnage. I've only done it once (I may have done it more but if so I've erased it from my memory). I have to admit I had fun when I rode it in 2008, but it was savagely intense and crashtastic. There are three reasons for this: it's flat, it's windy, and all the Classics riders (aka crazy bastards) go there. The Classics riders are so fucking up for it, there's usually a race to the start line. Rather than rolling up to the start line in the usual chilled-out fashion, the few kilometres from the neutral start to the *départ réel* were, the year I rode it, some of the wildest I've ever known. It was like being a junior again – that was the last time I felt I might lose the race by not being ready to race from the gun. The official start line became a finish line; the neutral zone became a battle royale in slow motion because, as in every neutral zone, we weren't allowed to overtake the controlling lead car whose job it was to limit our speed in a manner that had us crossing the *départ réel* on the exact scheduled time. Never before had I been in a race situation where we were racing before the race.

Then there's the empty desert landscape, literally in the middle of nowhere surrounded by flat deadlands – no spectators, no buildings, no vegetation and, worst of all, no team buses; just a weird, random castle in a desert, which apparently features every year.

Challenge Mallorca

This is like a drop of early season heaven compared to the other three options. For starters, the genius organisers made it five one-day races instead of a five-day stage race. Meaning we get to choose which days we race – it's a total luxury.

I chose four of the five races, or, should I say, 'we' decided. The team are fully aware of my disdain for the early season and spare me the suffering of the hardest day. Fabian Wegmann and I both skip that particular race, yet we're such dorks we still go with the team on the bus to the start and hang out and then ride eighty kilometres back to the hotel. (After all, we didn't have anything else to do.) More importantly, it alleviates the guilt of not racing by sort of being there with the team. As soon as we set off ahead of the race we feel like naughty school boys skiving a day off school. Like I said, dorks.

Ryder

When I arrived at the hotel in Mallorca at the beginning of the week I experienced something I'd never felt before. I felt out of place. It was the strangest thing. Walking past all the team trucks, buses and cars parked up out the front of the hotel I had the sensation that I no longer belonged there among them. Then entering the hotel and looking for the room list I realised that for the first time since 1997 I wasn't excited – even when I was in bad form and hating January I would always feel a spark of something inside me when I got to that first team hotel of the year. There was simply nothing now, it felt like an old routine, which wouldn't have been a problem if I didn't suddenly feel very old.

This was accentuated by the fact that when I did find the room list I became suddenly aware that Christian Vande Velde and Dave Zabriskie were no longer on it, and that two of my other friends, Andreas Klier and Robbie Hunter, had moved column from 'Rider' to 'DS'. I looked closely, sliding my finger down the column reading through all the names. I didn't recognise a bunch of them. This made me feel even older, so old that I started checking the list again to see who else was old, in the hope I was younger than someone. Then it happened: I realised I'd become the Oldest Rider On The Team. Fucketyfuck, not good. I can still remember vividly being the youngest rider on the team, and, by a long way, I'd never imagined I'd be the oldest on any team.

Thankfully one name was still on there: Ryder Hesjedal. Ryder and I had become close friends over the years. The first time I'd spoken to him was at the Vuelta in 2006 when he was riding for Phonak. He was telling me how he was going back to the States as he was over the European scene. I can remember telling him to stick at it, that he'd regret giving up. He stopped the race that very day, so I'm guessing my motivational talk tipped him over the edge. He went back to the US and rediscovered his mojo, so much so that Jonathan Vaughters signed him up along with me, Christian VdV and Dave Z among others at the start-up of Slipstream Sports.

Ryder comes from the west coast of Canada. I was never aware this was such a big deal until I heard Ryder forever remind people of the fact. Evidently the west coast crushes the rest of Canada – at least that's how it is to Ryder anyway; he doesn't speak French and is proud of it, *chapeau*. He comes from Vancouver Island, which is a pretty epic place – big trees, bears, that sort of thing. Last September I spent a week with Ryder on Vancouver Island and I began to understand why he is the way he is from that trip.

Ryder's nickname is 'Legend'. It was created in a mildly sarcastic tone, the same way Little John was actually a really big dude. Ryder has always acted as if he is a legend, way before he had legitimately claimed the right to use the title. He was a big deal in mountain biking at a young age. The best way for me to explain Ryder is to give his life story in cars.

AMC Concord Wagon – $500, sixteen years old: This was his first car. When staying with Ryder I got to see where he comes from and got to know his friends. It was the first time I understood his background, as it's not something he ever talks about. Langford is their home town; it had suffered economically in the 1980s, resulting in high unemployment to the point of becoming a fairly destitute and desperate area, in other words a tough place to grow up. Although Langford seems to be putting those times behind it now, there are still signs of what it had once been, most poignantly visible in the derelict remains of the secondary school Ryder and his friends went to. They didn't have much, they were 'grinders' as Ryder would say. Cycling was his only opportunity to escape.

Subaru Wagon – $300, seventeen years old: Ryder funded everything himself at the time. He'd more often than not find himself racing against kids who could afford the best equipment. He was already trading down so he could afford to race.

Merkur XR4Ti – $2,500, eighteen years old: This was the first time Ryder started to have some financial control of his own life, thanks to winning money from races and getting small sponsorship deals. One of the first things he did was buy himself a 'nice' car.

Acura Integra (Purple/Slammed) – $10,500, nineteen years old: He gets his first big sponsor in Gary Fisher Mountain Bikes and with it enters the Poseur Period. Here the Legend starts to emerge. Slamming meant having the car's suspension lowered to a degree that more often than not made the car totally unusable in normal circumstances. This was a small price to pay for the level of supposed coolness attained.

Lexus IS 300 (Canary Yellow/18" Chrome wheels/Slammed) – $50,000, twenty-one years old: The poseur progresses to what is commonly known as 'pimping'. Most easily displayed by the fact he spends $8,000 on a set of chrome wheels for a car so slammed it can barely get off of his driveway. In fact he has to ask his friends to wait until he's out of the driveway in order for them to get in the car or it won't make it out.

Lincoln Navigator (White/24" Chrome wheels $14,000) – $100,000, twenty-three years old: This is the zenith of the Pimp Period. Ryder had become one of the best mountain bikers in the world, dominating the scene in the US and becoming a regular presence at the front of World Championship races. His crowning achievement in vulgarity was fitting this car with Gucci (fake) upholstered head rests that he collected personally from New York.

Chevy Avalanche (Fully Blacked-out/24" Chrome spinners) – $40,000 AND Ford F350 (Black/Full-size Turbo Diesel) – $40,000 AND Chrysler 300C (Hemi/22" Chrome wheels) – $50,000, twenty-four years old: Ryder trades in the Lincoln for two cars and buys a 300C for his home in Vancouver Island. He keeps the 24" chrome wheels and adds spinners to them, which is probably the most ridiculous thing he's ever done, although it doesn't last long as he has a near fatal crash in that very car. Him and his friend Seamus are thrown out of the car while it's flipping and find themselves twenty metres from the eventual wreck. He doesn't replace the Chevy and he sells the Ford, and keeps the Chrysler at the house he has bought for his parents in Langford. He moves from mountain biking to road cycling, the big pimpin' life comes to a close. He is paid a fraction of what he earned as a top mountain biker, taking minimum wage from US Postal in pursuit of his Tour de France dream.

Isuzu Trooper (Rent money) – twenty-six years old: He acquires this car in lieu of rent from his friend, Nigel, who has been staying in his house in Victoria. He is in his second year of racing in Europe, with none of the success he is accustomed to. He returns to the US to race for a domestic team on the national scene and leverages himself to the max, buying a small place in Maui in a last-ditch attempt to reinvent himself.

Opel Monterey (Bought in Girona, identical to Isuzu Trooper) – €3,200, twenty-nine years old: Back settled into Europe with Slipstream, he's now made it, the reinvention has worked. Girona will be his seasonal home for the years ahead, so he buys himself an Opel Monterey, which is the same car as the faithful rent-traded Isuzu Trooper he has in Canada, just branded differently. It's even the same colour, a sort of army green. The least pimping car imaginable. We nickname it 'The Unit'.

Mazda 5 (bought from Hertz 'Rent or Own' in Maui) – $12,000, thirty-two years old: Ryder wins the Giro. Buys his teammates a Rolex each as a thank-you. Returns to Maui and buys himself a Mazda 5 from a rental agency. All four cars he now owns are worth less than $30,000. When people call him 'Legend' now there is not even the slightest hint of sarcasm.

So Ryder has had a fairly unorthodox climb to the top of cycling. He will be the first to say he is a frugal man, and even when he was going through his Pimping Period he was always careful with his money – he may have been driving some ridiculous cars but he also bought his parents a house and has always invested conservatively. Behind the façade there is somebody who has a deep-down, inherent respect for money. This isn't surprising when you know where he comes from – he knows all too well what it's like not to have money, and it's clear he can never forget that.

In many ways he encapsulates what pro cyclists used to be like: they weren't middle class, as is so often the case these days, they came from poor backgrounds and saw cycling as their only escape. He loves cycling more than any other pro I know. For him it's more than just a hobby that turned into a passion and from there to a profession; it's been a vehicle to a life he could have never imagined without it. Maybe it's for this reason he loves his bikes so much – they are always in perfect condition and he is obsessive about their set-up. I've never known a pro who will spend so much time and money on their own bikes.

All of this makes him one of the few truly interesting characters in modern cycling. He treats being a professional as more of a lifestyle than the science it seems increasingly to resemble. Even when he's at his best, before his big objectives, he won't think twice about having a beer in the middle of a ride if he feels like it. That's just the way he rolls: he's super-focused and dedicated, yet he still allows himself to be who he is. He'll send me video clips of himself in the off-season in Maui – bearded, shirtless, riding his favourite old mountain bike to a bar in cut-off jeans, just cruisin'. That's Ryder.

All of this helps make him a great roomie. He's so goddamned relaxed about everything, it never really feels like he's trying, and yet you know he is, because everything he does has a level of detail applied to it that belies the surfer-stoner attitude he radiates.

The Princess

Ryder's latest thing is juicing. So this first training camp of the year in Mallorca becomes a juice extravaganza. His juicer is called 'The Princess'. We go nuts on it. We're convinced it's working miracles – or we trick ourselves into believing so; either way it's a good way to kill some time in the afternoon. We have to go and buy the vegetables and then make the juice, and then clean up the inevitable mess. It becomes a fixture, something to look forward to. We feel like proper athletes. Then we go and have a beer at the hotel bar because we feel so amazing about ourselves.

Loose Ryder

Ryder shows me his ever-growing catalogue of selfies with cycling stars. It's become his thing, he's got some beauties – a particularly amazing one with Nibali – all of them taken while on the bike. I don't know when he does them. And without fail whoever the victim is, be it Contador, Sagan, Cancellara or the like, they all look a little confused, not sure whether Ryder is being serious or not, because Ryder is so loose at times you might just think he's serious about a fansie selfie, which explains the often perplexed looks and uncertain smiles he captures.

Ryder and Vincenzo Nibali (Alberto Contador photo bombing)

Ryder and Alberto Contador

Ryder and Fabian Cancellara

Even the way he races is loose: there is no other rider of his stature in the sport who does what he does. That is, to race from the back. He cannot fathom why everybody fights so much to be at the front of the peloton, it makes no sense to him. In most races he'll spend the four-hour preamble that the leaders have to endure before they battle it out firmly ensconced at the rear of the peloton. I personally cannot agree with this tactic, and yet he proves over and over again that it works for him.

There are a few problems with sitting at the back, the biggest of which is the fact you are at the whim of nearly 200 riders in front of you. For example, if you have your team controlling the race, you sit up there with them. If you're a team leader you'll be in the protected position near the rear of your team's formation, never the last position, because you always need a buffer of a couple of riders between you and the mêlée behind you fighting for position. You also need the security of having a teammate or two on your wheel who can see if something happens, rather than having you try to shout ahead if a problem occurs – more often than not you won't be heard.

This means that if you're in this position you only have five or six riders ahead of you, and they are your teammates, whose job it is to take care of you; behind you are the 200 or so other riders fighting for position. That's 200 things that could go wrong behind you versus the five or six things that could go wrong ahead of you. It's simple risk analysis.

But Ryder doesn't give a shit. He'd rather deal with the randomness than live with the permanent stress of constantly fighting for position in the first part of the peloton. Because that's what it is; there is only one team that can actually sit on the front, and they have that privilege because they have the leader's jersey, or they have the favourite to win that day. Everybody else fights behind.

This is something I have seen change over my career. When I started in the late nineties the peloton was quite an organic, flowing thing. There would be one team on the front, then the leaders from other teams staying up there in relative safety, with two or three of their loyal *domestiques*/bodyguards protecting them – and then everybody else doing their thing behind. It's not that it was less stressful, it was simply a different, more independent stress. Each one of us decided how much we wanted to fight.

Nowadays it's robotic. All team *directeurs* are on the radio telling their riders to get to the front and ride as a tight unit. Fair enough, I can see what they're trying to achieve, but it ends up being counter-productive, as with so many teams trying to do the same thing it turns into a total clusterfuck.

If left organic then the guys who are at the front want to be at the front, and have the awareness and will to remain there; they flow freely and without stress, forever maintaining their presence at the front while never letting you know they're there. It's a remarkable thing when done well, and a very rare thing to behold in the modern peloton. These days flowing is difficult because you'll come up against racers who have been ordered against their will to be there, often young guys who are so scared of not doing what they're told that they end up fixated on their teammate's wheel in front and will be knocking into people and creating conflicts at what is a essentially a peaceful moment in the race. They've never been given a chance to learn how to flow.

This permanent and unnecessary stress leads to more crashes as people get more and more desperate to maintain their position, the desperation leads to careless and disrespectful riding . . . and all it takes is one flick into an unsuspecting rider who happens to be relaxed, in that particular peaceful moment of the race, and bang, a crash begins. I can understand where Ryder is coming from.

Of course, there is a flipside to the Ryder style of racing. You open yourself up to being stuck behind crashes that happen ahead, and more often than not left isolated from your team, because, contrary to the front, no team will risk having all their riders at the back – if we were all back there and there was a crash that left the road blocked we'd lay there on the floor watching the race ride away from us with zero of our team in it. This is exactly what happened in the 2012 Tour de France Stage 6 mass pile-up when our whole team got caught up behind what was the biggest crash I've seen in my career (see the Theory of Crashes, p.85).

Artá
MALLORCA

Dear Archie,
    Finished the last race in Mallorca
yesterday, I'm not exactly flying but
I'm not creeping so I'm taking that as
a positive! I hit 190HR in the first
two races helping Fabian in the sprint.
didn't even know my HR could go that
high anymore! Not bad for an old man.
Recovery day today so we rode to Arta
for a coffee, your Abuela lives only a
few kilometres from there. Training camp
now for nine days, time to get good!!

13/2/14

ESPAÑA   CORREOS
                            0,75€

ARCHIBALD MILLAR
CAN CRUSIC
PUJALS DE PAGESOS
CORNELLA DEL TERRI
17844
    ESPAGNE

Artá - MALLORCA

37

Challenge Mallorca (2)

All in all it's the perfect re-entry into the peloton. Contrary to other years, and most other teams, we follow up the five days' racing with a ten-day training camp. This is part of the deal for the team gaining a place in Challenge Mallorca: we also have to hold our training camp there. Team training camps have barely changed in the twenty years I've been doing them. The hotels are almost always nearly empty as we're staying in holiday resorts in their off-season. The weather is normally good but not good enough to actually be there unless you're a professional cyclist escaping northern Europe. The food is normally quite average, although compared to the food we'd get served back in the nineties on similar training camps it's Michelin-starred.

Calpe, north of Benidorm, is the favourite of teams – sometimes, in December and January, it's possible to find five of the best cycling teams in the world staying there at the same time. I've spent months of my life in Calpe. It's why I'm thankful to be in Mallorca for this, my final pre-season camp. At least it's different from what I'm used to, makes it feel a little bit unfamiliar.

The routine, on the other hand, is always the same:

08:30 Breakfast
10:00 Leave for training
15:00–16:00 Lunch
17:00–20:00 Massage (45 min)
20:00 Dinner

There will be a day with physiological testing, another for the team photo, but, all in all, that's it. The training will vary but not significantly. Ryder and I have, of course, added juicing to our daily schedule, and a pre-dinner beer if our massage rotation matches up. Apart from that it's general skulking around. I used to read, now I waste time on my computer or phone, surfing the web. I miss the days when we didn't have internet or smartphones. I actually used my brain.

As usual I build my form up slowly through the camp, then on the final day we're split up into groups for team time-trial training. Rohan Dennis and I find ourselves in the smallest group, going off last. We're probably the two purest time triallists on the team, he young, me old. We both raise our game and I find myself doing what I do best and loving it. The two of us together go faster than the two groups of eight that are chasing. It makes me feel young again, and reminds me of what I'm capable of and why I do it. It is the perfect way to finish the camp.

Stage Racers

You've got the crazy bastards, the Classics racers, frothing at the mouth, champing at the bit for early season form in Qatar. Then there are the stage racers, capable of winning the general classification/overall of any stage race without ever actually crossing a finishing line first. The stage racer's primary objective is damage limitation through racing conservatively and minimising time losses; aggressive racing is only encouraged if there is near certainty of gaining time. It's for this reason general classification racers will only dare to spread their wings close to the finish line – that way if it does backfire they can limit their losses because they are so near the finish.

It's also why whole teams are used up on the front of the race before a leader will show himself. In an ideal world the leader would never actually be seen exerting himself at the front – he'd always be there, yet invisible, economising as much energy as possible in preparation for the following day's racing. It's a numbers game: everything is measured and calculated in order to generate the most efficient result. To put it simply, discretion is the better part of valour.

I had, over the years, grown a stage-racing mentality. I would assess all the applicable factors and decide what was the most efficient and effective way for me to race; the only time I would take risks was if I was in a winning situation, more often than not during a time trial. Even then they were calculated risks, as I would have done sufficient reconnaissance to allow me to corner faster – so although from the following car it might have looked like I was hanging it all out, clipping barriers and basically being a maniac, from my point of view I knew exactly what I was doing. And therein lies the biggest difference between a stage racer and a one-day racer.

A stage racer is always trying to control the variables – if risks are taken, they are calculated – whereas a one-day racer essentially knows they can't control the variables, so they reduce them by racing aggressively, fighting each other to be at the front of the race in order to enter a particular corner that leads into a narrow road, or smashing each other to be the first into a dangerous section of cobbles, and demanding their team sacrifice themselves in order to be at the front in crosswinds. The closer to the front they are the fewer riders they have to deal with – for a one-day racer the biggest variable is the number of racers in front of them. Classics turn into wars of attrition, they become elimination races. It doesn't matter how strong you are, if you're not in the right place all the time you won't win.

Classics Riders

I had made an early career choice to avoid the Classics: they were so long and hard, and I'm not ashamed to say that, at the time, I didn't have the skill set for that. I spent my early years targeting races that I could win clean. In my mind Classics were up there with Grand Tours in their necessity for perfomance-enhancing drugs in order to compete. That was what I'd convinced myself anyway.

Now, looking back, with all the knowledge I have I can believe that a few special guys did compete and win clean against the dopers in the Classics (I don't believe it was possible in the Grand Tours during that time), but they were a minority. Of course, I didn't know that at the time (well, why would I?). Even the clean guys couldn't allow themselves public pride in winning the right way. Which, in a way, sums them up: the few that could do it were made of a different stuff, they were secure in themselves, they weren't affected by peer pressure, so at the same time they never needed to convince people of anything. They did it for themselves. It was never *omertà* for them, it was simply their nature. For a time, I was one of them

Classics riders are what we call 'one-day racers'. This title alone pretty much sums them up. They are obliged to be more aggressive in their style of racing because, contrary to stage racers, there is no tomorrow. Crossing the line in first place on that day is the only thing that matters. They have a 'he who dares wins' attitude. Every generation has its greats: the seventies had Roger De Vlaeminck; the eighties Sean Kelly; the nineties Johan Museeuw; and the peloton of today has Tom Boonen and Fabian Cancellara sharing the honours.

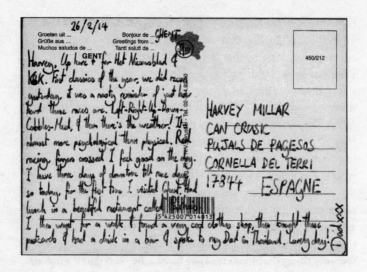

There's Nothing Quite Like Racing in Flanders

The first two Classics of the year are Het Nieuwsblad and Kuurne–Brussels–Kuurne. They're the first test for all the one-day specialists whose principal goals still remain a month away. The same guys whom I'd perceived to be trying to kill each other in Qatar all those years ago were actually just sparring in preparation for this opening weekend a few weeks later.

The races are mostly held in the Flanders region of Belgium. They do, on occasion, find themselves further afield, yet are still referred to as Flandrian in style. These are a particular type of race; they involve cobbles, small country lanes, steep hills, bad weather, muddy roads and about 342,105 corners. All one-day racers dream of one day being referred to as a Flandrian. This means you're one of the hard bastards who excels on that terrain.

The essentials of the Flandrian calendar are:

Omloop Het Nieuwsblad
Kuurne–Brussels–Kuurne

Dwars door Vlaanderen
E3 Harelbeke
Gent–Wevelgem
Three Days of De Panne
Tour of Flanders aka Ronde van Vlaanderen
Paris–Roubaix

Some professionals will base their whole season on this racing block alone – these are the proven and recognised Flandrians. Once Roubaix is completed in mid-April they will effectively end their season; they'll keep racing, but with none of the impetus, aggression or motivation that they showed from Qatar to Roubaix. Those of us who stage race through the summer find their lacka-daisical behaviour for the rest of the year near incomprehensible. It's as if they're in hibernation until they arrive on that start line in Qatar in January, ready to begin their annual three-month crazy-batshit phase.

The Flanders specialists seem to enjoy bad conditions; they have a skip in their step and a sparkle in their eyes when they wake up the morning of one of their beloved races and see wind and rain. Their enthusiasm for those six weeks of the year is uncontrollable and made all the more annoying by the fact you know that once Roubaix is done and dusted they're going to spend most of the rest of the season whinging about everything when everybody else has to keep their head in the game. It's clear their season's worth of mental energy burns brightly, and violently, for a very short period of time. The rest of us have to spread it out till October – we don't really stand a chance on their terrain. There are a few of those mad bastards who can spread it out through a whole racing season, but they're rare beasts, certainly not the norm.

I've grown to love the Classics. After spending so many years repeating the same races, season after season, it was a joy in 2010 to find myself thrown in among the Flandrians. I won the Three Days of De Panne and was racing the finale of Tour of Flanders with the favourites, something I had never thought I'd be doing. I discovered too late what I was maybe most suited to. Of course, the problem was my disdain for winters, which meant that truly I was never meant to be a Classics rider, no matter appearances.

There is nothing quite like racing in Flanders. I do believe it is the home of professional cycling. The atmosphere is unique – the enthusiasm the locals have is contagious. I get the impression that little has changed in decades; the fans are from all ages and backgrounds, and the races themselves are as chaotic and nonsensical as cycling. It beggars belief how it's possible to organise and marshal a Flanders race, for they go round in circles, figures of eight, back and forth. To quote Churchill, they're like a riddle, wrapped in a mystery, inside an enigma.

In order to be a specialist Classics rider it is not enough simply to have the right genetics and work ethic, and hit the right numbers in training then turn up as a contender – you have to know the roads intimately, much like a London taxi driver must possess the Knowledge. And not only do you have to be familiar with the route – you must be aware of every road that leads to and from it, the corners and turns, the cobbles and climbs. Each year the races will use these roads in slightly different combinations, and being able to know exactly where you're going next is a key ingredient to success.

For the uneducated, you will feel like you are trapped in a labyrinth, all sense of direction lost and absolutely no idea where you are in relation to where you have been or where you are going. You won't understand why all of a sudden everybody is racing like a maniac at what appears to be a random moment in the race, far from the finish. Then you'll see the lead cars and motorbikes far ahead veer to the left on to a single-track country lane, the front riders will follow close behind, sprinting out of the same corner in a scattered single file . . . while you're still braking in a densely packed bunch that feels miles behind. You may as well not be in the same race. That is what racing in Flanders is like.

Het Nieuwsblad this year lives up to its reputation: the weather is atrocious, barely going above five degrees all day and raining the last two hours. In these conditions there is very little you can do to prevent yourself getting cold – well, there is: you can wear a big jacket, but then you'll be dropped because the terrible aerodynamics will slow you down too much. I am far from setting the world on fire but manage to complete my assigned job and continue on to finish, which, considering the conditions, I am satisfied with. Ian Stannard of Team Sky, and a Brit no less, wins it, in the process becoming the latest pro to earn himself the moniker 'Flandrian' – something that Ian has always dreamt of the way others dream of winning the Tour de France.

The next day is Kuurne–Brussels–Kuurne. Although I've done Het Nieuwsblad in the past I have never doubled up and done Kuurne, too. I don't really know what to expect. In the end it's anti-climactic, as our leader for the race, Tyler Farrar, is involved in a crash and I am the man to get him back on, which involves a ten-kilometre chase back to the peloton to drop him off just before a key moment in the race, meaning my race is over. This isn't ideal, but it is often my job to fix things that go wrong for our leaders, and frequently that means sacrificing my own race in order to save theirs.

Road Captain

My role within the team has become more and more that of a road captain as the years have gone by. This is a natural progression that happens to many professionals who pass their peak yet are still capable of competing in the biggest races. I may have lost my ability to consistently deliver results, but at the same time I have such a depth of knowledge that I can read races better than anybody else in the team and have never been afraid to make decisions and call the shots on the road. Most importantly, at this point, I am still strong enough to be at the front of the race in key moments when the most important decisions have to be made.

In a way, I have always been a road captain. Even when I was a young pro at Cofidis I would be the one who made the tactical decisions on the road. The difference then was that I also had the responsibility to get the result at the end of the day, so most of the decisions I made were for my own benefit rather than the team's. Now, all the decisions I make represent what is best for the team rather than individuals. If we go to a race and we have a stand-out leader then we dedicate all our resources to him. But if he crashes or falls sick or simply isn't as good as expected, I have to come up with a plan B quickly.

When I was younger, and both leader and road captain, if things went wrong then there was no plan B. It was a two-edged sword: if I was going well and was motivated I lifted everybody up; but if I wasn't going well and wasn't motivated then everybody came down to my level, and there was nobody there to step in and take over the situation. For this reason it's always good to have a leader whom you can count upon to get the result and a captain to manage plan A and create plan B if necessary. Those decisions have to be made on the bike rather than from the following car because, more often than not, they unfold very quickly at key moments in the race, to the degree that the *directeur sportif* in the following car is unaware of what's happening.

There's also the fact that a good road captain stays on top of how his team is shaping up. It's all well and good having radios but they can't be trusted to work all the time, and you can't trust your riders to use them in the way they should. It's common practice when in bad shape during a race to simply ignore the radio – also, if you're feeling terrible the last thing you want to do is broadcast it to all your teammates and the following car. It's embarrassing to be the one who says, 'I'm not feeling good.' Without fail, you know all the other guys will be thinking, 'Of course you don't feel good, dickhead. It's fucking hard right now.' Plus every single one of us knows what message we'll get back from the *directeur sportif* in the following car if we admit that. 'Everyone feels bad, just hang on, it'll get better.' That's why a racer going through a bad patch will disappear deep into their pain cave hoping to be left to suffer alone in silence.

So, as a road captain, if you notice that one or more of your teammates aren't where they're supposed to be (i.e. near their leader or at the front of the bunch) then you go looking for them and talk to them and make a decision on what to use them for before they give up completely and are totally useless to the team.

More often than not when you feel bad in a race the best thing you can have your road captain do is come up and empathise and then give you a job. Simply being sent back for bottles can sometimes give a new lease of life, but more often than not riding on the front is the best solution because, psychologically, it's ten times better being at the front of the peloton – riding in the wind, controlling the effort and dishing out the suffering – than being back in the wheels feeling like you're being pummelled by everybody else, while listening to your internal monologue telling you repeatedly how much you suck and how it's just a matter of time before you're dropped like a stone.

It happens at the other end of the scale as well. Sometimes the leader will come up and tell the road captain they're not feeling good and that it's not their day. Often this has to be ignored. If they're a climber and the tactic is to place them at the front for the last climb then you simply tell them, 'Everyone feels bad, just hang on, it'll get better.' Then continue setting them up for the final climb. If it's a sprinter who comes up to you and tells you they're feeling terrible and the tactic is to chase down the break and set up a bunch sprint, you tell them, 'Everyone feels bad, just hang on, it'll get better.' Then continue chasing down the break to set up the bunch sprint. Generally you have to ignore how people feel, because even though we're elite athletes there are times when our perception of effort in a race is completely wrong. It's not unusual for the guy who wins to have endured a moment in that very race where he was convinced he'd get dropped and not even finish.

So my job in almost every race I go to now is road captain. It's good, up to a point, but there are times when it would be nice to just switch off from the race and be able to hide in the peloton. I appreciate now how easy I used to have it when I was younger, calling my own shots and not answering to anybody. Of course, being younger, I had no idea of that at the time.

Being Older

Making it through the first weekend in Belgium unscathed is a relief. We go up there prepared for the worst, be it weather or crashing. I wasn't very affected by the cold on the Saturday and avoided crashing on both days, which feels like my own little victory and means I head home in jubilant spirits. I've been away for almost a month. In the old days that would have been no bother whatsoever – it was part of the job and lifestyle. Since having children that's all changed. I'm now that old guy who says he wants to retire to spend more time with the family. Not so long ago I could not even begin to fathom why anybody would say that, let alone do it. I just couldn't believe that could happen. Racers can't talk about missing their wife and children, it's not very racer-like.

I remember being told by an older Italian pro back in my early years racing that he'd been advised by the legendary team manager Giancarlo Ferretti to marry and have children as soon as he could because it would give him a solid and stable home life, and therefore make him a better professional. Let me be clear that the only thing Ferretti was interested in was his rider being better on the bike, not being a wonderful family man; he wasn't exactly known for his warm and loving heart. For many young professionals this has been something they've done, and many still do. Getting married young is almost *de rigueur* in cycling.

There are a few reasons for this, I think: being madly, deeply, in love comes into it, I'm sure. But then there's also the fact that the mentality of many professionals is one that is attracted to stability and normality on the home front. It offers the perfect counter-balance to the professional life. So, in a way, Ferretti had a point. Certainly his motives were somewhat self-serving, but he wasn't exactly pushing water up a hill.

I got married later than most professionals, which was mainly to do with me taking longer to sort my shit out than others. I had never been a big fan of stability or normality. I didn't meet my wife until I'd totally burnt out the first part of my life and was at rock bottom. She was there when I began to reboot as a stand-up member of society rather than the twisted and damaged doper I had previously been. I was thirty-two when we got married, which is near retirement age in cycling years, and thirty-four when we had our first child, Archibald. In other words, I was totally off the back compared to my peers.

In hindsight this was a good thing because, in contrast to the ascending performance spiral most racers enter when they have children, I had entered a spiral that was slowly descending. Everything that I had thought was so important seemed far less so, now that I had this little miracle in my life.

I had always been the guy on the team up for anything. I had raced a crazy amount the previous years, I was one of the few riders who could be sent to almost any race and be relied upon to perform. I considered it my duty to always be there for my team and give them my all; that was my job and I would do it to the best of my abilities and be respected because I could be relied upon. I had become a bona fide jack of all trades and enjoyed it more than ever before. I couldn't really imagine a time when I'd stop, and found it mind-boggling that any professional would retire from the sport when they were still physically capable of doing the job. Hearing of guys who were tired of being on the road and losing the drive to race wasn't unusual, but it was a completely alien concept to me. Then I became a father and it all went pear-shaped.

No matter how much we're told having children will change us I don't think we can ever prepare for it. I always presumed I'd be able to manage it, yet I had forgotten that presumption is the mother of all fuck-ups. In a nutshell, I gradually began to enjoy being a father more than I did being a pro cyclist.

Being a pro cyclist is never a smooth affair. When we're healthy and fit and motivated we're able to revel in our job, the training is challenging, and even when the racing is stupendously hard it can be fun. From the outside people probably think it's like that all the time. It isn't. If it were I wouldn't get annoyed when people say, 'It's not a job! You get to ride your bike every day.' Somehow I don't think professional cycling would exist if it was simply done for the fun of it.

Most of the time we're chasing form, living in constant pursuit of maximal fitness and ideal race weight, walking a tight-rope between fuelling and dieting and training and recovering. It breeds neuroses. And that's just the training. I've seen more than my fair share of pro cyclists develop eating disorders or overtraining syndrome. I've suffered from both in my time but, fortunately, having done it for so long, what was once a regime has become a lifestyle. But therein lies the problem for every older pro: finally, just as we begin to master our profession, we run out of time. Becoming a father at the end of my career put everything into perspective, when the last thing I needed in my life as a professional cyclist was perspective. The racer in me was much better off living in his little bubble, floating around unaffected by the world at large and all that went with it.

When we are younger and at the foot of the mountain, like Tao Geoghegan Hart, we only care about one thing: and that is to climb the mountain. Everything else in our lives is there to aid us on our journey, we make choices that some would consider sacrifices but in truth are nothing of the sort. They are decisions, each one helping us further on our way – they only start to be thought of as sacrifices when things start to go wrong, because if you make it to the top then each decision will have proved to be the right one. Our perspective is narrow, and it is almost always completely selfish. I have seen it time and time again: the best pro cyclists have an incredible ability not to deviate from their own personal goal, nothing can interrupt them, they're simply not affected by their environment. They only do what needs to be done in order to achieve what they're focused on. I suppose this is the same with the majority of very successful people. Unfortunately, it does often make for quite odd individuals who start to live in a tunnel of their own making.

I have no doubt I have been that sort of person in my life. I owe much of the success I've had to that type of behaviour. The problem I have now is that being a father has made it very difficult for me to be the selfish, crazy person I need to be in order to operate at my highest level as a pro. Over this last winter I've beaten myself up for not having the same drive I'm accustomed to. I couldn't motivate myself to be the self-serving professional I needed to be. I presumed I'd just let myself go, and yet that didn't add up because I'd never felt more in control of my life. So I must have been doing something right? I got myself into such a state of confusion that I came to the conclusion I needed to talk to the man who always has the answers for me: the psychiatrist Dr Steve Peters.

Dave Brailsford was the first person I spoke to on leaving police custody in Biarritz in 2004. He was there waiting for me when I left the police station having confessed to doping after forty-eight hours locked up. Dave realised he couldn't help me, so he flew Steve Peters over from the UK to spend a day with me, as he didn't know what else to do. After the police, and then Dave, Steve was the first person I spoke to in depth about everything I'd done. We spent a full day together. I spent the morning answering his questions, and then the afternoon listening to him. He explained to me that the person I was and the life I'd lived – the circumstances I had found myself in – had resulted in the decisions I'd made, good and bad. It didn't justify anything, but it was a massive help for me to be able to look back in a rational manner, to understand for the first time the hows and whys of my life up to that point.

That has been something I've carried with me ever since. I'd only spoken to Steve twice since then, but both times I'd learnt things. He'd taught me to recognise the difference between my emotional feelings and my rational thought – something I'd been clueless about in the past – and I was suddenly able to see that many of my decisions had been purely emotion-based. Our relationship started with him helping me understand my past; since then it's been about handling the present and preparing for the future.

So, I trusted him, and he'd always made sense. This time around, in 2013, I explained everything I was going through, and asked him why I found it so difficult to do what in the past I'd found so easy. His answer surprised me in its simplicity: 'David, you're not the same person you were before, there is absolutely no point in comparing yourself to him. Your brainwaves and chemistry are no doubt different. It has been shown to happen with age, and especially fatherhood.'

That's that then. I'm old.

Postcards/Killing Me Softly

Now one of my biggest focuses when away racing is tracking down postcards to send to my sons. This is harder than it sounds as postcards aren't found quite as easily as they once were. It's become my thing, the team staff know to keep their eye out if they get to a stage start or finish and have a bit of spare time, and the bus driver is now accustomed to me occasionally having the team bus pull up outside a shop that I have an inkling may sell them. It's also a common occurrence to find me wandering around some random village or town the evening of a race in my team tracksuit postcard hunting. It's bordering on obsessive behaviour. It's probably the last bastion of obsessiveness in my pro cycling. I do it because I've faced the fact that my boys will never remember seeing me race, and yet this part of my life will be what shapes much of our futures. I thought the closest I could come to having them there with me on the races would be to send them postcards from every race I went to. This ended up going beyond that and becoming a ritual where I would send them postcards whenever I left home. It's become something unexpected: a diary of my final years as a professional. Writing them allows me to stand back and see where I am in the here and now, but also where I have been, because I've already been to every race and place I send them from.

Archibald has nearly a hundred postcards, and not many among them talk of me dominating the race. There are a small handful in which I get the opportunity to regale him with my exploits, but they are few and far between. During these last two years I've spent more time being made to suffer than making people suffer. I'm slowly, and softly, being killed off. I can see it when I read through all the postcards. The decline is apparent.

Film (1)

When I'm not hunting down postcards, or writing postcards, I'm thinking about film. There is a project I've been working on for a while – with the Scottish director Finlay Pretsell – making a film about professional cycling. Myself and Finlay both share a similar vision in wanting to capture what it's really like in the modern peloton. On top of this, over the winter I've been involved as a consultant on the Lance Armstrong movie, *The Program*. On a slightly melancholic drive up Alpe d'Huez with the director Stephen Frears, and over the course of a subsequent two weeks' shooting, I began to see how the world I lived in, and had grown up in, appeared through the eyes of an outsider. I began to see how much everything had changed. It was wholly weird, watching everything my generation had been through condensed down to its essence in order to tell the story in the simplest way possible. In many respects the time I spent working on that movie was more cathartic than anything else I'd done – but it was also like watching deforestation. Unlike books, this is what film does: everything has to be cut back. There are weeks, months, sometimes years of preparation, of writing, planning and filming; growing the forest in other words. Then, the moment the last tree is planted, the cutting begins. All that time and effort succumbs to the brutality of reduction. The bare minimum is left: you can watch a film and be totally convinced you have understood the story, then you read the book and realise there were a thousand other components.

The Race to the Sun or the Race of the Two Seas?

March, the final month of preparation for many, brings two key races used for the final polishing of form. In France there's Paris–Nice, 'the Race to the Sun'; in Italy there's Tirreno–Adriatico, aka 'the Race of the Two Seas'. Most people try to get on the Tirreno programme, which is perceived to be a better experience than Paris–Nice. This is mainly a weather-based preference, because more often than not the weather is properly shite at Paris–Nice: cold, wet and windy. To add insult to inclemency the hotels and restaurants are the bad side of mediocre; the final slap in the face being the fact we race it so hard, it can hardly be called a preparation race any more – it's very full-on, borderline heart-explodingly intense at times. Post-race analysis of the previous years has shown that on occasions Paris–Nice has generated some of the biggest power files of the season.

Tirreno, on the other hand, has managed to maintain some sort of decorum. The peloton is mainly made up of one-day specialists who are there to add the final touches to their condition. Normally the weather is good and the hotels are the better side of mediocre; compared to France, we eat like kings.

This doesn't mean Tirreno has always been my natural port of call come March; my career has seen me start a near equal number of times in each race. Although Tirreno would be the natural choice for any sane person I have always preferred Paris–Nice. For some reason I get some allergic reaction to Tirreno. Four times I have stopped it on the first or second day – once I didn't even start – each time due to me developing some strange respiratory reaction which leaves me with all the symptoms of bronchitis. It's an allergic reaction I only get in Italy. As my career has gone on I have learnt to use antihistamines and Ventolin when going there, but even then it doesn't always prevent it. So, the horrors of Paris–Nice are more appealing to me than the risk of turning into a coughing and spluttering mess in Tirreno–Adriatico.

So why on earth did I choose Tirreno–Adriatico for my final season? Well, that had more to do with film.

Finlay and I had approached the UCI in the winter about using onboard cameras – essentially having our own camera motorbike in races to follow me and capture images that haven't been seen before. Up to this point onboard cameras hadn't been officially used in a top-level UCI race, so we were the first to gain dispensation for this and paved the way for the more wide-spread use of them. We were essentially the UCI test project. And Tirreno–Adriatico was the proposed stage. We had two more hurdles to overcome before being able to begin filming: the first was getting permission from the race organisers to film in their races; and the second, surprisingly, was permission from my team to allow me to do so.

Big Money C***s

The race organiser decides everything that happens within their race except the TV rights, which is dependent on the deal they have struck with the company that will produce and broadcast the images from the race. Most of the big races in France are owned by the ASO (the Amaury Sport Organisation) – they are part of a larger media group and have an exclusive deal with France Television who own, along with ASO, all images captured within their races. To the point that if you were sitting in a following car at the Tour de France you are not allowed to film or take pictures without having come to an agreement with ASO and France Television. This would normally be a very expensive agreement.

This is one of the fundamental problems with professional cycling today: there is no revenue sharing between teams and race organisers. Each team is its own island within the sport. There is very little if any money coming in from outside of what the team itself can generate.

Merchandising isn't exactly the money-spinner it may be in other sports. Each team's identity is changing on such a regular basis – new sponsors require the team they sponsor to adhere to their corporate colours and use their name, making it difficult for a fan to show loyalty and long-term affiliation when there isn't really any of that on display in the constantly changing landscape of team identity. Why would you buy a jersey to show support for a rider or team when for all you know the next year that same rider or team will more than likely be sporting a new, completely different kit?

Another big problem often forgotten about in professional cycling is the fact it doesn't take place in stadiums or closed circuits but on public roads, so teams and race organisers can't sell tickets, one of the reliable revenue streams in other sports. A few teams are now majority owned by bike manufacturers, but again this is financed out of their marketing budget and is at the whim of the commercial marketplace: if they stop selling enough bikes to fund their team they will simply shut it down or make it smaller. There is very little structure within professional cycling to look after the common good and long-term existence of teams. For this reason rider contracts are commonly short term, and the culture is a mercurial one; ultimately it's in everyone's interest to look after themselves rather than each other. Add to that the fact there isn't a strong rider union and you find yourself understanding a bit better the reason why professional cycling is very much a dog-eat-dog world.

Teams are therefore funded by sponsors alone, or, more commonly these days, a rich benefactor, the ultimate example of this being BMC, which stands for Bicycle Manufacturing Company; or, as Ryder and I christened them after spending an afternoon sitting by a pool on a Tour de France rest day staring at their truck in the car park, discussing their existence: Big Money Cunts. They have one of the biggest annual budgets in cycling, around thirty million euros, courtesy of Andy Rihs, the billionaire Swiss owner who happened to have a bike manufacturer in his portfolio and so made it the title sponsor, something no other bike sponsor was capable of doing at the time.

More than a quarter of the teams in cycling's uppermost echelon, the World Tour, are backed by what are, frankly, billionaire fans. This isn't much different from football, although unlike football there is next to no equity in a cycling team. You will put more money in than you take out unless you are benefiting directly from the increased brand awareness that a successful team can produce for its sponsor. So Andy Rihs was slightly ahead of the game, his investment having turned a relatively small bike company into a global player. Unlike other billionaires who will put one of their companies on the team jersey and in the team name but then hope to amortise their spending by bringing on another outside sponsor, Rihs went the whole hog, in for a penny in for a pound. It would appear he doesn't see why anybody else should benefit from the significant sums he has personally chosen to invest in his passion. Fair enough, if you have the means.

As a result, cycling, even at its highest level, is forever at the whim of a handful of individuals. There is no clear long-term system in place that allows for teams to be sure of their continuation. Therefore the same is true for the cyclists, and even the races. More and more races are disappearing off the calendar as local government backing is withdrawn due to the economic crisis or because long-term sponsors can't increase their funding in direct correlation with the constant increase in costs. When I turned professional in 1997 it would have been possible to race a full season in Spain, as their race calendar was spread across the year and, amazingly, almost all of those races were shown live on national television. Now there are but a handful of races in Spain, and many of those are in a precarious financial state.

The paradox in all of this is that cycling is perhaps more popular than it has been in decades. The level of participation is up, and in the English-speaking world it is beginning to challenge, if not overtake, golf as the corporate sport of choice. The professional racing side of the sport has not kept up with this boom in the recreational and business side. The calendar is disjointed and confusing to say the least; it has become a global sport and yet remains far too provincial in its workings.

The most obvious and easiest way to witness this is in the way cycling coverage is produced for television. Onboard cameras have become the norm in almost all 'wheeled' sports for years now, yet had been banned by the UCI until Finlay and I negotiated our dispensation. Of course, this was mainly due to the technology not existing until recently as, contrary to motor sports, for cycling use everything must be very small, lightweight, extremely robust and, most importantly, rely on its own battery. Yet no research and development had taken place in anticipation of what was inevitable. Professional cycling until now has only ever been seen through the lens of a cameraman perched on the back of a motorbike or an overhead helicopter. Most races will have only two, maybe three, TV motorbikes; the biggest races will have five. There will be a fixed camera beyond the finish line to capture the final sprint, and maybe one or two more in the final 500 metres if, again, it's a big race. In other words everything the viewer will see is from a distance; there is no real sense of what the sport actually entails. Watching a bunch sprint from an overhead helicopter image or a long-shot fixed camera is all well and good but it doesn't really capture what's going on: the proximity of the riders, the jostling and shouting, the panic of some and the coolness of others in among what is, at times, total chaos. A bunch sprint appears to have some sort of natural order when watched from afar, but when you're in there it's like being on the scariest roller coaster known to man, and there's not just one but dozens of roller coasters, careering along next to each other, and they're not on rails. I think it's a shame people don't get to experience that. I've seen Mark Cavendish do things in the chaos leading into a bunch sprint that defy belief.

Cav

Mark's ability to maintain his cool when all around him lose theirs is, next to his innate natural speed, the reason he is one of the greatest sprinters in the history of the sport. It is extremely rare for him to make a mistake, which is all the more remarkable when you've experienced how frantic and uncontrollable it is up there at the front of the peloton in those final kilometres leading into a *sprint massif*.

Most sprinters spend most of their career making mistakes and rarely finding themselves in a position to actually sprint for the finish line. They will have been quacked off a wheel or have chosen the wrong tactic or simply panicked and got it wrong. That's the difference between the good and the great sprinters: the great are consistently finding their way through the mêlée to fight it out between each other for the line. It doesn't matter if you're the fastest sprinter in the world, if you can't be where you need to be when the sprint begins with 250 metres to go then you don't stand a chance.

All we see on TV is the final sprint, not the battle that's been going on during the preceding kilometres, where all the interesting stuff happens. Often by the time the final sprint begins most of the riders are already at or near their maximum effort. If you're not a sprinter you simply can't comprehend how those guys are even capable of going faster. For the majority of the peloton it would be impossible to even get out of the saddle at that point, let alone sprint out the saddle and increase the speed. It's a particular physiological gift being able to sprint like that; you have to possess the human equivalent of a nitro button – they hit their VO2 max and then sprint.

It's for this reason Mark is infamous for being 'himself' when he is interviewed immediately after a bunch sprint. The moment he crosses that finish line all the rational thinking is thrown out the window, and he becomes the irrational, emotional Mark that he was holding at bay those final kilometres in order to remain lucid and make the right decisions. The floodgates are opened the moment the line is crossed and he can flip the kill switch.

Neither of those personalities are truly representative of Mark. He exists most of the time closer to the rational side rather than the emotional side, but the racing brings out the extremes in him, as it does most of us. Fortunately most of us aren't Mark Cavendish, or there'd be a whole peloton involved in a mixture of mass brawls and group hugs immediately after every finish line. One thing's for sure: if we were all like Cav the journalists in the finish zone would be sporting full riot gear and trained in hostage-negotiation techniques in preparation for the spitfire interviews, each one a book in itself.

Film (2)

It was to capture all this – the jostling, the shouting, the panic; what goes on, what you can't catch from a helicopter – that so motivated us to make a film. We considered there to be so much that people still didn't know about cycling. The preparation had gone on between Finlay and me for years, ever since I'd seen his short film *Standing Start*, about the track cyclist Craig MacLean. Although barely fifteen minutes long it felt closer to the reality of cycling than anything else I'd ever seen; it felt like a first-person experience, the intensity of it all counter-balanced perfectly by the poetic narration. It made me believe Finlay could do the same for road cycling.

Finlay had already visited races and had filmed here and there, experimenting with the director of photography, Martin Radich, to get a feeling of what would and wouldn't work. The financing phase had been accelerated with the knowledge that this was my last year racing; there was no longer any time left to talk about it, it now had to be filmed. We had an opportunity to capture footage nobody had ever seen before and with Finlay and Martin's skill make it into something that was different from your usual fly-on-the-wall documentary, something none of us were interested in doing.

We quickly learnt the reason why so few films had been made about cycling. Corralling all the relevant parties and getting them to agree to anything was unbelievably difficult. This was mainly down to there being so many unrelated stakeholders – the teams, organisers, governing bodies, cyclists, sponsors, media – each one stands alone and we had to get permission from each group separately, and inevitably each group would be different for each race. It was a challenge to say the least, and it would have been impossible if I hadn't been so involved and wanting the film to be made, because at times it felt like nobody in the world of cycling was interested in the slightest. Even my own team made it as difficult as humanly possible, enforcing a very strict contract limiting what could be filmed and demanding control of the final edit. They only delivered that contract a few days before we were to start filming at Tirreno, adding that little bit more stress that all of us could have done without.

Team Time Trialling

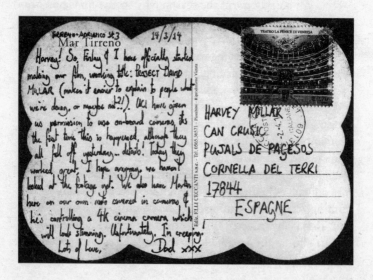

Tirreno started with a team time trial. Unfortunately my team didn't allow us to use onboard cameras, as they thought they would compromise the aerodynamics, which was a shame because the least of our problems was lipstick-sized cameras attached to handlebars or under saddles. It wasn't a surprise to me that we were less than average in our team time-trial performance. The team was no longer what it once had been.

We used to be amazing at team time trials at Garmin; there were only really two places we'd consistently finish – first or second. From 2008 to 2011 we were the gold standard to which other teams would aspire. It was thanks to Jonathan Vaughters' recruitment policy of signing time-trial specialists that we had built such a strong group those first few years. Our greatest ever team time-trial performance was no doubt the 2009 Tour de France, Stage 4. I say 'greatest', but I also mean the hardest and most disappointing.

It was a thirty-nine-kilometre loop starting and finishing in Montpellier. The first twenty-one kilometres were super-technical, mostly on a country road that twisted left and right, with barely a section of flat. This was very un-Tour de France-like; in the past the majority of Tour team time trials I'd done had been point-to-point on big roads, and mostly flat. This was much different. The final eighteen kilometres were more traditional in that they banged it down a *route principal* straight back into Montpellier.

Leaving Montpellier was already a challenge; it was twisty, as you would expect a ride out from a small city to be – in other words, a bit shit. Already, even before breaking through the suburbs the route was taking us up and down, left and right, then only a couple of kilometres after leaving town we tackled the longest climb of the course. It wasn't actually that long, only 1.5 kilometres or so, but long enough to basically rip our team to pieces and leave us with the bare minimum of five riders at the summit.

The only way to stand a chance of winning a team time trial at the highest level is to go very fast right from the beginning.

This means that the weaker guys in the team are going to be over their limit and in the red zone almost immediately – which can be managed if the course isn't very challenging. The problems arise when the road starts to go uphill or there are lots of corners. Corners involve deceleration followed by acceleration. In Grand Tours there are nine-man teams; that makes for quite a long line of riders, enough to make for a considerable concertina effect through tight turns. The goal is to be fast and smooth through corners; a mantra we would always be repeating to each other in training was 'Remember – Truck and Trailer'. This would remind us to think about our trailer, to try to choose the smoothest line possible: not necessarily the racing apex you'd use in an individual time trial but a line that wouldn't be so extreme as to force errors behind, which would lead to sudden braking and gaps being opened up.

Whoever takes the team into a corner is responsible for taking the team out, so you'll often see the front rider in a team time trial exiting a corner looking over his shoulder making sure everybody has made it through safely and the team is in tight formation before beginning the acceleration back up to speed. The bottom line being that the further down the line you are the bigger the acceleration you'll have to make because you'll have lost the most speed through the corner (although the lead rider won't have to brake much, if at all, the no. 2 rider will brake a bit more, no. 3 a bit more than no. 2, and so on). The best teams are made up of guys who have trained together on their time-trial bikes and trust each other implicitly, because ultimately that's what it comes down: you have to believe the guy in front of you is not going to fuck it up and cause you to crash or force you to brake abruptly. The final time is taken from the fifth rider to cross the line, which means you can afford to drop no more than four of your team along the way.

Within that 2009 Tour de France team we had four pure specialists: Bradley Wiggins, Dave Zabriskie, Christian Vande Velde and myself. The four of us were at the top of our game;

it meant that we absorbed the first few kilometres of corners and up and down roads without much problem, although VdV was already smashing it on certain sections, which filled me with dread as normally he always erred on the side of caution for the first half of team time trials.

It was no time until we were at the bottom of the longest climb, which would lead us into the really technical hilly section. Already at the bottom two guys peeled off, then halfway up Danny Pate pulled off (we had expected him to be one of our stronger riders). I can still remember him switching to the left side of the road and giving up and Christian shouting: 'Don't you fucking dare, Danny!' To all intents and purposes it was going pear-shaped. A couple of hundred metres later we lost another rider. Whitey came on the radio through our earpieces, 'Ryder, you're number five now. You gotta stick with them. COME ON, RYDER! All right, boys, this is it, it's just you four now.'

I'll never forget that moment. We all had a split second to soak it up and accept we now had thirty kilometres to race as four riders, plus Ryder, against mostly nine-man teams. As we passed each other in the rotation we gave each other looks of 'How the fuck are we going to do this?' There wasn't any talking because we couldn't talk. I, for one, was already peaking out. I'm guessing we were all the same.

That's the thing with team time trials: it's horrible for all of you. People tend to think it must be easier for specialists but, in truth, it's the other way round. The specialist has to lift the team, do longer turns on the front, bring the speed back up when it's dropped, and not miss a turn; that's what's expected of them, it's their responsibility to not flake out. Now there were four of us having to shoulder all hopes, and no way out. Ryder was our fifth man. We didn't expect him to ride with us as he isn't a specialist, and we couldn't risk blowing him up and losing him. There was also the fact that the four of us were so equally matched that bringing Ryder in would have unbalanced our rotation.

Being down to effectively four men with so far to go was horrible – at least when there's more of you it's possible to trick yourself into thinking there's a chance of escape. But we were now committed, the clock would only stop when all of us including Ryder crossed the line. Whatever happened we were now stuck together – crash, puncture, blackout, didn't matter, we'd have to bring it home.

Each one of us started doing longer turns. Whitey stayed calm on the radio, controlling what each of us did: 'Take them to the top of this one, Dave. Get it over the crest, come on, GET IT OVER! Nice work, Dave. Now you get it up to speed, Zab, you know what to do. Ryder, just stay where you are, we need you.' Whitey is the guy you want on the radio when the shit hits the fan. He always keeps it calm and knows each of us well enough to know what needs to be said and when.

Going under the twenty-five-kilometres-to-go banner was soul-destroying. It seemed impossible to think we could keep doing what we were doing for that long. It was then that we were all thankful for the technical country road, because it allowed us to focus on something else beyond the effort – the pace was constantly changing, we were moving from one end of the block to the other on our gears, some of the corners were sketchy enough to actually spike us with a tiny bit of adrenalin, the technical and handling aspects were almost requiring as much application as the physical effort.

Then, with eighteen kilometres to go, we turned on to the big road that would take us home, and the purgatory truly began.

The road was the straightest route back to Montpellier. The only obstacles in our way were some large roundabouts, which barely slowed us down. The latest time check indicated we had the second fastest time on the road, eighteen seconds behind Lance Armstrong and Alberto Contador's Astana team. It made no difference what the time check was; we couldn't do anything about it, each of us was giving our maximum – it even felt more than our maximum because we would never be able to go so hard on our own. We were raising each other to a level we didn't know was attainable.

In an individual time trial you have to constantly monitor your effort and avoid going too far in the red, otherwise you risk blowing up and losing power while your body recovers itself back to a manageable state. In theory a perfect effort is where you have been sitting on or just below your threshold the whole time, only daring to push yourself over it when you are sure there is a descent coming up which will allow you to recover, or the finish is near and you can time the explosion within sight of it.

This isn't the case in team time trials. Every time you hit the front you go into the red, because the power you have to produce is above and beyond what you would do individually. I may be putting out around 450 watts on the flat in an individual time trial, compared to 550+ watts on the flat when hitting the front in a team time trial. The only reason this is possible is because the effort lasts approximately forty-five seconds to one minute each time. Then there is recovery time while in the slip-stream of your teammates; in practice you are on the cusp of exploding when you latch on to the back of the line and only recover once in position two or three. For this reason it's better to have a complete team for as long as possible; this allows for more recovery time from the moment you latch on to the back of the line and slowly move up positions protected by the slipstream of the riders in front of you, until it's your turn again to hit the front and begin the horrible effort once more. With only four out of five of us rotating we were never fully recovering. There was never the feeling you come to expect in team time trials of being over and under your threshold – we were either over it or on it. We were going very, very deep.

On the way back it was more a case of holding our momentum. There were no technicalities on that return stretch of road to rub our speed off, so we each knew the only thing we could do was keep our heads down and refuse to let the speed drop.

On the right day each of us individually had proved to be one of the fastest bike riders in the world. We'd all won major time trials, all been part of winning team-trial squads. I'm quite sure that's what made us believe we could do it against all odds. I think that's what each of us was thinking – there weren't three other bike racers in the world I'd have rather been with for those final twenty minutes.

What was weird was how similar we all looked on the bike. Each of us had worked hard to develop our aerodynamic speed, none of us were big fans of wind tunnels, we just had the feel for it. We'd learnt to hide from the wind, tucking our heads down, rolling our shoulders in, and tucking our arms and hands as narrow as we could, all in order to shrink our frontal area. Beyond the actual positions each of us had we also pedalled with the classic old-school time-trial specialist's smooth style, always keeping our cadences high even when entering a state of total fubar. Poor Ryder, on the other hand, was in a world of hurt at the back, the fifth man hanging on for dear life.

In an individual time trial we have an empty road in front of us, and we only have to apply ourselves on corners, where the entry/apex/exit are all-important; the rest of the time we can pick and choose our own line on the road without any undue concern. But in any team time trial a racer's visual point of reference continually changes; in the final phase of a team time trial it becomes completely narrowed to the smallest of areas. Once our turn is done, and we begin the horrible process of dropping down the line readying ourselves for the explosion of effort to latch back on to the rear, we count the riders who pass us (so far we have only had to count three for the majority of the race, so that bit is relatively easy). As the second rider passes we prepare ourselves to accelerate so we can make it back into the lineout without missing the third rider's slipstream, which means beginning that move as soon as the second rider comes by. This is when you hope beyond hope that the rider who has taken the front isn't accelerating at the same time, otherwise it will be even more difficult to slot back in as you're already at your maximal effort. We all know this, and so, if we accelerate, we only do so when we know everybody is in formation.

Once you latch back in you are so blown to pieces that the only thing you care about and focus on is that precious wheel of the rider in front of you. The first minute is excruciating, as you're still putting out near threshold power, so it takes your body that much longer to recuperate. During that time you just stare down at the gap between your front wheel and the back wheel you cannot – will not – lose. There's probably only an inch or so separating the two wheels, and we don't have the option of braking as we're in our aero tucks, where there are only gear shifters rather than brake levers. We're near delirious from the effort, while teetering on the edge of a crash, so that first minute all you think about is that tiny gap, and trying to keep it as small as possible to reap maximum benefit from the slipstream. By the time the next rider drops back and makes your rear wheel their focus you already begin to feel like you're not going to die. You begin to lift your head a little in order to catch in your peripheral vision the rider two positions in front. Readying yourself for the cycle to begin all over again.

But in 2009, on those final five kilometres, Zab and I were beyond fucked. We didn't miss turns, but they became shorter; Christian was as strong as he had been from the beginning, while Brad had been doing longer and longer turns, lifting the load Zab and I could no longer carry.

With two kilometres to go we went up a very little hill. We were still on the main road we'd been on for the previous sixteen kilometres – normally the slope would have been a bump rather than the wall it resembled as we approached. As I peeled off from my turn at the bottom and Christian came by me I managed, in total desperation, to order him, 'Don't stand up, Christian.' I knew he had the power and wherewithal to stand up out the saddle and smash on the pedals in one final take-it-home effort. I knew that would send Zab and me out the back. We were completely broken by this point.

I can't remember those last two kilometres. We crossed the line and I didn't even stop. I was too dazed and didn't have the strength to unclip, let alone get off my bike, so kept rolling through all the people and past all the teams and out into the non-Tour de France part of the world. I think I was gone ten minutes. Again, I can't remember much about that. Finally, I got back to the team, where all the guys were sitting there at the side of the road by the team cars with wet towels on their heads, as it was so hot and we were so overheated. They all looked like me: none of us could quite register what we'd just done. I wasn't able to eat anything for seven hours, my body was in such shock. I think it was the deepest I ever went in a race.

Astana ended up winning by eighteen seconds, putting us in second place. With a full team they hadn't taken back one second from us in those final eighteen kilometres. Few things I've done as a professional cyclist have left me feeling so proud. And we didn't even win.

That Was Then . . .

That team is gone now, and we have a different team, one that is better at other things. Unfortunately the team management hasn't quite accepted that team time trialling is no longer 'our thing'. So

71

they expect the results of old yet don't have the specialist riders required. What's most ridiculous about it is that almost no training is done to make the team better. It's almost become a self-fulfilling prophecy; as the team has slowly declined in team time trials, less effort has been put into recruitment or specific work in training, and the only thing that we have left from our golden years of team time trialling is the expectation. So for some reason beyond my comprehension, Garmin's Charly Wegelius and Jonathan Vaughters still think we're going to do well, and are shocked when we don't.

We definitely sucked at Tirreno this year – eighteenth out of twenty-two teams. We could have crashed and done better than that back in the day, not that we ever used to crash in team time trials – that's something the team does quite often of late – so, in a way, eighteenth without crashing is a bit of a bonus (it's clear our standards have fallen). It's for this reason I was a little angry about not being able to have cameras on the bikes for the team time trial, because at least then we'd have felt like we got something from the day's racing.

The bright side of a poor performance in a first-stage team time trial is that there's really not much to do the following days. There are enough teams ahead of us with bigger responsibilities and the right to assume position at the front of the peloton that we're left to scuttle around keeping out of trouble and awaiting the next general classification shake up. This suits most of us as we're only at Tirreno to get ready for the remaining, and most important, Flanders Classics, so we don't have the pressure of protecting a general classification rider or controlling the race.

And, anyhow, my biggest motivation was making sure I got some decent material for the film, which first of all meant getting used to having my very own camera-equipped motorbike following me around every day; on top of that I permanently wore a microphone, while my bike was carrying onboard cameras. I wasn't exactly keeping a low profile.

The motorbike itself was impressively set up, cameras fixed to the front and sides and a fully stabilised cinema-quality camera on the back on a rig so that Martin could position himself facing backwards in order to control it. The motorbike pilot – 'pilot' because that's what he resembled: 'rider' simply doesn't do him justice – is a Frenchman called Patrice. He has more than twenty Tours under his belt and is sporting the sort of moustache last seen in the RAF during the Second World War. He sings (in French) through the helmet intercom, only breaking it up when catching sight of something at the side of the road that reminds him of an adventure that Martin absolutely must be told about. His English is perfect, made all the more so by his fantastical French accent. He is from another time, an absolutely brilliant *pilote de moto* and, most importantly, has no fucks to give.

Martin on the other hand is a very quiet man; he would have happily sat on the back of that motorbike in complete silence for the duration of even the longest day (Stage 4 – 244 kilometres); he's a studious listener. Cinematography is his primary love, but his passions encompass books, film, music and art. Somehow he gets bike racing very quickly. Having had no previous knowledge, he is seeing it all with fresh eyes and no preconceptions. He is seeing it and filming it in a way that none of us has ever witnessed before.

It takes me a couple of days to get used to Patrice and Martin hanging around all the time. The first day was a bit embarrassing, as the motorbike was carrying so much electronics that it created a blocking signal around it, meaning that everyone in the vicinity stopped receiving data on whatever device they were relying upon. I was sitting not too far from the front, hovering around, making it easy for Martin to get me in shot. Cav had his team riding up there, as he had the leader's jersey and wanted to win the stage. After a while I could see discussions beginning up and down the line of his team. Cav being Cav, he figured it out pretty quickly. He went and 'had a word' with Martin. The next day they disconnected some of the radios on the motorbike. Nobody likes being told off by Mark Cavendish – the only saving grace is he'll always come back later and apologise profusely, so Martin and Cav were friends for life by Stage 3.

Fortunately, I'm big enough and old enough not to worry too much about what people think. The younger me would have been far too concerned about having the piss taken out of him, or, worse, bullied out of it, to have thought it was a good idea. In truth there was nobody left to take the piss or bully me. They'd all retired. I was at the top of the food chain.

Fortunately for me, although not so much for Martin and Finlay, the race as a whole was fantastically uneventful. I switched my head into using the race as a training exercise and made sure I did just the right amount of work to have me coming out of it feeling good for the following month. I definitely wanted to avoid doing so much that I'd weaken myself sufficiently to succumb to illness as in previous editions. All of which was frustrating for Finlay, as he wanted to get images of me off the front of the race, but I couldn't do it. I knew my primary job was to think ahead – no matter how much time, effort and money had been put into the film, I still had to do what was professional.

To complete the race feeling healthy and in form was a major success. I'd almost go as far to claim it to be the greatest

Tirreno–Adriatico of my career. I finished eighty-third. Success comes in all shapes and colours.

La Classicissima di Primavera

Milan–San Remo is the first of the five one-day races held throughout the season and referred to as the 'Monuments' of cycling. They've all been around for more than a century, and if you can win one of these in your career then you will be considered a great of the sport. As successful as British Cycling is we have only won four Monuments in those 100-plus years; three of those were won by Tommy Simpson in the sixties, the other by Mark Cavendish – and those two are also the only British riders to have won the World Championships Road Race, arguably the sixth Monument. (The other Monuments are the Tour of Flanders, then Paris–Roubaix followed by Liège–Bastogne–Liège to close the start of the season. The final Monument of the year, and considered by many to be the final race of the year, is the Tour of Lombardy in October.)

Apart from their longevity, the Monuments all have one thing in common: they all have distances of over 250 kilometres, which is a remnant of ye olde bike racing when the distances were massive – for example, the first Tour de France in 1903 was just under 2,500 kilometres and consisted of a scant six stages: that makes for an average of just over 400 kilometres per stage. That's what cycling was originally: expeditionary in its nature.

Milan–San Remo takes the biscuit for the modern era, with its 294 kilometres, a long way to drive a car let alone race a bike. And yet it's considered the easiest of the Monuments to finish. This is because the majority of the race is on big, flat, straight roads, and, because of the length, everybody is scared to make any effort until it's absolutely necessary, as the race is almost always decided in the final thirty kilometres, and more often than that in the last ten.

Milan–San Remo has always been one of my favourite races to watch – it seems so perfect in the way it has such a clearly defined finale. Yes, the race is 294 kilometres long, but ultimately there are only four kilometres that matter, and they begin after 284 kilometres, at the foot of the final climb, the Poggio. As a teenager beginning to follow pro cycling from Hong Kong (on a video, months after the actual race, of course), I remember Maurizio Fondriest winning, and that was it: he was my hero and stylistic role model. I spent that first year on a road bike trying to mimic his position and form on the bike.

That all said, the first 130 kilometres of flatlands, heading south from Milan to the foot of the Turchino, are mind-numbing to the point of inducing sleep. The first stress point of the race comes at the Passo del Turchino. It's not a particularly hard climb, but it is made difficult by the battle for position in order to pass the summit at the front of the peloton and so begin the long, fast and technical descent in a relatively safe position. Milan–San Remos have been lost on the descent of the Turchino due to splits in the peloton that were never regrouped.

Once off the Turchino Pass the mood changes as much as the landscape. We arrive into the Mediterranean azure and on to the corniche road that will take us the final 150 kilometres to San Remo. The cold, grey flatlands are now a thing of the past, the leaders start peeling off clothes item by item, and *domestiques* are seen laden with gear descending through the peloton to hand it all off to the following car. The final calls of nature are made and the peloton begins to feel more alive as tensions rise.

Now the wearing down begins. We fly up and down hills, strung out through coastal towns, all similar to each other, the speed gradually increasing as more teams ride on the front, positioning their leaders. Around here the day-long breakaway will begin to haemorrhage time, their 200-plus-kilometre escapade beginning to take its toll. While they are slowing down the bunch is speeding up, and all of sudden minutes are chopped off their gap. Then we hit the first true obstacle of the race, the Cipressa climb, right off the coastal road and up the side of one of the many hills that rise up off the seafront. The positioning into this is frantic, and it's very easy to waste too much energy in the battle leading up to it, as many riders do. Not much happens at the front of the peloton up the Cipressa; almost all the action is at the back, as riders are spat out one by one. The summit is at 272 kilometres – for the many riders taking part in Milan–San Remo for the first time this will be the furthest they have ever raced. Much like the Turchino, the motivation for being at the front over the top of the Cipressa lies in being positioned well for the descent. With almost 280 kilometres in your legs as you rejoin the coastal road it's nearly impossible to close the gap. This is probably the spot where the most racers watch their chances of success evaporate.

The final and deciding climb is the legendary Poggio, with its summit at 288 kilometres, yet only six kilometres from the finish. And so the whole day comes down to this point. There will be teams who are there to try to control the race by keeping it together and making sure their sprinter makes it over at the front and in a position to sprint for victory. There are other teams whose job has been to disrupt the race, making it harder for the sprinters' teams to control and thus allow their leader to attack and solo to victory. Ultimately each team's tactic is dependent on their leader's abilities. A climber will attack on the Cipressa, a *puncheur* will attack on the Poggio and a sprinter will try to survive the Cipressa and Poggio and win the sprint finish in San Remo.

My final Milan–San Remo is something of a damp squib. I don't even make it to the Cipressa. The weather has been bad – not as bad as the winter wonderland we had experienced in the 2013 edition, but still unpleasant. In my usual role as road captain it has been upon me to cover the first part of the race then make sure our leaders are looked after. We have two in Sebastian Langeveld and Tom-Jelte Slagter. It has rained for much of the race, from Milan to the Turchino, then, descending down to the Mediterranean, it seems to clear up, and so, following tradition, everybody starts to remove the extra clothes, convinced that the worst is behind us. Unfortunately, it isn't.

A mere handful of kilometres later it begins chucking it down again. With nearly 140 kilometres still to go this means we can't risk getting cold, so back to the team cars we go to get the clothes we've only just removed. I spend nearly an hour in the convoy trying to organise who needs what and then ferrying Sebastian or Tom back and forth. At one point Tom finds himself totally out the back of the convoy – I actually thought he'd stopped the race – so there I am out the back looking over my shoulder and asking other team cars if they've seen him. It would be funny if it wasn't so unfunny. (It turned out his hands were so cold he couldn't actually get his gloves on, so had slowed to a stop in order to get them on. Even then it took him an age to get them on, then he couldn't get his jacket fastened, which he probably should have done before putting the gloves on – but when you're that cold rational thinking isn't readily available.) It's a black comedy of errors.

And so my lasting memory of my final Milan–San Remo will be of racing rain-blind with numbed, useless hands, dodging cars, off the back looking for Tom-Jelte Slagter. Just before the Cipressa, I'm a broken man. I make a last delivery of bars and gels to Tom and Sebastian and then let the race go and climb into the next team car I see, frozen and tired to the bone. I wasn't alone. Nathan Haas was already in there having been in the break all day before being dropped due to near hypothermia. He'd been in the car long enough to return to life and know exactly what I was going through. Without asking, he began to help me out of my clothes, knowing my hands were useless to me. La Classicissima di Primavera, my arse – wet and cold misery-fest is more like it.

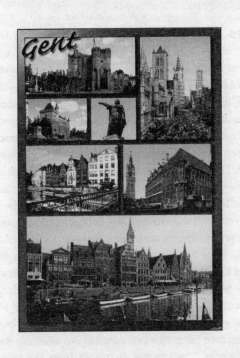

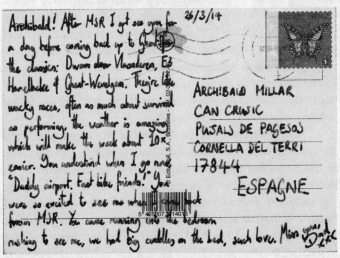

Archibald! After MSR I get see you for a day before coming back up to Gent for the classics: Dwaan door Vlaanderen, E3 Harelbeke & Ghent-Wevelgem. They're like wacky races, often as much about survival as performing. the weather is amazing which will make the week about 10% easier. You understand when I go now, "Daddy airport. Fast bike friends." You were so excited to see me when I got back from MSR. You came running into the bedroom rushing to see me, we had big cuddles on the bed, such love. Miss you. D♥xxx

26/3/14

ARCHIBALD MILLAR
CAN CRUSIC
PUSALS DE PAGESOS
CORNELLA DEL TERRI
17844
ESPAGNE

Flanders

The Europa Hotel in Ghent is our home for three weeks. This is the Tour of Duty for the Classics team, staff and riders alike. Most teams will fix themselves a hotel as a base camp for the Flanders campaign; those riders who don't live in Belgium or Holland will stay there for the duration. There's no going home between races. When we aren't racing we're either resting or doing reconnaissance. The recon ride is done by all the teams: it allows for the experienced riders to refresh their knowledge and learn of changes to the route since the previous edition. For the inexperienced riders it will more than likely confuse and scare rather than educate. Everybody gets something from it, though.

We have two days' rest between Milan–San Remo and the first of the six one-day races we'll do over the following three weeks. It's held on a Wednesday, and it feels like hump day. It's called Dwars door Vlaanderen, which translates as something like 'Through Flanders'. That sums it up. It's not a particularly challenging race but it's a good reminder of what awaits us in the following weeks. I feel totally recovered from my recent efforts in Italy, so much so that I make it into the first selection of the day. It isn't long before I regret being so eager. I average 153 heart rate and 340 watts for nearly four hours; banging my head repeatedly against a wall would have been more enjoyable. Once we're caught I accept that my race is over and roll back to the team bus, my DNF in the results not telling the full story of my day in the saddle.

The next day we recon the critical fifty kilometres of the race we'll be doing on Friday – E3 Harelbeke. E3 is the old name of the motorway that runs next to the town of Harelbeke; it's maybe one of the least glamorous race names on the calendar. The race itself is better than its name would have you believe, and because of this has attained World Tour status, meaning there are precious points up for grabs. I should have been saving myself for this rather than getting carried away and head-banging my way

Through Flanders. It's too late for me to learn from this. All I can do is accept it; the phenomenon of knowing this is my last year racing means this has become a regular state of mind. No longer can I say to myself, 'Well, I won't do that next year.' It's more like, 'Well, I won't ever do that again.'

E3 is referred to as a mini Tour of Flanders, which is a fair description as it tackles all of the climbs (referred to as *hellingen* by the locals) that will be used in Flanders, although its distance of 210 kilometres means it's fifty kilometres shorter. This doesn't make it easier. In fact, it can be harder because there's none of the inherent fear of distance that the Monuments can instil in the peloton, therefore there's little trepidation about racing it hard and fast from early on. The favourites for Flanders will be out to prove themselves and earn the right to leadership within their team for the upcoming Monuments. All the ingredients are there for a great race, and it rarely disappoints.

Unfortunately, it is disappointing for me. The team decide to save me for the finale, yet when it comes to crunch time I'm not good enough, the efforts of the previous week finally rearing their ugly head. There is only one day's rest until the next big one: Sunday's Ghent–Wevelgem. Hardly enough time to fix me, but enough for me to recover sufficiently to do my job as road captain.

Ghent–Wevelgem is one of the few Classics that often finishes in a bunch sprint, hence its reputation as the 'sprinter's Classic'. This doesn't mean it's an easy roll around the Flanders countryside – far from it: it can be as hard as any Classic. The key difference is that it is relatively controlled because of the many teams having the same objective: to have the race finish in a bunch sprint. There is only one thing that is almost guaranteed to spoil their monopoly over the tactics, and that is bad weather, especially wind – if it's blowing then all bets are off.

This year we don't have any wind. In fact, we have beautiful weather, something that is to last the whole Flanders campaign. This makes all of the races easier, hence why the specialists prefer bad weather, because when that's the case they're already winning before they even get to the start line. While they're wringing their hands with excitement others are wallowing in self-pity in anticipation of what awaits them; the psychological warfare begins the moment the morning curtains are opened. This year the concern isn't the weather, it is the crashes.

The Worst Crash Ever

We found out later the crash began right at the front of the bunch when Alessandro Petacchi handed his teammate some clothing he no longer required. While the teammate put the clothing in his back pocket he clipped the wheel of the guy in front of him and lost control, and with one hand on his handlebars and the other in his back pocket he could do nothing to stay upright. The ensuing crash was brutal. We know from the post-race data analysis that the first guys down were travelling at 78 km/h. It was about twenty-five kilometres from the finish of Stage 6 of the 2012 Tour de France. We had a tail wind and were going down a slightly descending, dead straight, road. Anybody who wasn't at the front was trying to move up to be at the front, meaning we were packed like sardines, riding dangerously close to each other. Concentrating on the riders surrounding you 360 degrees meant we didn't have much perception of the speed we were travelling as a whole. I remember it clearly. First there was the noise: metal and carbon grinding and smashing, tyres skidding, brakes screeching. Then there were the impacts. I started seeing them from a long way out: bikes and bodies were going everywhere, some were piling directly into the centre of it all, others were taking evasive action either to the left or to the right, disappearing off road. The tidal wave of peloton debris was approaching at an unavoidable speed; we became all too aware for the first time of just how fast we were travelling. There was zero hope of escaping it, so then it became a case of braking as hard as you could and rubbing off as much speed as possible before the impact. To say I 'chose' the lesser of the two evils by deciding to head for the verge would be an overstatement. My avoidance plan took me off the road into the unknown, at which point my bike got caught up in other bikes and bodies and I continued on my own through the air, bike left far behind. I landed on other bikes and bodies and came to a stop.

Unfortunately, once your crash is completed you are at the mercy of those careening in from behind, many of whom aren't as skilled or aware as you'd perhaps like them to be. The best thing to do is cover your face and close your eyes. If you're not too fankled up then naturally you'll curl up into a fetal position. The fear is primal. Then the blows land. They're coming in, skidding and dodging and smashing to a halt from behind. Some go over you, some land on top, some stop right next to you. For others, you're the point of impact.

One of the strangest things about crashing with professionals is the fact that they never scream or shout. All we hear are the machinations of the crash; the racers themselves don't make any noise until they know it's over. Total silence. Perhaps it seems quiet because moments before everything was so loud. Or maybe it's because everybody is dazed. Then you hear the groaning from those injured, and the shouting from those trying to help. There's angry swearing from those who came out unscathed, and occasionally screaming from somebody who has got himself really fucked up.

For me, there is no acute pain immediately. I'm shocked – sometimes like a white pulse through the body, electric but bigger, on the point of impact – but I don't ever really know in those first few minutes after a big crash how hurt I am. Our bodies are protected by the adrenaline. If there is immediate pain it tends to be the surprise of the massive impact. It's like walking along a street and somebody comes sprinting out of the blue and body slams you. You'll lie on the floor writhing for a bit but then, a minute or so later, you realise nothing is actually damaged. I don't get scared when I hurt myself, which I think is the main reason we cry or scream or groan: it's a fear of the unknown. We are conditioned to be scared of hurting ourselves and rightly so. As professional cyclists we are conditioned to accept hurting ourselves. The longer we've being doing it, the better we become at controlling it.

Yet despite all this conditioning, Stage 6 of the 2012 Tour was the worst crash I'd been involved in. Once it had all stopped I started to untangle myself. I realised I was one of the lucky, unscathed ones and started looking for my bike. My whole team was in a thirty-metre radius of me, but everyone seemed so messed up that each of us had switched to survival look-after-number-one mode. I found my bike under Christian VdV. I asked him if he was OK. He said, 'I think so.' I checked the wheels spun, and that nothing was inoperably bent, and started picking my way through the carnage, carrying my bike over everyone and everything, trying not to look or listen too much – all this wasn't something I wanted to register. I left my whole team behind knowing there was nothing I could do to help them and that maybe if Ryder, our team leader that year, was OK he'd be better off having me wait up the road, ready to ride for him rather than standing around here trying uselessly to help.

Aftermath of 2012 TdF Stage 6 Crash

Tom Danielson post-crash   Ryder post-crash

I set off up the road, barely pedalling as there was no point until I could see Ryder coming. There were other guys doing the same; everybody was too shocked to really know what to do. Some were arguing whether they should wait for teammates; many were clueless as to whether their leader was in the crash or up the road. It was a slow-motion bamboozled chaos.

After a kilometre or so I realised blood was pouring down my arm. I hadn't even noticed I'd hurt it. I sat up and twisted the arm around so I could see it. It looked like I'd been swiped by a big cat, five perfect knife-like cuts – clearly a chainring had 'broken' my fall. I just shook my head. If that was it, I was one lucky bastard. Ryder eventually made it to the finish but was too injured to start the next day. Everybody else in the team was messed up. It felt like a mobile emergency unit in the bus after the race. That crash was one of the main instigators for the Tour de France having an X-ray machine at the finish line soon afterwards – the hospitals in the area couldn't handle the influx of professional cyclists that day.

That night we stayed in a converted monastery and dined in the adjacent abbey, no longer the place of worship it had once been. There were no pews, an empty stage where the altar had once stood and temporary tables laid out for the two teams dining there that evening. We arrived one by one, the gravity of the injuries dictating our time of arrival. I was one of the earliest. I spent five minutes walking around taking photos. I love cathedrals, abbeys and churches; their architecture has always amazed me, how such monumental things could exist in such apparently basic times. There was something quite perfect about being in a place of such surreal grandeur, made all the more beautiful by the fact that it was stripped back and free of any religious connotations. It was one of those evenings where we all let go, released from the pressure we'd felt to fulfil expectations, but also by the fact we'd escaped the biggest crash of our careers without very serious injuries. It felt mischievous having so much fun in a church. We took the piss out of each other chronically: the worse you were injured the bigger the target you were. No one was spared. Ultimately it was probably the fucking strong painkillers and wine. The other team dining there watched us like we were deranged. I think we were.

The Theory of Crashes

There are always crashes in the Classics. We all know that and are prepared for it. There are even certain races we start where we take it for granted we'll be involved in at least one crash – it goes with the terrain. Yet over recent years crashes have become something of a more regular occurrence. At first I wondered if this was simply me seeing the sport through the more safety conscious eyes of the older pro I'd become. I began to see certain young pros as reckless kids. However, after a while I realised it was not just a case of hot-headed younger pros cycling impetuously, but also of older pros who should know better.

As professionals we have a duty to respect each other. We are completely reliant on this in the peloton. We shouldn't be squeezing through gaps that are too small, or slamming on our brakes without a care for the riders behind us, or taking unnecessary risks in descents. In fact, we should be involved in nothing that could provoke an unnecessary crash. Yes, there are moments when we're all flat out, taking risks – but those moments usually occur under truly high-pressure racing conditions and none of us will reproach somebody who crashes because it was a genuine accident.

There are six primary causes of crashes in a bike race. I made a fairly close analysis of this after Stage 4 of the 2009 Vuelta a España:

1. Mechanically induced (puncture at high speed, snapped chain, etc.).
2. Slippery surface.
3. Contact with other rider in peloton leading to loss of control.
4. Individual rider taking risks and losing control or grip.
5. Loss of concentration, leading to distraction and loss of control.
6. Close proximity to anybody going through the above five.

The number and scale of the crashes that day at the Vuelta were primarily due to number two, although the origin was almost always a number four. Unfortunately, number two, by its very nature, would cause number threes and, as a result, plenty of number sixes.

The reason a slippery surface has such an overbearing presence in the anatomy of a crash is easy to understand when you think about the basic physics of bicycle road racing, which involves, on average, seventy-five kilogrammes balanced vertically four or five feet off the ground on roughly three square inches of inflated rubber. That's a lot of stress to put on those three square inches of rubber in dry conditions, never mind in wet. When it's wet, avoidance braking, or simply turning, can result in loss of grip and control, and inevitably conclude with a crash.

For this reason Stage 4 of that year's Vuelta was scary. Coming down into Liège (the Vuelta a España had started in Holland, then descended into Belgium), I could barely see anything through my filthy glasses. The only reason they were still on my face was for the protection they offered me from the dirty, high-pressure water spray that was being thrown up. We were ripping along, close to 80 km/h.

In such circumstances we are more reliant on each other than at any other time. There are 200 of us, and yet it takes just one to think he's Valentino Rossi then lose control and cause the chain reaction that can take down dozens of us. It's scary having to rely completely on your peers' mutual respect and care for each other. I do not implicitly trust them in those conditions. I've been around long enough to understand that pro cyclists aren't particularly blessed with a common love for each other.

Yet the thing is, as pro cyclists we have to trust each other an enormous amount. After all, it's the only reason we can race for so many kilometres together under often extreme circumstances and not crash more often. But what follows is not about a lack of trust – It's an accident. Racing downhill after 200 kilometres at 80km/h in heavy rain was one of those times. What happened at the end of that stage in the Vuelta was a crash of quite horrible proportions.

Our leader was Tyler Farrar, who was on top sprinting form, and I was his lead-out man – the two of us were on a mission as it appeared to be a perfect stage for him. We had gone through the finish line on the first circuit and got a good look at the last kilometre. We had the nineteen-kilometre lap to negotiate with the gentler side of the Côte de Saint-Nicolas to be tackled, although this wasn't too complicated as both of us were feeling well in control. When we got to nine kilometres to go we found each other.

'OK, Ty?' I asked.

His reply was so matter-of-fact it could be nothing but the truth: 'Get me through that last corner first and I'll win.'

That was it. That was all that was said. We made eye contact and I nodded. Our teammate Svein Tuft got to the front with about six kilometres to go and lifted the pace. For the majority this was too high to allow them to move up, making it easier for Ty and me to pick and hold our position. Our plan had been to let Columbia and Quick Step do the lead out, then, inside the last kilometre and leading to the final corner, I would come over the top of them. So we were sitting near the front, but not right at the sharp end. We really were picking and choosing what we were doing – lucidity at its best. Unfortunately, we weren't quite the masters of our own destiny that we thought ourselves to be.

We were starting to string out into single file as the speed increased and the finish approached. We came under the three-kilometre banner and entered a big roundabout – not something that should have caused much of a problem, even in the wet, as we were battle-hardened to the conditions by this point. That's when the human factor kicked in. To this day I don't know the initial cause – I'm presuming a number four in the list above, which led to a number three and, because of number two, caused a massive number six – but I lived the effect.

Like the Tour de France crash three years later there was the familiar nasty noise that we all come to recognise and fear. It's a horrible sound because of what it represents: shoes being ripped out of pedals, metal dragging, plastic and carbon grinding; it's a cacophony in the truest sense. When it's wet there is little hope of escaping. In the dry there's a chance you'll escape it right up until the last second, because at least there is some grip on the road for the braking tyres to hold on to. Often in the wet the moment you touch the brakes the bike disappears from under you as the tyres slide out. You'll normally hit the ground before making contact with anything or anybody, simply because even the mildest evasive manoeuvre means a loss of grip and subsequent crash. This is what happened in Liège. I heard the crash ahead, then I saw a guy about five or six riders in front of me hit the ground independently of whatever the noise had been. And then it began. Every single racer in front of me hit the ground, like a dozen bowling pins. You see it happening and are powerless to do anything about it. I knew I was going down. I simply waited. In the moment, it feels like a long time – but is actually probably no longer than a second. THUMP. I'm on the ground.

Then comes the really horrible bit. I'm sliding in the middle of the cacophony and I know there's a concrete barrier that I'm going to hit at speed. The impact of this is not a concern, it's the incoming impacts from behind that I'm scared of. At least when you crash in the dry there's a small chance you won't get hit from behind; in the wet there's no such luck. There's no pain, just fear. So as I slide along the road I try to curl up and close my eyes tightly.

Then, BANG! Followed by silence.

Everything has stopped, and at first it seems nothing really bad has happened. I barely even notice the secondary impacts from behind. Then the relief is replaced with a burning sensation – not anything in particular, just everything sending out alert signals. The only way it's possible to trace most of the injuries in the moment is by checking where my kit is ripped up. All I want to do is lie on the ground, but I have a feeling there are some properly hurt guys around me so I get up and sit on the concrete barrier to show I'm relatively unscathed.

Sitting there, looking around, I realise the scale of the crash and notice there are a few guys not getting up. Ty, who was on my wheel at the time, is on the ground behind me. To my relief he's OK. Less than ten seconds before we'd been at near peak heart rates, adrenalin-filled, fully in the zone, preparing to take ourselves to our maximum. It's amazing how much can change in a handful of seconds. If ever there is a moment of being dazed and confused, this is it.

That type of crash is part and parcel of being a pro; we'd go as far as referring to it as a 'race incident', implying that it happened at a heated and intense moment of the race where risks have to be taken. Those who choose to be at the front, where the stress increases the chance of crashing, do so at their own risk, fully aware of the possible outcome. These crashes will always happen in cycling. The more worrying phenomenon in modern cycling is the higher frequency of stupid crashes – not so much race incident as rider incompetence, something that is starting to happen at every race, but is all the more obvious in the Flandrian Classics, where the stress is constantly high and the roads narrow and technical. There no longer seems to be any real tactical skill in positioning; too many riders want to be in the same place at the same time.

And where historically this occurred only at critical moments in the race, now it seems to happen all the time: instead of having the strongest guys who have the requisite skill and experience battling for position when it's a recognised and important moment, we have inexperienced guys stressing at uncritical moments. This is a recipe for disaster because in order for a peloton to flow at its best it requires everybody to be in the same mental state. This is the most common cause of a crash: a stressed, inexperienced rider coming into contact with a relaxed rider who isn't expecting it. When we're relaxed we're not gripping the handlebars as tightly and we're not fully focused and so are unable to react at the split-second speed required to avoid a crash. These are the stupid crashes we're seeing more and more of. They occur at unexpected moments in the race for no apparent reason. Everybody who witnesses one of these unfortunate events will look at each other, shake their heads and say, 'What the fuck just happened there?'

Tour of Flanders

Ghent–Wevelgem was full of these stupid crashes. Coming into the final obstacle of the day, the Kemmelberg, I was caught up behind one such nonsensical crash. We were on a big straight road going slightly uphill, so not exactly a high-risk zone. One minute I was racing along, the next I was in a pile on the floor. I wasn't even hurt. I just lay there on the floor thinking, 'I'm too old for this shit.' By the time I was up and rolling again the race was long gone. I rode over the Kemmelberg and stopped at the top, where I saw one of our team staff and told him I was done for the day. The Australian Matt Goss, who rides for Orica-GreenEDGE, pulled over with me and asked, 'How you getting back, Dave?' I told him, 'I'm not riding back, that's for sure. We have a team car here, you need a lift?' This was an unnecessary question as it was obvious he needed a lift back to the finish. So the two of us cruised to where all team cars were parked and loaded our bikes on to the roof and sat on the bumper and whinged about how many stupid crashes there are these days in pro cycling.

We must have been a sorry sight. The fans kept double-taking as they walked past, returning to their own cars, seeing us perched there in full race kit, not exactly radiating excellence. We didn't care by that point, we just wanted out of there.

It's an interesting phenomenon in the Flanders races that when you're dropped out of the front groups you may as well be completely out of the race. Due to the crazy nature of the race routes there are rolling road closures, meaning it doesn't take long before you find yourself back on open roads with traffic. When the weather is bad, which it often is, you risk being abandoned in Flanders farmland – wet, cold, exhausted and with no idea of where you are or where you need to go, like a wounded animal left behind by the herd.

It's for this reason the Flandrian fans are accustomed to rescuing random stray pro racers and piling them into their cars to drive them back to the finish. The fact that this process is so normal for them is always a little unnerving – being such avid fans they often know more about you than you do yourself, so it's actually like being picked up by an old friend. Well, if that old friend knew everything about your cycling career and also had strident opinions about every other cyclist, team or manager and wanted to share them with you and ascertain your opinion on each matter. Reminds me of the film *Misery*. Only in Belgium.

After Ghent–Wevelgem we get our first real rest since before Tirreno–Adriatico. It's not long, only six days, but it's needed in preparation for one of the biggest races of the year, the Tour of Flanders. This is the race that all the smaller Flanders Classics have been building towards, the results of which will be dictating each team's leaders and tactics, as well as the journalists' and fans' expectations.

It's a race like no other. The word epic gets bandied about way too much in cycling these days, but Flanders deserves that description. Every pro racer who takes part in it is left with a sense of awe. It's the second Monument of the year, and couldn't be more different from the first. The only thing Milan–San Remo and the Tour of Flanders have in common is the fact they both start and finish in different towns. A map of the route for Milan–San Remo it pretty straightforward, easy to understand; the route map for the Tour of Flanders, on the other hand, looks like a two-year-old has been left alone in a dark room with some paper and a pen.

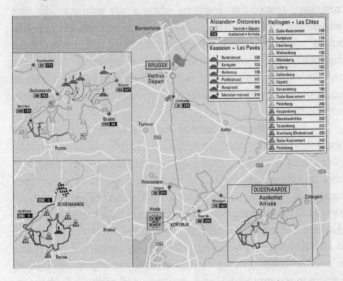

Our final Flanders recon takes place on the Wednesday of the preceding week. It's now we realise why we've been doing so many recons and races in the same area the previous weeks, because what was once confusing and disorientating is now clear and concise – well, until you enter a state of delirium. Those of us who don't live in Belgium need all the time we can get there to imprint the roads in our memories. Each year it takes a few recons and races to refresh it anew, and with each year spent repeating this, the easier it becomes to recall the detail. For the Belgian racers it is a given to possess this knowledge – they will have been racing on the same roads since they were juniors; for them it's their back garden. It's one of the reasons they always excel here; it's the greatest of home advantages.

We have our team meeting in the conference room at the Europa Hotel. We've turned it into our communal room for the duration of our stay. It has sofas, and two tables filled with healthy snacks – biscuits and Nutella, etc., were banned a couple of years ago after a rider put on five kilogrammes during the Classics campaign; that's what happens when a pro cyclist's addictive personality uses food for comfort – and boxes of cereal, protein powders, recovery drinks, a coffee machine, and a fridge with yoghurt, milk and pomegranate juice or whatever else is the latest trend. It's where we go to sit and nibble on nuts or dried fruit or bowls of cereal when the cabin fever of our hotel rooms becomes too much.

We sit there in silence looking at our phone or the computer we've brought down with us. Maybe while we're doing that one of our teammates will come in and quietly mull over what to eat or drink, trying to decide whether they are actually hungry or not. They come to the conclusion they're not, so have a yoghurt and make a coffee before sitting down to stare at their phone. Then one of us will get up and return to the sanctuary of our hotel room, realising solitary confinement is preferable to what feels like a communal prison. By the end of the Classics campaign we are institutionalised: our hotel rooms have become our homes; the communal food area becomes a dangerous place, the risk too big that you might actually have to talk to someone.

The team meetings are the only time the communal room has any sense of actual community. It's certainly the only time all the riders are in there at once. Andreas Klier and Geert Van Bondt are our *directeurs*. They have two different roles: Andreas dictates tactics, while Geert directs logistics. Both are ex-professional racers, as is almost always the case with *directeur sportifs* in cycling. There are two principal reasons for this: the first being that it would be very difficult to make tactical plans for a race that you have never actually competed in, and, secondly, bike racers don't like being told what to do in a bike race by somebody who has never done a bike race. We're a bit small-minded in that regard.

Andreas has become a good friend since he arrived on the team in 2011. He's German (although he'll correct that quickly to Bavarian), now lives in Mallorca and has more of a Spanish than Germanic attitude to life. He was a Classics specialist, to the degree that when he first turned professional he decided he would move to Flanders in order to completely immerse himself in the region, to become a true Flandrian. He learnt Flemish and got to know all the roads so well he ended up being nicknamed 'the Human GPS'. As for the races themselves, he has done them so many times he can predict outcomes in advance: depending on the weather, the course design and the teams and riders present he will be able to deduce incredibly closely how the race will unfold.

He retired in 2013 after Paris–Roubaix, which, being a Classics specialist, he considered to be the end of the season anyway. I think it's for this reason that, although Andreas and I had been professionals in the same era, we'd never actually said a word to each other until he arrived at Garmin. I'd usually be starting my season properly just as he was winding his down; we were on different teams racing different programmes and we didn't have much in common apart from being called professional cyclists. That is quite normal: it's possible to go through a decade of racing against guys you've never spoken to.

It is Andreas' job to select the teams for the Classics and decide on the tactics. Without fail, no matter what my physical condition, he makes me road captain, trusting me to action his plan and keep everybody on a tight leash and lead by example by always doing what he asks. Almost as importantly, he can rely on me to report back to him objectively when we debrief a day's race over a pre-dinner beer. I always tell him exactly how I was, good or bad, and I can also tell him how the rest of the team were, because, no matter how much experience Andreas has or how perceptive he is, he can't see much from a car in a convoy behind the race, and he certainly can't completely trust what each rider will tell him. Some guys would rather blatantly lie about their day's racing than admit they've had a shocker. Others are so delusional they will be convinced they had a great day when they were at best average. Then there are the guys who are amazing and are totally oblivious to it – the Ramūnus Navardauskases of this world.

Our team is not very stacked when it comes to leaders. This is both good and bad. Obviously the more great riders a team has the more chance there is of success, but this is a two-edged sword, because a team with all chiefs and no Indians can potentially be its own worst enemy. *Domestiques* are a necessity in cycling. *Domestiques* shape the race, controlling the situation by neutralising threats, or tiring the peloton until their leader is ready to do battle with the other leaders in the finale, when it becomes *mano a mano*. Some teams are powerful enough to have super-*domestiques* or loyal lieutenants to chaperone their leaders, even in this final stage of the race. This isn't as common as you'd think, though, because the likelihood of having two riders from the same team make it into the finale is small, no matter how strong they are. The simple laws of probability reduce the numbers; for this reason it's all the more remarkable that the same riders are racing for the win without fail year after year. Tom Boonen and Fabian Cancellara are the kings of this. By the time Fabian finished his 2014 Classics campaign he had the ridiculous stat of having been on the podium in the previous eleven Monuments he had finished. That was a phomeral feat.

Our team for 2014, with roles allocated by Andreas, is as follows:

Sebastian Langeveld, Leader (Netherlands)
Johan Vansummeren, Protected Rider (Belgium)
Tyler Farrar, Protected Rider (USA)
Dylan van Baarle, Protected Rider (Netherlands)
Jack Bauer, *Domestique* (New Zealand)

Raymond Kreder, *Domestique* (Netherlands)
Steele Von Hoff, *Domestique* (Australia)
Me, Road Captain (GB)

It is Raymond and Steele's job to cover the first fifty kilo-metres of the Tour of Flanders. This is where attacking will take place, with certain teams trying to get in a break while others are more concerned about preventing a dangerous group slipping away. We fall into the latter category. This means choosing two or three important teams and marking them. We choose Quickstep and Lotto, so if one of their riders attacks off the front of the race we go with them. We know that if those two teams aren't in the break then at some point later in the race they will assume respon-sibility to chase it down. With both teams being from Belgium it is their most important race of the year, and we'll play on that fact.

We have been using a similar tactic in the Classics leading up to the Tour of Flanders. I've been teaching Steele the art of covering attacks in this manner, something he has never done before. It's pretty simple: all you have to do is switch your brain to a defensive style of attacking, which means always reacting and never acting. You surf the peloton, flowing from one wheel to another without ever actually putting your nose in the wind, yet always being near enough to the front to have open road to launch off if required. If you relax a bit you'll find yourself sucked further back in the bunch, surrounded by riders, unable to react when you see one of your targets move. By keeping it to two prominent teams it is relatively simple: you stop thinking about individual riders and only concentrate on the jerseys of those teams. If a Lotto jumps, you jump; similarly with a Quickstep. The most important part of this is never to hesitate, because if you hesitate the gap will open and you'll have to work harder to close it down. The faster you react, the easier it is. It takes a few races to get good at this, and it hurts like hell at first, but if you're fit it doesn't take long for your body to adapt to the repeated sprint efforts.

The majority of big teams will be employing a similar tactic. They'll have two, or maximum three, riders assigned for early duty, and each big team will have identified teams to neutralise. Lotto will be marking Quickstep, and vice versa; both of these teams will be marking Team Sky and Trek. Team Sky and Trek will both be marking Quickstep and Lotto and each other. So it will end up being quite a protracted shoot-out until finally a move 'slips' away, minus the key teams and of the right size. That will be another order given to the *domestiques* on this early shift: do NOT let a group of more than ten riders go, no matter what team is in it. Anything over ten riders can become difficult to bring back – like a team time trial, the more riders in a group working together the more recovery time they get, which will make it easier for them to ride faster for longer and stand more chance of making it to the finish.

It's fair to say that the majority of riders in this initial battle will not be interested in actually escaping; their job is to make sure the right breakaway goes. On average, after forty-five minutes, they're all quite fucked from marking each other out, and an invisible white flag is flown and the perfect small group will get its gap and begin its long day out, destined to be reeled back in before the finish. It's because of this inevitability that the last order for the *domestiques* will have been not to be in a break of five riders or less, because of it having almost zero chance of success. The team would rather have that *domestique* back in the peloton working for his teammates than up the road on a hiding to nothing.

While Raymond and Steele are covering this first part of the race it's mine and Jack's job to look after our four protected riders. We are split into two groups of three; it's my responsibility to look after Sebastian and Dylan, while Jack has Tyler and Johan. Groups of three are easier for us to manage, as the start is always frantic. Three of us makes for a tighter and more organised group; it's also less demanding mentally in this early part of the race, as we can flow easily within the peloton. The first feedzone comes at 100 kilometres, and from that moment we're to ride as one united team.

Our first danger point comes at 109 kilometres – the Oude Kwaremont, one of the most famous climbs in cycling. It's only two kilometres long but is cobbled the whole way, and is as iconic in Belgium as l'Alpe d'Huez is in France. Approaching the Kwaremont, Raymond and Steele join Jack and me to protect our four other riders. This, like the Turchino in Milan–San Remo, is a moment when we try to avoid incidents and accidents rather than expect action.

Like all Flandrian races the focus is on positioning. We have grown accustomed to this in the Classics leading up to the Ronde, but then it becomes even more extreme on this: the big day. This is due to the climbs being cordoned off to prevent the vast number of fans at the side of the road infringing on the racers. So the smooth gutters at the edge of the road that we've used when racing the same *hellingen* in the weeks before no longer exist. Now the peloton is bigger, the pressure higher, the rewards greater, and the roads narrower. For this reason it's of even greater importance than normal to be well placed into each and every key moment.

When Andreas was racing he was the absolute master of being in the right place at the right time. Nobody thought of him as the strongest, yet everybody considered him to be the smartest. His was the wheel to have – that is, if you could get it. Some riders and teams would base their race on marking Klier; he was the ultimate guide through the bedlam. This skill was the fruit of his Flemish labours – he had taught himself to be more of a Flandrian than any other, born or bred.

Unlike many, he has always shared his knowledge with teammates. To the degree that in the second half of his career, and while still a rider, he found himself effectively leading team meetings and calling the shots. Everyone bowed to his knowledge. When it came to the Flanders Classics he was constantly the smartest guy in the room. The reason he was allowed to lead team meetings while still a rider was because he never posed a threat to anybody. This was due to him being a lovely man: there is little to no ego and he genuinely cares about people which, considering the domain he excels in, is something of an exception.

Most *directeur sportifs* forget within a matter of months of retirement from racing what it was like to be a rider. I've only known two who have remained truly empathetic to what it's like to be out there doing it: Matt White and Andreas Klier.

This is what makes Whitey and Klier so much better than everybody else out there: they remain fully aware of the difficulties involved in being a pro bike racer *during the race*. As racers we always joke about how easy it must be to make decisions in the team car – some *directeurs* order us to act as if it's a computer game, oblivious to the fact that's the easiest way to lose the respect of your riders. Whitey and Klier are, suitably, the only two *directeurs* I know who we've given nicknames to: 'Whitey' because he's Aussie; and 'Klier' because we needed to give him a nickname and the only thing we could think of was his surname, which makes him sound hard and German, which mostly he isn't.

Yet when it comes to strategy Andreas is so German. He'll break the race up into sections and give them different levels of difficulty. He'll allow us moments to relax and others where we have no choice but to be fully engaged at the very front of the race. There are even moments in the first 100 kilometres where we congregate at the front as a team at a relatively non-stressful moment, preventing us from slipping into complacency or switching off completely in the calm before the storm, and so reminding us of what's coming. This is where both Whitey and Klier are different from all other *directeurs*: they remember we can't be switched on all the time; they remember what it was like to be out there on the bike, in the race.

We have moments in the race that Andreas refers to as 'red alarms'. He doesn't use yellow or orange: it's straight to red. These are pivotal moments where the race won't be won, but it could most certainly be lost. We have had three red alarms before we get to the holy mother of moments: the Taaienberg cobbled climb at 223 kilometres. This is crunch time. Being such an important moment it can be called only one thing on Planet Andreas Klier: a *dark red alarm*.

Unfortunately, before even getting there we already have our own dark red alarm. Sebastian has been caught up behind a crash just as the final phase of the race is beginning. I wait for him and call on Steele to do the same. Eventually we get him going again, and I start to bring him back in as controlled a manner as I can. The nature of the Flanders roads means we're already losing sight of the front group we're chasing. Then things get worse when Sebastian's rear derailleur snaps. It has obviously been hit in the crash, but not enough to break at that moment: now it gives way under the load. He raises his arm and starts to pull over, all three of us slowing to a stop. I look behind and can't even see the lead following car coming up in the distance – that could at least give me some hope of the team cars arriving before long. All I can see are random stragglers from the crash scattered along the road, some chasing desperately while others have clearly given up, almost thankful to be out of it.

It seems the race is over for Sebastian – all the support cars are still clogged up behind the crash and, being single-track roads, have no way past. We have no idea how long it will take for the car to get up to us. I look at Steele, then I look at Sebastian. I realise they're a fairly similar size. I shout, 'Give him your bike, Steele!' Steele doesn't hesitate, he hands it over. Sebastian doesn't really know what to do, so I tell him, 'Seba, you have to take his bike or the race is over. We'll get your spare when we can.' His head is clearly shot. He must be thinking, 'That's it, my race is done.'

He throws his bike in the ditch and jumps on Steele's. Steele gives him a running push-off and Sebastian and I set off again, with Steele shouting, 'Seba, my brakes are the other way around!' We leave Steele to walk back to fetch the broken bike out of the ditch and wait for the team car, his race now finished.

We have a fairly long chase, mainly due to me wanting to pace it as steadily as possible in order to stop Sebastian making too much of an effort on my wheel – but also to show that I am calm and in control, knowing this will rub off on him and allow him to get his head back in the game. Eventually we make it back to what is left of the peloton – then, just as we join the back, there is another crash. Neither of us are involved but it blocks the road in front of us. I make it through on the grass but Sebastian is well and truly blocked behind. I continue to roll along, waiting for him to pick his way through and catch up so we can begin the chase anew.

It's like Milan–San Remo all over again. I'm off the back doing an effort that would have taken me off the front of the peloton. Once we make it back on I wait until our team car is behind us and then drop back to explain what is going on. In these circumstances I always prefer to speak to Andreas directly rather than over the radio, and tell him we'll change the bike as soon as the moment is right. This means the next big road, and when it's clear the peloton is grouped and in a steady state. Sure enough, the moment comes and I tell Sebastian to stop, and we change his bike. Then, out of the blue, the peloton starts stretching out again, making it a total bastard to get him back on and up to the front. I drop Sebastian off a handful of kilometres before the second time up the Kwaremont. I'm deep in the red from the repeated chasing. I watch the race disappear up the road before we've even reached the dark red alarm. I've done my job; I can't be too upset that my last Flanders is ending this way.

It's quite an experience riding the next ten kilometres with my head disengaged from the race, because I get to look around and take in the carnage. There are riders everywhere. I catch up with guys who've had mechanicals, others who are injured from crashes. I see two riders who've missed a fast corner on a descent and are now sprawled in an adjacent field. Then there are guys flying by me, chasing like I was not long before. The motorbikes and official cars are screeching and honking, squeezing by all of us, while the whole time the buzz of overhead helicopters and nearby screaming fans fills our ears. I haven't really paid attention to any of these things while in the race.

Before long there's a little group of us riding along. When we get to the bottom of the next climb, the Koppenberg, there isn't any hesitation: we all file left instead of right. I didn't even know there was a short cut back to the finish. I look right, think about it, then go left with the others. I don't need to finish. I'd rather keep the memory of the good times at Flanders than a long, lonely, sad slog to the finish. That isn't necessary.

At the finish Finlay and Martin are waiting to film me as I cross the line. They follow me back to the bus. They aren't expecting me so soon, but fortunately they get me arriving at the bus, so all isn't lost. They then film a fair amount of footage of me sitting out the front of the team bus in my tracksuit, talking to fans and getting my photo taken a lot. Which is better than nothing, I suppose. Sebastian ends up finishing tenth, a brilliant result in the circumstances. It makes me feel like my final Flanders hasn't been entirely wasted.

Scheldeprijs

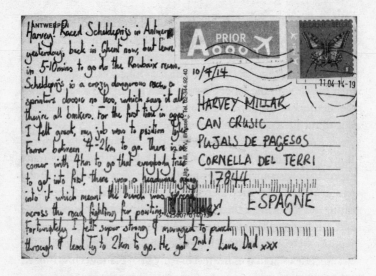

Scheldeprijs isn't much of a race, although saying that it must be something because this was the 102nd edition. It's a 200-kilometre loop that starts and finishes in Antwerp. If there's a flatter race in the year I don't know it. Most of the peloton is lethargic from racing Flanders and weary at the thought of the following day's Roubaix recon, so all in all it's a fairly mundane day out. We have an out-and-out leader for the race in our sprinter, Tyler Farrar. He's won it before, and with it almost always coming down to a bunch sprint he's the obvious candidate for us. We have a fairly simple plan: do nothing, then position Tyler for the sprint. Easy.

Only it's really difficult, because everybody has the same plan, and I mean *exactly* the same plan. I've been put in my old faithful lead-out position: penultimate lead-out man. It's my job to place Tyler and his final lead-out man, Raymond, in the perfect position, as near as I can to the finish. I've done this countless times for Tyler in the past. Most of his biggest wins have come off the back of such a lead out, only instead of Raymond there has been the Kiwi Julian Dean in the final position.

We've lost our touch somewhat of late. First of all I've been finding it harder and harder to motivate myself to do lead outs and, secondly, Tyler isn't getting the results. It's a vicious circle: the less I believe in Ty the less I am willing to put on the line for him. I've been unstoppable in the past – helping the climbers through mountains one day, trying to get in a break the next, and leading out Tyler the rest of the time, while going full gas in every single time trial. I'd considered that normal behaviour at the time. I took for granted my physical ability to do all those things, and so it hadn't been much of a demand, psychologically. But as soon as I started to find it harder physically I was affected psychologically. Yet the moment I'm strong physically all the enthusiasm and motivation comes flooding back.

I know I'm getting stronger with every race. Although I didn't finish Flanders I was confident I was going well: to have spent so much time out the back bringing Sebastian back into the race took some strength. And so it proved in the final of Scheldeprijs: I was able to revert back to my old self. Tyler knew when he saw me relaxed in the final, while it was going nuts all around, that it was like the old days. I, in contrast to many other sprint lead outs, like to sit a bit further back and await a moment to punch through. In other words, just doing one big and important move rather than a protracted drag race with other teams at the front. This has become a bit of a trademark of ours: we essentially hijack the work of other lead outs who've been slaving away on the front for numerous kilometres. This is mainly due to the fact that we were a general classification team with a small sprint train. We've had to find a method that works with our limited resources: we are a three-man band.

I'm told the most important moment in Scheldeprijs is the right-hander at four kilometres to go, which takes us off the road parallel to the canal and brings us back in through the suburbs to the finish line. If you find yourself badly positioned into that corner then you'll be sure to be terribly positioned coming out of it and can kiss goodbye to your chances of a result. Clearly everybody knows this, and so we have the whole peloton fighting to be first through – all of which wouldn't have been so bad if we hadn't had a headwind.

The headwind means that we are swamped across the road from left to right, because there is no way of stringing the peloton out – it's impossible for a team to stay united in the constant hustle and bustle, pushing and shoving, braking and accelerating. If you are on the wheel you feel like Superman because you are so protected from the headwind, so you think it's easy and try to get past. Everybody is doing this, then, when a rider gets to the front and faces the wind for the first time, they last a short amount of time before exploding and being swamped again. It is nigh-on impossible to hold a constant position; you just have to keep nudging forward. If there's a gap you jump into it; but even with this constant sense of moving up you are often just sliding back through. It's like walking up a descending escalator.

Riders are becoming stressed and trying dangerous moves, attempting to squeeze through gaps that clearly aren't there. If I see that happening I try to give them room in anticipation of the inevitable fuck-up. The last thing you want near you in a stressful situation is a stressed person.

I make the executive decision to stop fighting and to sit back a bit to wait for the unavoidable parting of the peloton. I figure the kamikaze peel-offs (when a rider literally rides so hard and fast on the front that when their turn is done they peel off and sit up having totally maxed out, to then have another rider begin what they'd just finished) will start in the final 500 metres before the corner and so stretch out the peloton a bit, allowing me to move up the side. Ty is on my wheel. I give him the sign to stay there, then I just relax and ready myself to go the moment it all opens up. Sure enough it does, not far from the corner, probably 300 metres, but enough for me to take Tyler right back up into the mix.

When we come out of the corner I see that we have limited options. The entire Giant team are forming in order to begin their lead out. Being such a well-drilled team Giant, I have no doubt, will nail it, which means we'll be stuck in the battle behind them for position. We've lost Raymond and the rest of the team in the mêlée leading into the corner, so can only rely on each other. I don't fancy banging around fighting for wheels behind Giant because, well, it's fucking dangerous and I don't want to crash.

So with four kilometres to go I take control of the race. With Giant on the left I start going on the right. They trust my ability to go long, so instead of drag racing me they swing across and get on my wheel, which gives Ty the opportunity to slot in among them, a chance that he wouldn't otherwise have got. This is in their best interest, too, as the pair of us aren't exactly a threat, and they can use me as an extra in their lead out and in the process save themselves two guys. I ride for two kilometres until I make my peel-off, then Giant begin their machine-like lead out with a full complement of riders thanks to my contribution. In the meantime Ty has been able to position himself perfectly on to Giant sprinter Marcel Kittel's wheel. Unfortunately Kittel is a giant of a man himself and proves unbeatable, but Ty gets a respectable second place, which turns a fairly shit day's racing into a good one. Good results tend to do that.

The Hell of the North

It's one thing to love watching a race, it's another to love doing it. Paris–Roubaix is an example of this: it's easy to love as a fan, much harder as a racer. I've started it three times and none of those times ended particularly well – which is another way of saying I didn't finish.

It's known as 'the Hell of the North', something people often mistake as being attributable to its renowned difficulty and the famous images of exhausted racers looking like they've been to hell and back. It actually originates from the 1919 edition, when it was held for the first time since the First World War had ended, and travelled through a devastated northern France – the journalists and riders who took part could only describe what they saw as 'hell'. Henri Pélissier, speaking of his 1919 victory, said, 'This wasn't a race. It was a pilgrimage.'

The recon on the Thursday before the race is, much like the Flanders recon, a tradition. Most of those starting Roubaix will have raced Flanders the previous Sunday and Scheldeprijs on the Wednesday, with the recon the day after that. In typical cycling fashion it's not exactly a light week; but there is a reason for this – the best performances at Roubaix are almost always achieved by the riders who have raced at Flanders and Scheldeprijs. The overload seems to do us well.

The Roubaix recon is a fixture in itself. There will be fans out watching, as well as photographers and film crews, all of which adds to the feeling that it's a race like no other. The recon is an opportunity to refresh our knowledge of the *parcours* – a necessity before Roubaix as it's the only time in the year we race on these 'roads'. (The only other time would be if the Tour de France decided to include some of the cobble sections in its early stages – it does once every decade.)

As we step out of the hotel, the bus is sitting out front, ticking over. It looks and feels like the morning of a race: all the team cars are lined up, loaded with bikes, and there is the general buzz of a big race day. This is the effect Roubaix has on everybody: it's still four days away, but we're all gibbering with a mixture of excitement and fear. Once we're on the bus and moving, everybody relaxes a little, remembering that we're not actually going to a race. Morning quiet descends. Headphones are on, phone calls home are made, a car magazine is flicked through; one or two of the young guys are studying maps of the course trying to memorise the sectors.

We park up in a supermarket car park in Denain, northern France. The Trek and Team Sky buses have chosen the same start location. This isn't a surprise: often these rally points have been used for years – many of the guys running the teams will have raced together on the same teams and learnt the same routines. Thirty years ago there was probably a friend of a *directeur sportif* who had a house near this supermarket where they would all get changed and have a coffee in the days before luxury team buses.

One by one we get off the bus. I tend to be first. I don't know why, because without fail I then stand around getting pissed off at everybody else for being so slow and not respecting the schedule. I'm of the school of thought that says you're not on time unless you're early – always have been when it comes to my racing life. This no doubt annoys everybody else as much their tardiness frustrates me.

There will often be a journalist or two with us. Little interviews will be done, photos taken, then we'll go and find our bikes among the ten that are lined up against the side of the bus (we always have two reserve riders in case of an accident during recon). We have special bikes for Roubaix that have larger clearance between the wheels and the frame so we can ride larger tyres that can handle the abuse that awaits them (28mm compared to our usual 25mm). It also allows us to be prepared for the eventuality of mud if it rains, because the bigger clearance will prevent mud getting clogged between the frame and the wheel. We've given these bikes the highly technical and innovative name of 'Mud Bikes'.

Some riders will place an extra brake lever on their handlebars next to the stem, because on the cobblestones the comfiest position is to grip the top flat section of the bars, where normally there is no brake lever. In Roubaix you never know what's going to happen in front of you, so some prefer to at least try to give themselves a chance. There will be extra rolls of bar tape, and some riders will even add some cushioning underneath that, all in an attempt to absorb the relentless shocks created by the cobbles.

As important as all those details are, they mean nothing if you don't have strong wheels and the right tyre pressure. Our usual lightweight wheels would be pummelled to pieces, so we use special wheels that have more spokes and stronger rims, which means not only will they survive the beating but they'll also have a higher chance of withstanding damage from a crash. Most of the equipment we use in modern racing is so lightweight that one crash is all that's required for it to be ruined; Paris–Roubaix puts more stress on equipment than multiple crashes, and that's assuming you don't crash.

Tyres

The tyre pressure is Andreas Klier's domain. Nobody questions his decision – not even the head mechanic, Geoff. The tyres we use are not those of our sponsors, they're artisan creations – most teams choosing those from the French maker François Marie, or FMB (the B standing for *boyaux*, French for tubular). They're wider and tougher yet also more supple, the finishing touch being the traditional natural cream-coloured side walls. If you're into tyres, these are beauties. I used to buy my time-trial tyres from François Marie, as he also makes lightweight silk tyres which really are something special, although they're so delicate they wouldn't even make it to the first section of cobbles in Roubaix.

These handmade tyres are one of the few things left in modern cycling that hark back to an earlier age, a time when artisans holed up in nondescript barns or outhouses were the go-to for the latest and best tech. Nowadays nearly everything we use is generic, almost all churned out by giant factories in China or Taiwan, whereas there is something so special about the feel, smell and look of these beautifully crafted pieces of cotton and rubber. It's ironic that perhaps the most carefully constructed and cherished piece of equipment we use all year will have the shortest life, because each tyre will race only once in its brief existence.

We run approximately 6-bar pressure – maybe a bit less on the front, and even lower in both when wet. The larger diameter of the tyre means there's more air volume, allowing us to run these lower pressures. The lower pressure gives us more shock absorption, and the wider diameter also gives us a larger surface area at the point of contact between the tyre and the ground, which means we're not ricocheting around so much and have more grip. It's also much more forgiving on the bike and therefore the body.

Cobbles

Nowadays nearly every team will supply their racers with this 'Mud Bike' set-up for Roubaix; the difference lies in how it is used. Having the set-up doesn't mean you'll go fast – ultimately, riding cobbles is an art form. It's not something I have ever truly mastered. I've had glimpses of it, and was certainly never bad, but I could never compare myself to the specialists. They appear to float over them with an ease that isn't fair to the rest of us, and tricks many – especially the fan on the sofa – into thinking, 'It doesn't look that bad.'

Every cycling fan must go and watch Paris–Roubaix one day, and take their bike to have a go on some of the famous sectors. Only then can you feel what it's really like. Only the actual reality of riding the *pavé* can do it justice. Roubaix specialists tend to have been good at it since their first attempt; they just got it immediately. In that sense it's more of a feel, a natural ability rather than a learnt one.

Every recon starts the same way: we set off as a team with lead and following cars and photographers or TV on accompanying motorbikes. The first couple of sectors we stick together, stopping a couple of times to adjust tyre pressures, because each one of us has a different style of riding and a different weight. There's always one rider who is totally neurotic and spends the whole day trying to find the unicorn of tyre pressures that will make them fly – which is normally a sign that they're *not* going to fly.

In this year's edition there are twenty-eight cobbled sectors totalling fifty-one kilometres of a 257-kilometre race. They're listed in reverse order, so it's a countdown from the first sector in Troisvilles (ninety-eight kilometres) to the final symbolic one in Roubaix (256 kilometres). Our recon will take us from Sector 19 (153 kilometres) to Sector 4 (240 kilometres), these are the eighty-seven kilometres that matter in the race. Unlike the definitive moments of Milan–San Remo or Flanders, Roubaix is a protracted war.

Each of the five Monuments in cycling has its iconic moments: in Milan–San Remo it's the Cipressa and Poggio climbs; in Flanders the Kwaremont and Patersberg; Liège–Bastogne–Liège has the Côte de la Redoute and the Côte de Saint-Nicolas; while the Tour of Lombardy features the Madonna del Ghisallo. There's also the Carrefour de l'Arbre in Paris–Roubaix. But for me the most memorable of all these is the Roubaix's Trouée d'Arenberg (the English speakers among us refer to it as the Arenberg Forest, making it sound like something out of *The Lord of the Rings*). It doesn't look like much – a 2.4-kilometre dead-straight road cut through a forest – but for a pro cyclist it is the most brutal 2.4 kilometres they'll ever race along. There is no hiding – in fact, if you try to hide you'll take a hiding. The race to be at the front entering the forest makes the Scheldeprijs positioning battle look like child's play, because although we're 100 kilometres from the finish, this is where the race finale begins.

There is almost always a decent-sized peloton entering Arenberg, but by the time it leaves it's in pieces. The compact group that enters the forest is stretched out and broken up over those 2.4 kilometres. Even those at the front will eventually find themselves beaten into submission, because Arenberg is one of only three five-star sectors in the race. All twenty-eight sectors are categorised, one star being the easiest, five the hardest. There's actually only one one-star sector, and that is the symbolic and specially made stretch a kilometre before entering the famous Roubaix velodrome. This is probably what people think of when picturing cobblestones, but it's actually quite smooth. None of the other sectors are like that.

The easiest way to traverse each sector is to go fast; the speed will allow you to skim over the stones. Well, that's not really true, but in comparison to what it feels like going slow it makes them feel like beach pebbles rather than ski moguls. The other problem, and the reason why positioning is so important, is the fact that there is only ever one good line on cobbles. Normally it's the central crown, as that's the strip of cobbles that hasn't had to endure the transit weight of decades of vehicles. It feels almost counter-intuitive to ride the centre like this, and there are always some riders who will decide it's a bad idea and instead try to ride in the gutter, or even off-road in the hard-pack dirt. It may seem safer there, but ultimately you run a much higher risk of a puncture due to the stones, dirt and potholes.

Arenberg doesn't even have a central crown: it's just shit cobbles the whole way, with one particularly bad section where it feels like you're being jack-hammered. It's slightly false: flat uphill means you're losing speed the whole time and, if you're caught up behind a crash or a slow rider, you'll lose even more speed. Only the very strongest riders can recover from that sort of situation, because once you lose speed you're not getting it back.

Jered Gruber
@jeredgruber

In the dust with @millarmind

In recon only the newbies actually ride on the cobbles through Arenberg; those of us with a bit more experience ride on the dirt path adjacent to it knowing it will do us more harm than good to ride on these harshest of cobbles in training. Unfortunately the dirt path won't be available on race day because, as in Flanders, they will barrier the road off, giving us no choice but to be beat up by the cobblestones.

From the Arenberg on we start getting more animated, testing ourselves. For the first time in my career I'm actually having fun on the cobbles. It feels effortless – even my hands are fine, whereas all the young guys already have blisters after only half the recon. I'm so relaxed that I'm barely gripping my bars, something that I'd never mastered before. It genuinely feels like I'm floating over the *pavé*.

Sebastian Langeveld and I decide to ride the last two sectors at full speed. Even Seba can't stay with me on our last sector of the day, the Carrefour de l'Arbre. Our bus is waiting, parked at the exit of this, the last sector. I'm the first rider at the team bus at the end of the recon. This is unprecedental. It appears I've finally hit form a few days before the last race of my final Classics campaign. Better late than never.

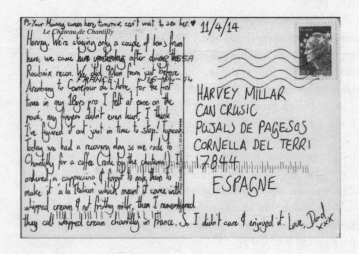

PS- Your Mummy comes here tomorrow, can't wait to see her. ♥   11/4/14

Le Château de Chantilly

Harvey. We're staying only a couple of kms from here, we came here yesterday after driving the SA Roubaix recon. We did 90km from just before Arenberg to Carrefour de L'Arbre for the first time in my 18yrs pro & I felt at ease on the pavé, my fingers didn't even hurt, I think I've figured it out just in time to stop! Typical. Today we had a recovery day so we rode to Chantilly for a coffee (code by the chateau!). I ordered a cappuccino & forgot to ask them to make it 'à la Italian' which meant it came with whipped cream & not frothy milk, then I remembered they call whipped cream chantilly in France. So I didn't care & enjoyed it. Love, Dad xxx

HARVEY MILLAR
CAN CRUSIC
PUJALS DE PAGESOS
CORNELLA DEL TERRI
17844
ESPAGNE

Don't Fuck This Up

I can't retire from pro racing without ever having finished Roubaix. I'd never forgive myself. I genuinely don't know if I can make it to Roubaix, but I keep telling myself I've never felt better on cobbles. It is truly now or never. Don't fuck this up.

Our plan for Roubaix is similar to what it was in Flanders in that Sebastian is once again leader, although he shares this responsibility with past Roubaix winner Johan Vansummeren. Tyler Farrar is having one of the best Classics seasons of his career, so we are giving him carte blanche and I am to make a call later in the race as to whether we back him or use him up to help Sebastian or Johan.

The race tactics are fairly simple in Roubaix: cover the early attacks and then prepare ourselves for the two red alarms in the first 152 kilometres and then a dark red alarm for the entry to Arenberg, followed by a dark red zone from 202 to 242 kilometres. We are to look after our leaders – unlike in every other race this involves riding behind them in key moments rather than in front. Andreas has given us strict instructions to make sure we are on the wheel of Sebastian or Johan whenever we hit a *pavé* sector, so we are ready to help them if they puncture or crash and don't hinder them if anything of the sort happens to us.

Apart from the final, symbolic sector, all other twenty-seven sectors will be covered by team support (in easy-to-spot team jerseys) with spare wheels and bottles. This will be the biggest logistical nightmare of the day. While Andreas plans tactics and speaks to riders, Geert is organising the team of vehicles, staff and volunteers whose sole job it is to be at their allocated sectors when they need to be – we'd had the same in the Tour of Flanders, with support at the top of nearly every *hellingen*. The reason for this is that the team cars are often too far behind the race to support the riders quickly enough to keep them in the race. Paris–Roubaix is the only race where the neutral race support is serviced by motor-bikes that can weave their way through the carnage and stay near the front of the race where they're needed.

Hitching a ride in one of the team support cars for Roubaix is one of the best spectating opportunities available in pro cycling. I know this from experience, having been picked up on the sidelines in 2009 with a broken collarbone (even then I wanted to go and watch a bike race). For this reason, and the fact she knows how important the race is to me, my wife Nicole has come up to watch – a rare thing considering she knows how much of a dick I can be at races. Having family or friends from my non-racing life visit me at races is strange. I get confused about who I'm supposed to pay more attention to. Unlike many, though, I do care about everybody on the team. I worry if somebody is having a bad time. I want to fix it. Similarly I get angry if some-body is disruptive in a negative or hurtful way. I have no fear of confrontation, which has served me for better and worse in equal measure.

Mechanics

The mechanics are the members of staff I get on best with. I'll often bring a tray of beers to the truck in the evening when they're the last members of the team still working, and sit and have a chat with them in the quiet and dark of the car park. Everybody else seems to forget about them. As I've got older I've always made an effort to tell my mechanic when my bike is working flawlessly – which means almost every day. The length of my career has allowed me to see trends. I've begun to notice things that I'd have taken to be anomalous moments if I'd just been passing through. One of these is the way mechanics always get told when things are going wrong, and very rarely when things have gone right. I've always thought it weird that they're treated as the bottom of the food chain when theirs is one of the most important jobs on the team. Then there's the way we take for granted that, when we wake up in our hotel rooms, the first thing we hear through our window is the truck compressor running and the compression hose hissing. Mechanics are the first up and the last down, nearly every day. Most pro cyclists will never wake up before their mechanics; they'll spend a career not noticing them already down in the car park at the team truck getting the bikes and cars prepped, often before sunrise; or that once the race is finished and we've had our massage and been down for dinner and returned to our hotel room and bed that they'll finally be putting our bikes back into the truck for the night, ready to repeat the cycle the next morning. It's easy to forget that they're at the hotel with our bikes when we arrive from whichever airport the day before the race. Then, the moment the race finishes and we leave in a mad rush to the airport to get home to our families, it's the mechanics who are left cleaning our bikes and packing the truck, with at least another day of driving ahead of them to get back to the *service course* where they will then have to unpack the truck. It's a metier far harder than being a pro bike racer.

Geoff Brown knows no other way. Geoff is an old-school pro mechanic and it goes without saying that he's as hard as nails, because for the majority of the time it's a thankless job. His hardness comes from his upbringing – he's not only a gentleman, he's also a gentle man, hence the fact he's lasted so long in such a hard job. He thinks it's fine, though. But that probably has something to do with him coming from Ottawa, where winters can kill you if you wear the wrong clothes. He spends the majority of his life on the road and has seen almost everything there is to see. In and among the twenty-one Tours he's done, he even saw a man win the Tour de France seven times.

This evening, the night before my last Classic, and Geoff's nineteenth Roubaix, I go down to the truck with a bunch of beers to have a final look at my bike and say thank you in advance. There's an incongruous calm about the scene; the bikes are all ready to go, an air of serenity permeates the air. Geoff is standing there with his apron on, packing the last little things back into the many drawers that riddle the rear of the truck; Alex Banyay is sitting in a fold-out fishing chair smoking a Marlboro Red, knowing there's no point in helping Geoff as he'll just tell him to sit back down, like every other time. Alex never leaves Geoff, though, even if Geoff tells him he's finished. They are near inseparable, which makes little sense as I don't think they have anything in common except their love of the job. Then again, that's probably the best reason, considering how all-encompassing their job is.

The easiest way to describe Alex is as a badass California skater/surfer. But there's nothing zen about him – he's like a coiled spring, tattooed up, permanently smoking, headphones rarely off his head; his fashion is the way California is supposed to be, not the diffused rip-off we're all used to. He wears clothes the way skaters and surfers who actually skate and surf wear them. It looks cool, he means it, there's not one iota of wannabe about him. He doesn't look loose, he looks a little fucking dangerous.

Alex is the mechanic assigned to my bikes. Geoff made sure of that the moment he realised he could trust him (I never asked). Alex doesn't do every race with me, but whenever he does nobody questions the fact my bikes are his property. We've grown to become friends over the last years of my career. That doesn't happen so often between riders and mechanics, which is strange, as it's such an important relationship, but I have good relations with both Geoff and Alex. This is made even odder by the fact that the two of them tend to avoid making friends. I take it as a privilege to have been let in.

The mechanics all take a beer and they pull out another fishing chair from one of the many compartments in the truck for me to sit with them. Alex is opening the beers and passing them around. Without even asking he passes one in my direction. 'Oh, man, I better not tonight,' I say, unconvincingly. Alex just looks at me not pulling back the beer: 'Fuck you, Dave, one beer isn't going to make a difference. We both know that.' I can't help but smile and shake my head. He's right, of course. 'Fuck, I know that, Alex, just let me pretend I'm being a pro.' He smiles right back at me, 'OK, you better be at the front tomorrow.'

Farewell, Roubaix

The nerves I've had in the build-up to the race dissipate the moment we roll out of Compiègne after the start. Immediately I'm feeling good. I surf the front of the bunch to make sure we don't miss a serious move, and then settle into the peloton and switch to energy conservation mode, spinning small gears, staying out of the wind, eating and drinking and trying my best to relax.

The first ninety kilometres are on big rolling roads. They're familiar to me as I lived in this region of France for a year back in 1996. We ride within two kilometres of where I lived – right past the supermarket I used to trawl of an afternoon in an attempt to fill the countless empty hours. It is bizarre to think of the nineteen-year-old me living there, fresh from Hong Kong, naïve as hell and more ambitious than perhaps I'd ever be again, clueless about what awaits him in the years ahead. A part of me wishes I could stop and warn him, just speak to him at least. Tell him it won't be anything like his dreams. Then it's gone, already behind us, in the past again.

Ahead of the first sector, things begin to get nervous; this is our first red alarm. Being at the front into this is so important, because we are still a complete peloton – more than 200 riders, and many among that 200 don't want to be here, and will be looking for a way out from the first sector onwards. Getting stuck behind a scared or unwilling racer is a bad place to be. These first sectors are very much where the culling takes place.

Something special happens when we hit the first sector. No matter how much you think you are prepared for the race, how ready you think you are, mentally, the moment you hit those first cobbles and you start to get thrown around, and the clattering and shouting begins, and the race stretches out, and the dust begins to cloud the air . . . you are hit by the fact you're racing Paris–Roubaix and, even if you're grimacing on the outside, you can't help but smile on the inside. The only other time I've had this feeling is when arriving on the Champs-Elysées on the final day of the Tour de France. For me, the sight of a peloton stretched out in a cloud of dust along a narrow cobbled road surrounded by fields is as magisterial as that most iconic of Paris boulevards. I think it's fair to say that the Tour de France and Paris–Roubaix are the two most iconic races in cycling.

For the first time in my career I am *totally* at ease on the *pavé*. I barely even notice those first sectors. I don't think about the line I need to be taking; I just can't help but be on the right line all the time. The sensation of floating is real, for a change I can't help but select the right gear – something that's not easy on the cobblestones as it's hard to judge gradients and anticipate or feel changes in speed. My cadence is always smooth, and not once do I feel like I'm fighting my bike. Most surprisingly my hands and wrists don't hurt in the slightest. I don't need to hold on for dear life, I have the impression of caressing my handlebars, guiding my bike through sector after sector rather than wrestling with it.

That's until the dark red alarm – the Arenberg Forest, where the floating is rudely interrupted for 2.4 kilometres. I'm caught up behind a crash a couple of kilometres before the entry to the sector, which means I'm going in badly placed – not that this makes any particular difference to me, it is going to suck hard even if I enter it in first position. I am prepared for it being bad, but it's worse than bad; it's horrible. At one point, where the *pavé* is at its worst, it feels like riding over logs; there is next to no sensation of momentum – if I were to stop pedalling I would come abruptly to a stop. I can see this happening to guys – either from puncturing, or other mechanical issues, or a crash, or simply having stopped pedalling and stalling on the spot. It is next to impossible to get going again; the only way I can describe it is to imagine emptying wheelbarrows full of bricks on to a road and then riding over them, on a road bike.

Coming out of Arenberg is a joy. In fact, from here on in, as the race gets faster and therefore harder, each of these transitions from cobblestones to tarmac elicits a moment of euphoria. Coming under the banner to signify the end of each sector we give ourselves a moment of respite, a drink from our bottles, a look over the shoulder to see how many have made it, then bottle back in the cage, head down and back into the race.

The crossing of the Arenberg is the first indication of who is strong. Without fail the best guys will be leading out of the forest – it's rare to see a Paris–Roubaix winner exit the forest far from the front, even though it's still 100 kilometres to the finish it's pivotal. Everybody considers the race to begin here.

Surviving Arenberg and still being in the front part of the bunch is a first for me. I begin to feel confident that, at worst, I will make it to the finish; at best, I could be with the leaders in the final. The relief I feel makes me realise how worried I've been. I now begin to enjoy the ride even more, able to really appreciate it without the fear of failure that has been dogging me – without me knowing it – for so long.

Right up until twenty-five kilometres to go I'm feeling good. There's only Sebastian and Johan left from our team, and both have told me to do my own race as they aren't feeling strong enough to be counted upon. It is beyond strange for me to be up there with the specialists, holding my own. I'm having one of those days where I don't understand why there are so few of us at the front when it appears to me we haven't really gone hard yet. Then on the sixth sector I make the stupid mistake of riding the gutter instead of the central crown. My front tyre punctures halfway through the sector. In hindsight I can see this was a clear indication of fatigue setting in, because it was the wrong line to take.

By the time neutral service get to me I'm out the back of the group. As often happens in these situations, the wheel change isn't the smoothest, yet it is still quicker than waiting for my team car, because by the time I'm on my way again there is still no sign of it. I set off in pursuit, with team cars and motorbikes flying by me. Once I get up to speed I jump in behind the first vehicle that is nearby to get some respite in its slipstream. We are on a small country lane, weaving left and right. I'm trying to keep a cool head. I keep darting looks over the roof of the car or through the rear window in order to see what is coming up. This isn't the safest of manoeuvres at the best of times.

This is not the best of times.

I can see a ninety-degree left-hander coming up and know the team car I'm following will try to hold its speed in order not to hinder my chase. The *directeur sportifs* driving the cars in the convoy try to treat everybody the same – it would be considered incredibly bad form to compromise a rider's chase because they're from a different team. This is also the reason to try to keep friends among all the teams. Although none of the *directeur sportifs* will treat you badly behind the race, if you have friends you'll see the benefits when you're in trouble. I've been racing for so long that many of my peers have retired from racing and are now driving the team cars. Fortunately, I'm on good terms with all of them, some of them even being great friends, so this is never a bad thing when you're in trouble, behind the race.

I come into the left-hander at full speed. I'm fairly confident of my ability to make it round, which is stupid as I don't take into account I have a new front wheel, with a different tyre at a different pressure. I have no idea how I stay upright as the front tyre has no grip. My front wheel slides across the road, and I only just manage to avoid going down hard, but in the process I lose all my speed and veer off the road.

My team car finally makes it up to me. The timing is good, yet also bad, because if they hadn't been here at this exact moment I would have had a few moments to regroup and would have forced myself to adapt to the front wheel. As it is I'm so shaken I tell them I want to change the front wheel back to a trusted one I'm familiar with. It is the wrong decision, as stopping for a second time effectively ruins my chances of making it back to the group I'd been in. It's only six kilometres to the second most important sector in the race, Carrefour de l'Arbre, and the race is at full tilt up ahead.

I realise I've made a mistake quite quickly, and as soon as this hits me I become aware of the fatigue I've been hiding from myself up until that point. The moment my head goes my body follows suit. Knowing the front group is disappearing up the road I sit up and wait for the next group – all hopes of being in the final with the leaders gone, I go back to the best of the worst-case scenarios: simply finishing.

Then it all goes wrong. The next group catch me and I don't even try to fight for position. I drift to the back and think, 'I'll just ride in.' With my head disengaged from the race I lose the focus and ability to float that I've had up to then. I find myself in last position going over Carrefour de l'Arbre, feeling like the fish out of water I've been so many times before at Paris–Roubaix. Coming round a nondescript right-hander at a pitiful speed the bike disappears from under me, I smack down on the floor, legs and arms everywhere. I lie there on my back for a moment and can't help but smile. For a moment I'd thought I was a Roubaix hero – now I was back to zero. The tables had turned unbelievably quickly.

I can't even describe it as a crash, it's more like the cycling equivalent of tripping up. I get back on the bike and receive a push from one of the spectators. It takes me a while to clip into my pedal – the cobbles are bouncing me around so much, by the time I lift my head I can see the group I'd been with has gone. I decide there and then that I'll ride to the finish solo, I'm not interested in hanging on to any more groups that come up from behind – it feels more honourable to be riding in at my own pace, allowing myself the opportunity to appreciate my first and final arrival into Roubaix. Two more groups come by me, both of which I deliberately let go. I want to enter the velodrome on my own in order to give myself the chance to really soak it all up. It doesn't matter how far back I am now. It isn't just that it is my first Paris–Roubaix finish, it's also the fact it's my last ever Monument. I'm never going to race a northern Classic again. I won't say this makes me sad, because they're bastards of things, but it does make me nostalgic.

I enter the velodrome, and my vision of having a lap and a half to myself is just that: a vision. There's a small group who've come by me with a couple of kilometres to go. I let them pass, not wanting to have to speak to anybody or share the moment. Unfortunately I don't let them get far enough ahead, because as I'm coming round to complete my first lap they are blocking the track, having just finished. I'm going to have to come to a near stop and 'sorry, excuse me' my way through them in order to continue the final half-lap to the finish line. I can't bring myself to do this, and I've convinced myself that I'm so far back maybe I don't have to do the full lap and a half because of this back-marker confusion. I don't want to have the lasting memory of finishing Roubaix being me unclipping and politely asking some guys if I can squeeze through.

So I pull off the track. Nicole is in the centre waiting. This is possibly the only time that she has been right there, at the finish. Thank God she is – firstly, because it is such an important moment for me, but, probably more crucially, because nobody else has the heart or courage to tell me I still have half a lap to go.

After five minutes, and a couple of brief interviews, Nicole taps me on the shoulder and tells me I'd better put my helmet back on and get back on the track: 'You'll be DNF otherwise. Marya just told me.' Marya Pongrace is the team's press officer. I had noticed her being a little uneasy about me standing there.

Eventually I did it, all romance gone, nostalgia-free, just riding round that most famous of velodromes like a moron, wishing I could crawl under a rock. Farewell, Roubaix.

Not the Ardennes

Roubaix signified the end of the Flanders Classics, and the following week would see the Ardennes Classics begin – these run from Sunday to Sunday and include three races, Amstel Gold Race, Flèche Wallonne and the oldest Monument of them all, Liège–Bastogne–Liège, aka La Doyenne. These are hillier than the races of the previous weeks. Modern-day general classification racers will try to avoid the Flanders Classics like the plague, considering them too dangerous; completely unsuited to their more refined racing style. An arsenal of weaponry is required to win a Flandrian Classic, whereas, arguably, fitness alone is the key to success in the Ardennes. An Ardennes winner must be strong and light, yet have the confidence to hide their power behind their weight.

All three of the Ardennes are decided in a very intense and relatively brief finale among those who have endured the previous six hours of climbing and descending. There's little danger, and not much positioning; the roads are safe and fast. What the Ardennes lack in danger and madness it makes up for in workload. Liège is considered to be the hardest of all the Monuments because of the sheer physicality of it, but it's as safe as houses. Nobody goes to Liège thinking they'll crash.

This year I'm on a break during the Ardennes – this is the gift I get for having spent nearly a month in Belgium. The team is flipped, both staff and riders are rotated out, the stage racers come in for one of their brief forays into one-day racing while the rest of us head to our homes to rest and recover and prepare ourselves for the next part of the season.

Not the Giro

I'd had a few requests for my final season: Paris–Roubaix had been one; the Tour de France, the Commonwealth Games, Vuelta a España and the Worlds were the others. The final one – perhaps closer to a demand than a request – was that I had total, unequivocal exemption from taking part in the Giro d'Italia.

The Giro is a special race. I mean *'Il est spécial'* in the French sense; i.e. the 'I don't want to talk about it' sense. I'd done it for the first time in 2008, the Tour and Vuelta always having been my Grand Tours of choice. The Giro had never really held any great attraction for me, largely because I wasn't a big fan of racing in Italy, more than likely due to my nemesis, Tirreno–Adriatico. I never enjoyed the Giro the way I did the Tour and the Vuelta. The course was almost always the hardest of the three, and it often seemed the stages were mapped out to make our lives as difficult as possible.

Then there was the bad weather – almost a certainty considering we'd be heading into mountain ranges in May, where the risk of snow and rain was still high. There was also a constant sense of chaos about the whole organisation – much like Italy as a whole – we often felt like circus performers at the whim of a cruel ringmaster. It was the Giro that set the trend for having mountain stages right up until the penultimate day of the race, something that we have grown used to in all Grand Tours these days, yet is a relatively new development.

I came close to winning a road stage in my first visit to the race. I didn't because I snapped my chain one kilometre from the finish, when convinced it was wrapped up. I was so angry I threw my bike as far as I could, hurling it spinning over the barriers, ironically dwarfing any sense of achievement over the win I remain convinced was mine. It made me feel that Italy and I were truly not made for each other. I should have understood then, but I'm not known for my quick learning, unfortunately. And little did I know worse was to come.

Mainly due to the fact that I'd written a book over the winter, 2011 had been a classic slow start to the year for me. I was so bad I was sent home from Tirreno–Adriatico before the race started: a new low, even by my own low standards for that particular event. I returned home and trained with the sole ambition of being good for the Giro, something I'd never done in the past, as normally I arrived in Italy a broken man from the Classics.

We took a young team and unsurprisingly didn't display our usual prowess in the first day's team time trial, finishing what, at the time, was considered a lowly fifth, at twenty-four seconds from the winners. I'd been the strongest member of our team so knew I was ticking over well. There were only two stages I was aiming for – Stage 3 and the final day's time trial. Stage 3 was the perfect finish for me, hilly and technical, and I was reasonably certain a break wouldn't make it to the finish – on day three everybody is still fresh and motivated and the general classification is so close that the peloton will be under tight control. There was no point in going for a long breakaway. I decided to gamble everything on the finale.

I was so motivated I decided to wear the new speedsuit our clothing sponsor Castelli had developed. This went against everything I stood for, as it meant I was sacrificing style for speed. Back then these were the first-generation all-in-one road jersey and shorts combo. They're almost the norm these days, but back in 2011 they were still a little risqué in the looks department. I rolled up to the start in the piazza of Reggio Emilia. I was one of the last riders to arrive there. I saw my Girona training partner, Michael Barry, so parked up next to him.

'Hey, man.' Michael looked at me and immediately noticed the speedsuit. 'Whoa, you going for it today?'

'Yeah, I think I am.' I looked at the 200-plus riders parked up in front of us. 'Fuck, I can't believe I'm going to have to beat all these guys.' It was a weird realisation to have, but it was true: it was one thing lying in bed the night before studying the maps and profile and finish, planning how I'd win it; it was a completely different kettle of fish lining up and seeing what stood in my way.

One hundred and thirty-three kilometres later we crested the major obstacle of the day, a climb much like the Turchino Pass in Milan–San Remo. I'd never left the top ten on the ascent, and was in complete control of what I was doing, waiting patiently to attack in the last ten kilometres, where the last hills served as ideal launch pads.

The descent was fifteen kilometres and technical. The bunch was already broken up from the climb. At the very front there was no particular sense of urgency or danger, which is why I'd made sure I was there. It was easy to imagine how fast it would be behind, with the peloton being whiplashed by the concertina effect and the groups furiously chasing back on. I had no doubt the peloton was stretched over a few kilometres by the time we arrived at the bottom on to the coast. This was good for me, as already half the peloton were eliminated before I'd even done anything.

There were only two climbs standing between us and the finish. Both were relatively small, the first being three kilometres, the second just one. At the bottom of the first climb a strong attack went. I felt so good that I immediately jumped across with it – as is often the way when you feel that good, you don't panic. I sat on the back and spun a small gear, doing no more than the absolutely minimum required while my breakaway compatriots smashed themselves.

I could see the peloton was chasing hard and would probably catch us just before the summit – that would be my moment to go. The *domestiques* chasing us down would go deep in the red to bring us back, to the point of doing kamikaze peel-offs in the final closing metres of their chase. This would also put most of the peloton in the red. I could see this happening so stopped riding in the break, and sat in last position and began to take deep breaths in an attempt to recover, preparing myself to launch the decisive move and begin what would be a very intense nine-kilometre race for the line.

I pushed my left brake lever to change from the small ring into the big ring, readying myself for the attack. Only nothing happened. I tried again. And again. Nothing happened. I started flicking my other brake lever to move my chain down the cassette block on the rear wheel in an attempt to change the chain line and enable the front mech to have more tension on the chain. Still nothing. I couldn't believe it. What the fuck was happening? I'd had this problem occasionally before, the SRAM shifters and my oval chainrings were not a match made in heaven, but, seriously, not now, please, not now!

Sure enough I was stuck in the small ring. I couldn't do anything about it. The moment had gone. Guys from behind started attacking and coming by us and I was helpless to do anything. The front of the peloton swamped us over the top and the counter-attack of four riders was gone. The perfect moment taken.

Once we were on the descent I was able to get into the big ring. I was so incredibly angry, I couldn't believe my second Giro stage win had been taken away from me because of another mechanical issue. There were no *domestiques* left to chase; only the general classification leaders were left at the front, and they were perfectly happy to see the group of four ride away for the win, as it would make for a safer run-in if the win wasn't being fought out.

There was the one little climb left, less than a kilometre long, and I could see the break was going away; they already had twenty seconds. I was back at the front of the peloton. As we hit the bottom I looked around and saw that as far as everybody else was concerned it was over. It was probably obvious I was itching to go, as I was now in a big gear, out of the saddle in my drops looking around checking everybody out. Right next to me was Alberto Contador. I looked at him, and he looked at me and gave me the slightest of nods, as if to say, 'GO. NOW.'

I jumped as hard as I could. I knew everybody would watch me go and think twice, as it seemed a bit of a lost cause – and if Alberto was going to sweep behind me and not show the slightest inkling of movement it would cause a further hesitation. That was all I needed.

To this day I'm not sure how I did what I did next, but I'm quite certain much of it had something to do with how angry I was. I sprinted the whole way up the climb, bridging a twenty-second gap in a few hundred metres. I caught the back of the group over the top of the climb. I hovered off the back, knowing they weren't even aware I had made it across. I was confident I could win the sprint as the group was made mainly of climbers, and also because I'd studied the last kilometre and knew there was a corner inside the final 200 metres, which meant leading into it was the best option. I'd made sure this had been checked out by the staff at the finish, who'd then informed the *directeur sportif* in the car, who'd confirmed it to me on the radio.

Two things went wrong. The corner was barely a corner, more of a curve, and it had already straightened out before we got to the 200-metres-to-go sign. This meant I'd put myself in the worst possible position, giving whoever was on my wheel the perfect lead out. Then there was the second, and graver, mistake: I hadn't realised one of the four riders was Ángel Vicioso. He's a rider I knew was fast, but hadn't raced with in a long time: I didn't even realise he rode for a small Italian team these days so hadn't recognised him. I could have probably got away with my long lead out if I hadn't had a good little sprinter like Vicioso on my wheel. He fairly and squarely beat me into second place. I was even angrier now than I'd been about my chain only minutes before.

As soon as we crossed the line I was shouting down the radio, 'Who the fuck checked the finish? It's nothing like in the book. I just gave that away. FUUUUCK!' I didn't even stop. I just hissy-fitted it all the way to the bus, so incredibly angry at myself and anybody else who happened to cross my path at that particular moment.

Then a journalist literally stood in my way as I approached the team bus. 'David! Please, have you heard?' He seemed very wired, as if he had something really important to tell me that I needed to know. I didn't even care. I told him so, 'Jesus Christ. I'll speak to you later. Let me by.'

It didn't stop him. 'It doesn't look good for Wouter Weylandt.' Everything just stopped for me. 'What? What are you talking about?' It made no sense.

'He crashed on the descent. Really bad.' He'd calmed down a bit now. Even he realised that maybe he'd been a bit too eager to tell me.

'I'm going to my bus.' Anger had turned to confusion. What the fuck was going on? I was able to extricate myself from my own, oh-so-important drama and see that everybody was acting oddly. I stepped off my bike and leaned it against the bus. There was definitely an unfamiliar atmosphere. I got on the bus and collapsed in my seat. As usual the first thing I did was check my phone. There was already a missed call from Nicole. I called back immediately. She was crying when she answered, 'Why are they showing it on TV? They can't do that.'

Oh God, this didn't sound good. 'What's going on, babes? I just got on the bus. I don't know what's happened.'

'A rider crashed. There was blood everywhere and he wasn't moving.' I'd rarely heard Nicole so upset: 'They wouldn't stop filming it. Why would they do that? I don't understand why they'd do that. What about his girlfriend? They say she's five months' pregnant, just like me.'

I asked her who it was. I wanted to make sure this was actually happening.

'I don't know. Wouter Weylandt? Do you know him? It's so horrible. They're saying he's dead. Is that true? I've just looked on Wikipedia, it already says he's dead.'

There was nobody else on the bus. I got up to go and find out what was going on when my phone rang again. It was Whitey.

'Dave. You're in pink, mate!' Whitey didn't even work for the team any more, yet no doubt he was following my results and performances as much as he ever did, because that's just the way he is.

'What are you talking about, Whitey? How's that possible?' Now I was truly bamboozled.

'You had twenty-one seconds on the line, then, with time bonuses, you've taken the jersey. You did it, mate!' I could hear how happy he was for me.

'Fucking hell. This is mad. What's going on with Wouter? Have you heard anything?'

Whitey's voice changed. 'Doesn't look good, Dave. He wasn't moving. Last I heard they were helicoptering him outta there.'

I turned around and collapsed back down in my seat. I didn't want to go outside the bus any more.

Ten minutes later, when the last riders had crossed the finish line, it was announced that Wouter Weylandt was dead. He had crashed heavily on the long descent down to the coast, no doubt while chasing back on. They had attempted resuscitation for twenty minutes at the roadside before airlifting him out. He was pronounced dead soon after.

This official news spread like wildfire. Riders came on to the bus one by one, nobody said much. We all knew that Tyler would be arriving soon. Wouter and he were close friends, living near each other in Ghent, training and socialising together. They even had the same haircuts. None of us knew what to do, or what to say. We just sat quietly and waited.

Eventually Ty arrived crying as he got on the bus. He threw his helmet on the floor and went to sit at the back burying his head in his hands, sobbing. Everybody looked at each other; this wasn't something we knew how to handle. All other bad situations we simply bantered our way out of, that was the only way we knew how to remedy shit situations. This was way outside our bandwidth.

I was closest to Ty on the team, so it made sense that I should go to him. I got up and went to the back of the bus and put my arm around him. He leant into me like a child would. I didn't say anything as there was nothing to say. I just sat there until an official came and told me it was time to go to doping control. I told Tyler I had to go, that I was in the leader's jersey. He barely registered it.

The trip from the bus to the podium is normally one of those joyous back-slapping occasions, smiles everywhere, clapping, photos and autographs, a hug or two. It is a moment to be cherished because for most of us it is so rare.

This was different. There were a few gentle pats on my back, the occasional respectful handshake. It was exactly how you would expect it to be when somebody has died. It was a quiet and sombre walk with my French *directeur sportif*, Lionel Marie.

The podium area was already being dismantled, the barriers taken down; there were very few people around. We went straight to the doping control area where I signed in and sat down outside to wait my turn. We didn't speak much, probably nothings to fill the silence. What we did say was in French, which seemed appropriate as that had been the language I spoke when things had been bad in my younger life.

One of the Giro organisation came up with a bag, shook my hand and said how horrible it all was. He opened the bag and brought out the famous *maglia rosa*. Could I try it on, please? Just to make sure the size was right. So there I stood, outside a doping-control caravan, putting on the one jersey I had coveted for so long and had thought forever out of my reach. Having the pink jersey meant I had worn the leader's jerseys of all three Grand Tours, something very few people have had the honour of doing. I looked at Lionel and asked how it looked. He smiled sadly, '*Magnifique*, David.' I took it off and gave it back. The last thing I wanted was to feel like I'd gained something from the day.

Tyler didn't leave his room that night. Dinner was a subdued affair, as was to be expected. When I'd finished I made up a tray from the restaurant buffet and grabbed a bottle of wine and headed up to see him. Oddly, nobody knew what to do around him. It was almost as if they were afraid to be near him because it would make it more real. I stayed with him till he fell asleep, then returned to my room, fully aware of the responsibility I now carried the next day.

I didn't sleep much. I didn't know how to behave the next day. Should I assume the role of leader of the peloton? Or should I just let the organisation and Wouter's team decide how the day should be? Did being the *maglia rosa* mean I had to be the peloton's spokesman? Should I even wear the *maglia rosa*? What was expected of me? I didn't know, and the darkness of night didn't help me come to any conclusions.

As usual I was first at breakfast. I sat there and watched, one by one, other riders from other teams come in. Then a strange thing happened. Riders started coming across and shaking my hand, not to congratulate me, but out of respect. The ones who didn't looked at me and nodded with a smile, as if to say, 'Good luck.'

It was clear that what they expected of me was exactly what I would expect of the race leader at such a time – to lead. At that moment I decided there was no question of me not wearing the leader's jersey – and I would decide how we raced. One of my plans during my restless reverie of the night just gone was to have each team ride ten kilometres on the front, in reverse order of the team classification, with Wouter's team crossing the line first. That way there would be some method to the day. We could ride it in an organised manner, giving it reason and order rather than let it be a miserable march, or, worse, no start at all.

I called up the boss of Wouter's team, Brian Nygaard, and ran the plan by him. He agreed that it was the best solution. With that I called up the boss of the Giro and told him that that was how we would ride the day's stage.

When we arrived at the start I got kitted up sooner than I ever normally would, and left the bus to do the rounds and speak to the teams. The first team I went to was Wouter's team, Leopard Trek. I met Nygaard outside their bus. He asked me to try to persuade his riders that they were better off trying to finish the Giro, continuing the race than retiring and returning home as many expected them to. I told him I couldn't do that, and that I'd already told Tyler to go home. To this day I find it strange he would have asked me that. I entered the bus and paid my respects to each rider, wishing them luck and explaining how we would ride the day.

I went round a few more teams that had leaders who had influence in the peloton, and explained the plan for the day, so they knew it was coming from me, and therefore the riders. This, sadly, is the only way we get shit done, due to the absence of a strong union.

I then went to the sign-on podium. Behind that was a room where all the *directeur sportifs* had congregated for an emergency meeting with the race organisation. I could see and hear before I entered that it was heated, borderline chaos. Before entering I hesitated, the young neo-pro in me rearing his fearful head. Before I could turn around and leave I'd already opened the door. Then the strangest thing happened. I heard the words '*La maglia rosa*' ripple around the room. Within ten seconds there was silence and everybody was looking at me. I remember thinking, 'Fucking hell, didn't expect that.' I put my shoulders back, stood tall, ignored the fact I was wearing cycling shorts, cleated shoes and a pink t-shirt and told them the plan. Then I turned and left the room.

The day went as planned. The final climb, not far from the finish, saw me have recurring problems with my gears, which meant I was out the back of the peloton when my team was about to start doing the final pull on the front, before Leopard led us to the finish. This felt like a totally normal event by this point.

My team handed over to Leopard a handful of kilometres before the finish, and the whole peloton let them drift off the front in order to allow them to finish alone, together, across the line. Tyler went with them, because it was his best friend who had died.

For the first time that day I relaxed, relieved we'd actually done something that showed unity as well as dignity.

Then the third unexpected thing of the day happened. After the behaviour of fellow riders at breakfast, then the show of respect from the *directeurs* at the meeting, it was the peloton that made the loveliest gesture of the day. As we were being swallowed up by the peloton I allowed myself to stop feeling responsible. I began to feel hands on my back, stopping me slipping back. I lifted my head and looked around to find those nearby looking at me. Somebody who knew me well said, 'David, you have to go.'

So I finished alone, in between Leopard, Tyler and the peloton. I was so self-conscious I panicked and went as quickly as I could to the podium protocol next to the finish line, where nobody could get to me. To this day I regret that. I should have gone to Tyler, because he was a mess, but I thought that would look too contrived. I didn't want him breaking down in my arms.

Neither of us wanted that. Yet, in hindsight, I wish I had, because I know he needed me there. I got lost in what I was supposed to do rather than who I was – Ty's friend.

The day didn't end there. It was the eightieth anniversary of the creation of the *maglia rosa*. For some reason a special celebration of this had been organised at the Italian Naval Academy, not far away, so the day ended with me glad-handing Italian naval officers before being presented with a replica of the original *maglia rosa* on a podium in front of a dry-docked, tall ship. A weird ending to a sad day. I crashed the next day and lost the pink jersey. Ultimately I won the time trial on the last stage and promised myself I'd never return. Which turned out to be a lie, because I did, for the 2013 edition, leaving home only a few hours after my second son, Harvey, was born. I crashed the next day on the first stage and smashed my leg up, then suffered in the rain for two weeks before calling it quits on Stage 14.

Springtime in Catalunya

These days I consider May to be one of the most amazing months of the year: birds sing, fields are green and the sun is out. As long as I'm not racing around Italy life is beautiful. Living in Catalunya makes this feel particularly true. May is the lushest month of the year, cherished by locals in the knowledge that within weeks all will be arid.

I've never really experienced gradual changes. I always believed things passed without occasion: the fields were muddy when I went away and green to come back to; lush to leave and yellow wasted stubble when I returned. There was no gradual seasonal cycle in my world. I'd just turn up at different places doing different things in different moods. That was true of much in my life. I'd often forget the world revolved without me.

A prime example of this was life on the home front. My wife runs the house on her own. There is a routine in place and a system that she has created to sustain this lifestyle. This has been made all the more necessary with two small boys to look after. When I arrive back I spend at least a couple of days getting things wrong. I have to ask questions about what goes where and when we do what. I don't mind this in the slightest, but it took me a while to get the hang of coming back to my wife's home, because that is what it is for the majority of the year. It's the only way for Nicole to limit the constant disruption of my comings and goings. Although I spend a lot of time away, when I am back it's equally intense. I'm constantly around, and not the best of company – tired and useless most of the time. If I'm not tired and useless then I have to train so hard that I make myself tired and useless. It's a bit monotonous. Fortunately my wife is a very patient woman who understands that's part and parcel of being married to a professional cyclist.

The break after Roubaix had done me good. I was fully motivated for what was potentially the last big training block of my cycling career. I'd planned since the winter months to go on an altitude training camp the first three weeks of May, to set me up for the summer's racing. My planning involved asking the team a few times if they could organise something, which, as usual in the off-season, had seemed like a fairly simple thing to do and one which everybody backed as a good idea. At that point there was even talk of us having apartments permanently rented in Tenerife to allow riders to come and go as they pleased.

But, as often happens, this didn't come to pass. What had seemed like a fairly simple logistical plan became a total cluster-fuck. There was no accommodation available in Tenerife, and no support staff who could have come even if there had been avail-ability. With this plan A down the pan I didn't exactly try hard to find a plan B. I'd only been on a handful of altitude training camps in my whole career, none of which had done me any particular good, so after reminding myself of this fact I decided I could train sufficiently at home. This, on the other hand, had been something I had done the majority of my career.

The thing is, for the majority of my career I hadn't been the father of two small children, and neither had I been in my final year of racing. For some, those elements alone would have been motivation enough; for me, I felt more relaxed than ever. I trained well the next three weeks, but never really found myself in that totally committed state of mind where every part of my life revolved around training, eating and sleeping. I enjoyed being at home and being able to contribute to Nicole's household and life. Well, I say 'contribute'. I was probably still a massive burden, but I liked to think I was helping.

My training workload was huge, but what I was missing was the ability to hurt myself. I'd spoken to a few of the other older guys in the peloton, and it seems this is the first thing we all lose. I'd felt the same in the recent winter, but I'd always been like that in the off-season, so hadn't overanalysed it. Now was the time of the year when I needed to be outside my comfort zone, pushing myself to levels that were more akin to racing than training.

I simply lacked the necessary willpower. I was enjoying riding around Catalunya far too much. For the first time in my life I was paying more attention to the countryside than my power output. I'd become a cyclo-tourist, which is a wonderful thing. Unless you're paid to race a bicycle, that is. I'd embraced this attitude so much I even entered myself into a local cyclo-sportif with Nicole and my teammate and training buddy Lachlan Morton. I reckoned it was easier than having to actually think about where I was going or how hard I had to go. Nicole did the short version while Lachy and I did the long version, which was surprisingly hard – unlike everybody else at the front, Lachy and I were stopping at every feed station and having a drink and grabbing a bite to eat then catching them back up. This was probably massively annoying to everybody else, but it made for a good day out training for the two of us. We made sure we didn't win – that wouldn't have been cool.

I didn't fight it. I figured as long as I got the kilometres in and kept my weight down then I could use my next two stage races as fine-tuning events that would get me up to speed for the Tour de France. I'd done this many times in the past. It wasn't as if it was a new method for me.

Bavaria

The first of these stage races was Bayern Rundfahrt (aka Tour of Bavaria). Andreas Klier speaks of this race in the same way others would of Shangri-La. Something happens to Andreas when he arrives in Bavaria, or even talks about Bayern Rundfahrt. He lights up like the Munich Christmas Market. He's done it eighteen times and never won a stage. He is terribly proud of this fact – it probably has something to do with him having been on holiday since the Classics and the fact that it's considered a legal requirement to drink *Weissbier* in Bavaria (he would always be reminding us that workers were permitted to drink a litre of *Weissbier* at work. I don't know if this was true or not, but we were easily convinced). Andreas would vehemently deny that *Weissbier* ever compromised his performance – he has always been the most professional of bike riders when it comes to doing what's expected of him in a race, but he does have some bloody good stories of nocturnal escapades from his youth.

It is often the way with these smaller stage races: many of us have done them for years, so we keep returning because we've grown attached to them. The familiarity is a comfort. We know the roads, and often stay in the same hotels. There are stories and shared memories. They're like a home away from home, but not many of us can claim to have done the same race eighteen times.

It was because of this love affair that I was even going there. I'd promised Andreas that in my last year I would come and compete in his 'home' race. This meant more to him than anything else, and he'd convinced himself I was going to win the overall and we were going to rule like Bavarian kings of old. I didn't have the heart to tell him that I would be using it as a training exercise. I think he knew, but even he didn't let himself acknowledge it.

I'd convinced myself we'd be enjoying a *Sound of Music*-like experience, only instead of singing and evading Nazis there'd be bike racing and *Weissbier*. We'd have relaxed racing on beautiful German roads, hillside chalet hotels with beer gardens staffed with pretty German barmaids in traditional dresses, and men with big moustaches in lederhosen, slapping each other. Every day would be framed by a crisp blue sky, and we'd constantly be surrounded by rolling meadows speckled with blossoming flowers.

So I was a little disappointed when I got off the bus after the long drive from the airport to find myself in the pissing rain, standing in a miserable car park next to a supermarket, above which was our hotel. Julie Andrews would not have been impressed.

I eventually found my room. Our base for the night resembled an office tower block that had been converted into a hotel, only without imagination or money. My room just about accommodated my suitcase and me. I collapsed on my bed and rued the day I'd agreed to this.

A couple of hours later Andreas came knocking at the door having returned from the pre-race *directeurs'* meeting, where he'd been given the race numbers and race books. He entered quietly and sat at the end of my bed and put his head carefully in one hand, the other holding all the documentation that he was going from room to room handing out. He embodied the Klier version of *The Thinker*. 'I am sorry, David. We are in fucking East Germany.' He lifted his head and looked at me, eye to eye, serious, 'Really, we are. This is not Bavaria. There is no bar, not even a restaurant in this stupid hotel! I'm ashamed.'

He stood up and squeezed by my suitcase and my bed to get to the window, where he looked out through the rain-splashed glass at the grey town ahead and the supermarket car park below. 'I can't even see Bavaria through this shit.'

This is classic Andreas – he heads off my complaint by essentially pre-empting everything I want to say. So instead of me ranting about what a shithole we're in, I find myself consoling him. 'Ah, it's OK, Andreas, this is probably the worst of it. We must be in better hotels in the next few days?' I back that up with a pleading, 'Right?'

He sits back down. 'Yes, you're right. In fact in three days we have a very good hotel. This I am sure of. Tomorrow we ride south-west all day, then it will be better.'

Vilshofen an der Donau

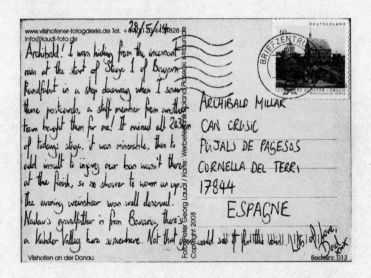

Archibald! I was hiding from the incessant
rain at the start of Stage 1 of Bayern
Rundfahrt in a shop doorway when I saw
these postcards, a staff member from another
team bought them for me! It rained all 203km
of todays stage. it was miserable, then to
add insult to injury our bus wasn't there
at the finish, so no shower to warm us up!
The evening weissbeer was well deserved.
Nadav's grandfather is from Bavaria, there's
a Kander Valley here somewhere. Not that I could tell ...

ARCHIBALD MILLAR
CAN CRUSIC
PUJALS DE PAGESOS
CORNELLA DEL TERRI
17844
ESPAGNE

Vilshofen an der Donau

Bestellnr. 013

The only good thing I could find to think about the race
was the fact that they'd given us permission to film, just as we'd
done at Tirreno, so I was back carrying cameras and a microphone, with Martin and Patrice as my guardian angel motorbike. Finlay was praying I'd do something so that he could catch
an exploit on film. I just couldn't do it, though. I couldn't bring
myself to hurt myself getting in a break. I no longer had the
crazy switch that allowed me to go and rip a race to pieces for the
sake of it. My motivation levels weren't helped by the fact that it
rained relentlessly the first three days. I was decidedly stuck in
a training mentality, not wanting to do more than I had to, my
grand plan being to get through Bayern with minimal damage
and then train immediately off the back of it leading into the next
race, Critérium du Dauphiné, effectively giving myself a three-
week block, almost like a Grand Tour simulation. I could then rest
properly after Dauphiné and be able to do the fine-tuning inten-
sive work needed in the build-up to the National Championships,
my final race before the Tour de France. It was a way of preparing
I'd used many times before in my career.

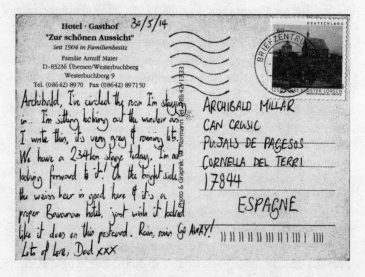

Hotel · Gasthof
"Zur schönen Aussicht"
Seit 1904 in Familienbesitz
Familie Arnulf Maier
D-83236 Übersee/Westerbuchberg
Westerbuchberg 9
Tel. (08642) 8970 Fax (08642) 897150

30/5/14

Archibald, I've circled the room I'm staying in. I'm sitting looking out the window as I write this, it's very grey & raining lots. We have a 234km stage today. I'm not looking forward to it! On the bright side the weiss beer is good here & it's a proper Bavarian hotel, just wish it looked like it does on this postcard. Rain, rain Go AWAY! Lots of love, Dad xxx

ARCHIBALD MILLAR
CAN CRUSIC
PUJALS DE PAGESOS
CORNELLA DEL TERRI
17844

ESPAGNE

The bad weather left its mark and the final day I didn't feel 100 per cent so I pulled out on the finishing circuit so as to minimise the risk of falling properly ill, which at this point in the year I couldn't afford, especially with my plan to give myself limited recovery time in the days following. I would have loved to have won something for Andreas, to have been able to celebrate with him. I wasn't able, though. I knew Andreas was fine with that, he understood; we'd become friends more than colleagues, we had many years in the future to visit Bavaria, and on our own terms. I returned home mentally ready for a good week of training pre-Dauphiné.

Early Summer in Catalunya

I woke up at home, the morning after Bavaria, with not even the slightest hint of the cold I'd felt coming on the day before. I felt incredible, which didn't make much sense, but I wasn't going to argue with it. After a couple of days' recovery I went full-beast-mode training with Lachy.

Lachy's one of those rare genetic freaks. He's a natural climber, a thoroughbred who already has massive endurance capabilities at a very young age. His freakishness doesn't stop there: he's about as nonconformist as anybody I know, more akin to an out-there artist than an elite athlete.

His training helmet is covered in dinosaur stickers and sharpie graffiti, his hair is from the Bob Dylan school of stylin', and he has a moustache like a Mexican drug dealer, while his tattoos look like dares. I enjoy hanging out with him; we train hard, and laugh a lot.

We decide it's time for us to be proper science monkeys, and plan out our week and make up what we think are Team Sky interval sessions. We really do just make them up (well, with my eighteen years of training experience) and tell ourselves that, for sure, this is what they do. We even name the ride on our training programmes 'Sky Shit'. This involves lots of intervals on climbs. We are both on our hands and knees by the end of each session. We are effectively racing each other, and using the intervals as an excuse to do so.

I'm not sure why we get on so well. An equal amount of disdain for normality, I'm guessing, and a shared love of disruption. I keep this bent under wraps most of the time; Lachy might just as well walk around wearing a sandwich board saying 'YOLO'. We make a fairly incongruous double act.

During this week Nicole has been planning her Big Camper Adventure. She'd always said that before I retired she wanted to hire a camper and take the boys to follow me at a race. Up until the previous year I'd been convinced I'd keep racing until I was thirty-nine or forty, so it had always been something for the future – a lovely idea with time to plan. My decision to stop racing this year means it is now or never. A lesser woman would have let it go – after all, Archibald is two and a half and Harvey has only just turned one. The two of them together are like a chaos machine. Then there is the small detail of Nicole never having been in a camper van, let alone driven one. Of course, she treats this as just that: a small detail. My mum, Avril, decided this was a great idea and joined in on the craziness. The race chosen was the Dauphiné, as it was the one that I thought would be most accommodating of such an adventure.

Nicole Millar
@lastfastbike

Well that is pretty cool and rather cute!

How to Race a Prologue

In June there are two stage races that are treated as the final Tour preparation races: the Tour de Suisse and Dauphiné. The majority of aspiring Tour de France winners will do one or the other. Tour de Suisse starts a few days later than its French counterpart. The fundamental difference between the two is their nationality. Both have very similar profiles, only one is clockwork, the other a little romantic. The Critérium du Daupiné is like a mini Tour de France. It has all the ingredients – a prologue, bunch sprints, big mountains, a time trial, it's in France – only instead of three weeks it's eight days. Often the Dauphiné will even replicate one of the big Alpine mountain stages that will take place in the Tour de France a few weeks later, and race along some of the same roads. For this reason it's considered one of the most important preparation races for *la Grande Boucle*. The Dauphiné is one of the first races of the year where the weather is almost guaranteed to be hot and sunny, although that doesn't mean I haven't experienced rain – and even snow during certain editions; even in June the Alps can't be trusted completely to behave when it comes to the weather.

This year the heat is a bit much, rarely dropping below thirty degrees. The prologue is the first day, except this is a ten-kilometre time trial – a prologue is essentially a time trial below eight kilometres in length, another quirky cycling nuance that few grasp. I used to find them so easy, placing outside the podium was a disappointment when I was younger; these days I dream of finishing inside the top ten. Now that I'm an old pro I appreciate prologues are generally a young man's game – they're the shortest races we do, and for that reason the most intense. And there's a certain art to racing them, because although they're short they're still an aerobic effort. Many make the mistake of thinking that because they're a few minutes long they can sprint them. In theory you only make that mistake once or twice, yet some choose to make a career out of going too hard from the start.

Unlike time trials, which can be anywhere from a ten- to a ninety-minute effort, a prologue rarely lasts longer than nine minutes. Starting fast in a prologue is imperative – there's no riding into it and finding your rhythm, as is more the norm in a time trial; the old adage of start fast, accelerate in the middle and sprint to the finish is actually appropriate in a prologue. Technical mistakes can't be made because the results at the finish are usually decided by the tiniest of margins. Detailed pre-race recon can often make the difference between winning and losing. I've won prologues in the past by less than one second, and I could have told you immediately after the finish where I gained that second because I will have practised one corner a dozen times in training beforehand knowing that was where it could be won.

I still carry my old habits of detailed recon, and I try to do the same protocol for every prologue or time-trial day:

07:30 Wake up
08:00 Light breakfast: fruit, yoghurt, croissant and coffee
09:00 Course recon if possible, or forty-five minutes on the home trainer, at 300–350 watts. Drink at least two bottles if on the home trainer, up to three or four if it's over thirty degrees
11:00 Lie in bed, listen to music, read the map and visualise the course – make notes in accordance with recon knowledge from previous day or the morning
12:30 Lunch: pasta, omelette and bread and Nutella as a little treat. I always amaze myself with how much I can eat at this meal, and I always make sure I eat exactly three hours before my start, no matter whether it is a four-kilometre prologue or a sixty-kilometre time trial
13:00 Leave for the race in team car. Listen to music, study my annotated course map
13:30 Arrive at start, drop bag off at team bus, get a ride in the following car of the next rider from the team to start. Each prologue or time trial will set riders off at one- to two-minute intervals, meaning there are hours between the first and last starters. I spent much of my career being in the final wave, where the favourites are all placed to start. Following in a team car allows me to see the course now that it's closed and fully cordoned off. This can often change things compared to when it was still an open road, as seen during the recon
14:00 Return to bus and chill out, listen to music, watch the race on TV, get feedback from teammates as they each finish in turn and return to the bus. The wind would be the only thing I needed to know, there's not much else they can tell me as I tended to already have my pacing strategy in place

14:30 An hour before my start I begin the ritual of getting kitted up and having my number pinned on. I always liked giving myself ten to fifteen minutes for this

14:45 Leave the bus and begin warm-up on my spare road bike which waits outside on the home trainer. I always warm up on my road bike rather than my time-trial bike, simply because my position is so extreme on the time-trial bike that I can't hold it unless I'm riding at full time-trial pace, which tenses my body enough to distribute my weight across all my contact points. I do the first five minutes easy, then fifteen minutes at 300–350 watts, then a four-minute-threshold effort, which is between 400–450 watts. One minute's recovery, then two ten-second sprints. I do the last five minutes just spinning my legs at 250–300 watts. That totals about thirty-five minutes. It's only in the last five years that I've done such a regimented warm-up; when I was younger I would hop on the home trainer, and if I felt amazing I'd do five minutes then get off and wait in the bus till I had to leave for the start, no warm-up required. It used to blow people's minds. It blows my mind now, looking back

15:20 Ten minutes before the start I get off the static trainer, step inside the bus, mop myself down with a towel, take a caffeinated energy gel, have a piss, do a final radio check, put my helmet on and leave for the start

I can vividly remember what it used to feel like when I was at my best. Everything felt controlled. I would spend much of the first half of a prologue trying to hold myself back, spinning a high cadence, awaiting the inevitable accumulation of workload that I knew would come. That's essentially the rule of riding a good prologue: never chase it, let it come to you. When we roll off the start ramp our muscles are fresh and fully loaded and we're pumped with adrenalin. That can only get us so far, so we have to anticipate that our initial sensations bear no resemblance to the reality. Even the most experienced elite athletes can fall into this trap. The perception of their effort is totally wrong due to their level of excitement and feeling of strength.

If you get that first kilometre wrong there's little chance to remedy it – because of the short distance of the event you're given no time to recover – so in an ideal world you ride a prologue as an exercise in accumulation: lactic acid should build in a steady curve over the duration of the race, peaking out as you cross the finish line, not after one kilometre. At my best I was able to hit almost 15 mmol of lactic acid at the end of prologues, which meant I was blowing up as I crossed the line. It took a lot of training, recon and discipline to be able to time an effort that precisely. For many years it was my speciality, if you can call nuking yourself to the point of collapse at the end of a bike race 'special' – well, it was my speciality when I won; it just sucked when I lost.

I can't do that any more. My body doesn't allow me to go so deep. I say 'my body', but I'm not sure if it isn't my mind playing a strong part in it. It's a strange thing that, even after all these years of training and racing, I can't tell whether it's my mind or my body that's in control. Sometimes it feels like they have to work in perfect unison; other times it's clear to me it's my mind making the difference – others still, it's my body. There have been plenty of races where I've been a mental milkshake, not possessing a gram of motivation or desire, and yet my body has been so strong that I've been forced into action. Equally there have been times when I've done everything right, am super-motivated and fit, race-ready, and my body has simply said, 'Yeah, not today, thanks.' I fucking hate it when that happens. Everybody would say, 'It's in your head, David.' Well, thanks for that pearl of wisdom, super-helpful. Why did nobody say, 'David, it's your body, it had a bad day'? That would have made much more sense to me.

Of course, if somebody said to me now 'It's in your head, David,' I wouldn't get so defensive. I can accept that now, but that's because my body is weakening. For the first time ever the two are in perfect unison. I don't have the same confusion that I did when I was younger, about what's affecting what, and how my body and mind are both in a descending spiral, dragging each other down. Finally, after all these years, they've lost their first love: time trialling.

The Dauphiné

Nicole and Archibald are in the following car of the Dauphiné's first-day time trial. I'd been feeling good in training and held a little hope I might get a reasonably respectable result – top ten was ambitious, anything in the top thirty would have satisfied me. I got seventy-fourth. That puts me just inside the first half of the peloton. I decide to take that as OK. It isn't reasonably respectable, more like decidedly average, which is better than terribly shit.

The week is better than that first day. We have a summit finish on Stage 2 and my fitness is good enough to see me through the day without issues, to the point where I am able to use the final climb as a training exercise. This is effectively how I am treating the whole race. I am covering attacks in the first hour, then working for our team leader Andrew Talansky the rest of the time, always in my role as road captain. This is exactly how I treated the build-up of the Classics campaign, only this time I'm getting fitter more quickly.

For the first time since Flanders I am feeling in control of things again. I just had to get through the week without any issues and now I've completed a big three-week block. The recovery period I've planned to give myself following the Dauphiné will see my body assimilate the workload, rebuilding itself into a state of full race fitness, ready for the Tour de France onwards. A lot of riders race Dauphiné with this attitude. Although the Dauphiné is very important for physical preparation, and a prestigious race in its own right, the final results don't carry much relevance regarding performances at the Tour – to the point that it's often said that if you have a good Dauphiné you're likely to have a bad Tour, and a bad Dauphiné means a good Tour. If you happen to perform well, everybody will say, 'He's ready.' If you go like a bag of shit, everybody will say, 'He's clearly training for the Tour, he'll be ready.' In other words, a win-win situation. There are exceptions to this rule, but it is a fairly accurate generalisation, and one that I'm always surprised people don't pay more attention to.

Having Nicole and the boys at the race has been magic, especially knowing it will probably be the last time they'll ever see me race as a pro. My whole family is planning on coming to Glasgow for the Commonwealth Games in August, but that will be a different experience, it will be a one-off. The Dauphiné is a race that has been around for decades, and will no doubt be around for decades more. I like to think that one day we'll all go back there together with shared memories, or at least photos.

There were two highlights. Getting to the bus after a particularly grim day in the heat to unexpectedly find Nicole and the boys waiting for me. All my disdain for the conditions disappeared. It reiterated where I found true happiness in my life these days. The second was riding to the start with Archie one morning between all the parked-up buses, the two of us getting cheered by teams and fans alike. Some folks even knew his name. 'Allez, Archie!' seemed so strange after so many years of hearing 'Allez, David!' Here I was riding next to my two-year-old son at a bike race and he was getting cheered for the very first time, while for me it was one of the last.

In typical Dauphiné fashion the final stage is a beast. They've always had a habit of doing that, it's one of their trademarks. I've never been a big fan, especially when at the back end of a three-week block of training and racing. I am semi-resigned to my fate before we even cross kilometre zero.

As a team we decide to engage super-offensive mode. Our leader, Andrew Talansky, is lying in third place overall behind Chris Froome, with Alberto Contador leading. Head to head against those two he doesn't stand a chance; Contador's team, Tinkoff, is weak while Froome's team, Sky, is strong. This means that Sky has to light up the race right from the get-go, putting Tinkoff under maximal stress in the hope they'll explode and leave Contador isolated without teammates early enough to force him to use up his own strength to defend his position, while Froome marks him until the last climb and attacks the moment he sees him weakened. The stage is mountainous, but not long at 130 kilometres. All this points towards anarchic racing, especially when everybody knows Tinkoff are going to have trouble defending and Sky are going to be offensive. Andrew agrees that he is better being part of the attacking than sitting behind at the whim of Contador and Froome and their teams, because when Contador and Froome decide to battle it out among themselves it will be a battle royale between the two of them – nobody else will be able to match their fire power, not even Andrew, who is the next best in the race. Andrew would be left to fight a new battle among the collateral damage inflicted by the two ahead. That would more than likely see him slide down the classification.

Fortunately Ryder is on one of his missions this final day, so our super-offensive tactical plan involves him single-handedly ripping the race to pieces. He becomes a one-man wrecking ball for three hours. A group of twenty-three riders breaks away on the first climb after only twenty kilometres – Andrew and Ryder are there. It doesn't take long until the gap goes up to 3:20, meaning the thirty-nine-second deficit Andrew had on Contador before the start becomes a 2:41 advantage before even half the stage is done, mainly thanks to Ryder driving the pace, not expecting help from anybody. That's what Ryder can do when he's in the mood: his only objective is to make sure that Tinkoff and Saxo use up their *domestique* arsenal in order to defend their first and second places on general classification from Andrew.

As expected, Tinkoff are in deep trouble. They can't control the race and the gap keeps getting bigger. At this point Froome is forced to go on the offensive and orders his team to take control, but not in the usual manner. They attack en masse, Froome plus three teammates. Meaning, they isolate Contador completely: he has no choice but to follow them without hesitation, knowing he can no longer rely on his team to bring them back.

I can see all this happening before it happens, and call on the radio to tell the guys to get ready. I know the moment Sky go my race will be over. I have nothing else to contribute to the team, my three-week block is complete, and I've overloaded myself to the point of exhaustion, which is exactly what I want. I don't need to bury myself to finish when I know it is no longer benefiting me long term. Now I needed to recover. As Sky and Froome attack, the peloton is ripped to pieces. I don't even fight it, I drift back through the convoy until I get to our team car. I lean in through the window and tell the *directeur sportif*, Geert, that I'm spent and am getting in the car. Immediately I tell them to radio ahead to the car behind Andrew and Ryder to make sure Ryder gives everything he has for the next forty kilometres, as it is of the utmost importance that Froome uses up his teammates as quickly as possible in the pursuit. That will leave Froome and Contador to do the work themselves.

This works like a dream: the three Sky riders chasing the Ryder-led group only take a minute back before exhausting themselves, and the two leaders have to go head-to-head. But then they start bluffing each other, neither wanting to help the other. It gets to the point where they are almost at a standstill on the road. Eventually, Contador takes matters into his own hands, leaving Froome in his wake, but the damage has been done. Ryder eventually pulls off, having ridden himself into the ground. That is the cue for Andrew to begin the ride of his life. He doesn't ask anybody for help; he sits on the front and begins a time trial to the line, his only objective to make sure he gets to the finish line forty seconds before Contador. Although Contador eats into the lead, Andrew crosses the line 1:06 ahead, meaning he wins the general classification by twenty-seven seconds. It is an incredible and unexpected day of racing, textbook in its execution and, of course, impossible without Ryder having been so selfless and Andrew being gutsy enough to attempt it in the first place.

Andrew has become the future of the team. Being an American in an American team he has assumed the mantle of Great Hope for the Future, and rightfully so after his results from his first two years at Garmin. Andrew is a nice, if at times strange, guy. At twenty-six he is entering his prime, a great talent, but a demanding guy and not a natural leader. He has a legendary temper. He's one of the few people who I believe do actually 'see red' when losing their shit – to the point he can't remember what happened. He's like Jim Carrey's character in *Me, Myself & Irene*.

Fabian

Ryder and I had been rooming together for the week. He'd finished the Giro just the week before the Dauphiné had begun. He'd had a tough time there, all due to the fact that the team had once again proved its new-found team time-trialling incompetence by crashing in the first stage – the crash was serious enough that two of the team broke bones and were out of the race.

The crash happened near the halfway point on a dead-straight section of road. The team was lined out in classic team time-trial formation, travelling at full speed. Dan Martin was in fourth place, moving up the line, readying himself for his next turn on the front when he hit a drain in the road. I don't know how, but he lost control and went down like a sack of shit. Fortunately the guy right behind him was slightly off the wheel and managed to get round him. The other three didn't stand a chance, they all went careening into him. It's spectacular to watch in the replays. I spoke to Ryder before I'd seen it. His description, in hindsight, was quite accurate: 'We got car bombed.'

The thing is, there had only been eight of them left when the crash happened. The ninth man, Fabian Wegmann, had been on a creeper and had been dropped a couple of kilometres earlier. When that happens in a team time trial you hate yourself, no matter how much you've given and how helpless you were to prevent it; you can't help but beat yourself up. So you roll along in a sad slow state, pitying yourself for being crap, riddled with guilt for letting your teammates down, waiting to be caught and humiliatingly passed by another team . . . all the time trying not to look at all the fans at the side of the road. It's rather demoralising by any standards, yet at the same time it's a massive relief to have freed yourself from the head-kicking you'd been receiving. So that's what Fabian was up to when he saw in the distance ahead the team cars pulled up in the road.

This in itself would have been a bit of worry, but not something he would have overly concerned himself with. Maybe there had been a mechanical or a puncture. When he got closer he'd have seen a teammate on the floor – 'Ah, shit, that's not good.' He'd have started to wonder what had happened, hoping they weren't badly injured, but probably also thinking, 'Well, at least I have somebody else to ride in with.'

He'll have then seen another body on the floor, another at the side of the road, and another trying to get back on his bike: 'OH, FOR THE LOVE OF GOD, NO.' At that same moment somebody in a team car will have seen him and thought the same thing, only instead of 'NO' it would have been a 'YES', and radioed to the guys who weren't in the crash, now probably 500 metres up the road, 'FABIAN IS HERE! HE'LL BE THE FIFTH MAN. GO, FABIAN, GO!'

So poor Fabian had to face the fact he was now going to have to get what was left of his head back in the game and endure another fifteen kilometres of horrible suffering, knowing this time he wasn't allowed to be dropped. It made a bad situation worse: the four who had survived were now totally reliant on a rider who they knew was in a bad way. For a professional cyclist that is probably the worst turn of events it's possible to experience. Being dropped from a team time trial early on, thinking your race is done and the suffering is over, only then to find half your team splattered across the road and realise you're now the most important man in the team. Poor, poor Fabian. The team chaperoned him to the line, losing nearly three and a half minutes in the process, effectively destroying any hopes Ryder held for overall success. His Giro was scuppered on that first day. He did well to keep his head about him and have a good race, but when he arrived at the Dauphiné he let the disappointment hit home. I spent most of the week being his roomie-psychologist.

Ryder (2)

Riders share rooms at nearly every race – mainly because there are so many people on a bike race that there aren't enough hotel rooms; and, more importantly, for organisers and teams it's a damn sight cheaper. This is not so much the case these days, as there are more hotels and bigger budgets, but, like many things, what was once a necessity has become a tradition. For the majority of pros the thought of rooming alone fills them with fear. Even our loner sensibilities have their limits. Personally, I'm a big fan of being on my own, and would almost always put my hand up to be the ninth man (who gets his own room) when on Grand Tours. Everybody is fine with this, as I'm always up so bloody early compared to everybody else – nobody likes a roomie who wakes up at the crack of dawn.

Ryder is the exception to my single-room rule. It's a much more enjoyable experience sharing the events of a day with him.

Ryder's slight insanity helps me feel sane, and I'm sure he thinks the same of me. This is often the case in a team: we find the teammates who we are compatible with, because sharing a room together for what can be a month at a Grand Tour means you need a certain chemistry from which you both benefit. You get to know each other well enough to read when things aren't going so well, which is when having a good roomie is most important. It can be an emotional roller coaster being a racer, not only because of the extreme nature of the sport, but also because we are pummelling our bodies so much that at times it has a negative effect on our minds.

At the Dauphiné it was my turn to keep Ryder's head above water. On Stage 6, the Friday, he was ready to pack it in and go home, his mind was completely shot. He was convincing himself he was useless and needed rest. There was no doubting he needed rest, but it became my job to persuade him he wasn't useless. He sat in the very last position of the peloton for most of the day. I had to keep dropping back to talk to him and make it clear he was not going to stop. We needed him for the final two mountain stages over the weekend, whether he liked it or not.

In that situation the only thing you can tell a rider, not just Ryder, is that they have to survive the day. There is never any point in telling them that they're going to be fine and it's all in their head – that's a surefire way to have them lose what little will to live remains. So that's how I was spending my Friday in the race: making sure my roomie stayed in the race.

It was a massive relief when we got through the feedzone at the halfway point and he didn't stop, because it was my biggest fear he'd quietly pull over and step off the bike there. As we approached it I dropped right back and rode next to him in order that he could see I knew what he was thinking. He wouldn't stop in front of me, because when we do quit a race we try to do it in a way that none of our teammates can see – it alleviates the guilt a little. I knew Ryder wouldn't even attempt it if I was present.

Once we get through the feedzone we find ourselves committed to making it through the stage, because if we've been feeling shit since the start of the stage the only thing we think about is the team car that will be sitting at the feedzone. We know that if we give up, we can climb in and fall asleep while being driven to the hotel, far away from the race. It can become an all-encompassing objective, like an oasis in a desert. Once it's passed we know if we stop we either have to get in the team car with the *directeur sportif*, or, worse, the broom wagon (literally that, the final vehicle in the race convoy, a bus with a broom tied to it, signifying it's cleaning up the stragglers). Nobody wants to be swept up by the broom wagon and endure that loser-cruiser trip to the finish before shamefully disembarking like a captured deserter.

Sure enough, Ryder came into his own the next day in the first big mountain stage. He went with the first attacks on the first mountain and was in the break all day, dropping out of it deliberately in the final in order to wait for Andrew so he could help him. In the space of twenty-four hours he went from wanting to quit on a relatively easy stage to sacrificing his own chances of a stage win in order to pace Andrew the final kilometres, in the process moving Andrew from fourth to third on general classification.

When I got on the bus and saw Ryder for the first time since the stage start it was clear he was a different man from twenty-four hours earlier, his exhaustion of the previous day a distant and foreign memory. He embodied the cliché 'back in the game'. That evening in the room he was telling me how he was going to rip the race to pieces the following day, just for fun. Which is what he did, in inimitable Ryder fashion: from the back, to the front, through the front, off the front, then a series of counter-attacks against himself. Full beast mode.

Ryder's day out ripping the race to pieces and setting up Andrew for the Criterium du Dauphiné win was a big boost for the team, and a career-defining result for Andrew. The euphoria of the win was slightly diminished by the fact that we faced an eight-hour bus ride home. At least it was in our bus. As a treat we got to stay in a motel en route in order that we could get some decent sleep. Little did I know this was going to be the last good night's sleep I'd get for a week.

Back Home

Nicole and the boys had stayed in Annecy the last couple of days of the race, deciding that going into the high mountains probably wasn't the best idea in the world. The camper van was to be dropped off on the Monday morning then they were heading back to Spain where I'd be at home to welcome them, which was a first: normally they were always at home waiting for me.

The damp squib of a bus trip home got wetter when I received a call from our cleaning lady telling me our house had been broken into. We were still three hours away when I got this uplifting news. I called Nicole to tell her, and found out that her engagement ring and all her other jewellery were in the house, as she'd taken nothing with her on the trip, a very sensible thing to do at the time of her departure. Those next three hours were interminable. I started racking my brains, thinking of everything that was in the house that could be, and probably had been, stolen. The list was sickeningly long.

Unusually the team bus took me right to my front door, another first, which made the whole thing even more surreal. Everybody on the bus shared my stress; none of us had ever had our houses burgled. There was nothing to be said: nobody knew what to say or do. I was prepared for the worst, yet couldn't stop myself from hoping it wouldn't be as bad as that.

I dumped my suitcase in the driveway and walked despondently into the house. It appeared that they'd done a thorough job: everything had been turned upside down. I went straight upstairs to find where Nicole kept her jewellery. Everything important was in a small ring box sitting on top of an antique miniature chest of drawers she used as her main jewellery box. The drawers had all been pulled out, yet remarkably the small ring box hadn't been touched. I daren't believe it was possible. I picked it up and opened it, wincing, preparing myself for the worst.

Everything was there. I couldn't believe it. I sat on the floor, and thought, 'OK, I don't care about anything else, at least Nicole still has her ring.' That didn't last long. The more I looked around the house the more I noticed missing. All the computers with their countless photos had been taken, each computer being a back-up to the other, our internet having been too slow to upload to any cloud. They'd taken anything they could sell: TVs, cameras, sunglasses, that sort of thing. In other words, all the cool shit, the luxuries. I told myself, 'It's probably a good thing I don't have TVs. I had too many sunglasses anyway. We have other photos of the boys. I've had worse shit happen to me. I can rise above this.'

Then I remembered I had a safe in my gym that was to be installed in our new house. It wasn't fixed down, yet stupidly I'd put my watches in there thinking it was a safe thing to do. I had a beautiful IWC Portuguese Chronograph that Mark Cavendish had given each of the Copenhagen Worlds team when he became only the second Brit to win the Worlds road race, engraved with my name, the race and date. Three other personal watches, one of which was my grandfather's. I reverted to the feeling I'd had when looking for Nicole's engagement ring. I went to the gym, not allowing myself to think the worst, hoping beyond hope the safe would be there in the corner where I'd last locked it shut.

I opened the door and turned the light on. It was a mess. I used it as an office as well as a gym. The filing cabinet had been rifled, files and paperwork were strewn across the floor. I waded through it all, not caring. I could see immediately the safe wasn't there. I kept looking for it, though. It didn't take long for me to accept they'd taken it. I felt myself shrink, my head hang, trying to tell myself, 'They're only watches, you never wore them anyway.' It didn't help.

I spent the next few hours tidying and cleaning up, trying to get the place as normal looking as possible in anticipation of

Top: Milano–San Remo
Below: E3 Harelbeke

Ronde Recon (above)

Ronde van Vlaanderen

Mechanical

The Hell of the North

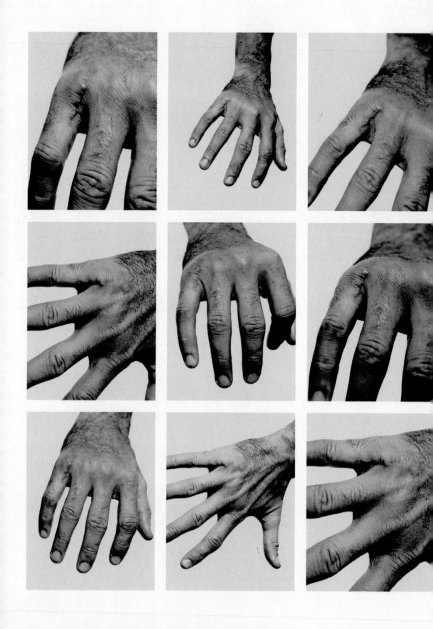

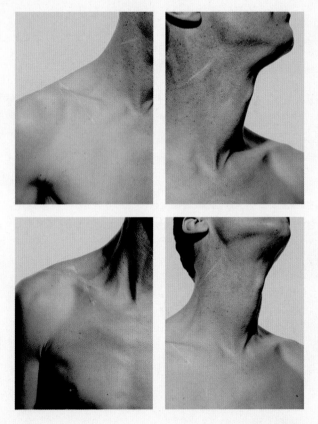

Scar tissue

La Vuelta

Gone biking

the arrival of Nicole, my mum and the boys. The thieves had even raided the kids' room – clothes and stuffed toys everywhere, as if the teddy bears had held a rave in the absence of their children, *Toy Story* on drugs and alcohol. I stopped being sad and sorry for myself and started getting angry. What sort of people did that to a kids' room?

The police came by and did their best impression of not being *CSI*. They were in and out in fifteen minutes, barely asking a question, about as useful as a chocolate watch. I can understand that: it's not as if a robbery like this is top of their list of priorities, especially as they expect everything to be insured. Which is when I realised I wasn't insured. I had let the insurance expire as I had presumed we'd be living in our new house by this point. That was unfinished, empty, yet fully insured. I felt queasy again.

For the next week I had to endure people saying, 'Well, at least the insurance will cover everything.' Or, 'It's only stuff.' Neither of which helped very much. I couldn't sleep at night, continuously waking up thinking about something else that I needed to get up and look for in order to be sure it hadn't been stolen, my paranoia growing ever worse as the days went by. It didn't matter how unlikely it was that the thieves would have been interested in it, I still had to check. One night was spent going through Velo Club Rocacorba clothing (high-quality kit from our cycling club), checking it was all there.

The theft of the Worlds watch from Cav affected me the most – it was what we had as a team to show we'd been part of something important. We'd always talked about the fact we'd wear them together, as a team, years in the future when we met up to remember that day. I don't have anything else like that from my career. I constantly remind myself, 'It's only a watch. It's only a watch.' It doesn't help, to be honest, much like the futility of telling myself 'I am light. I am strong' while racing my bike up a mountain.

All of this meant that the rest and recovery period I'd anticipated and based everything upon during my three-week block of training and racing never happened. It felt like I barely slept for days following the Dauphiné. Which was possibly the worst thing that could have happened considering how tired I was by the final stage. Sleep was all I needed, yet I couldn't manage it. I got more tired by the day. I knew I was becoming weaker rather than stronger; the weaker I became the more susceptible I was to sickness. This led to stress, which made me worry and find sleeping even more difficult; it was the most vicious of circles. Then it happened. My glands went up and I began to feel sick.

Tour Preparation

Being sick just over two weeks before the Tour de France is the nightmare scenario. It's the most important race to me. I've based my whole season on being at my best from this moment on till the end of the year: Tour de France, Commonwealth Games, Vuelta a España, World Championships. That was my racing block; that was where I would come into my own. It has almost always been that way in my life as a professional cyclist. I am a man for the second half of the year. I do what I have to do the first half, then do what I want to do the second.

Falling sick at this point in the season meant even the most confident version of myself had doubts. I needed somebody to trust me, to tell me what to do.

I'd been in a similarly sorry state leading up to the 2013 Tour de France, to the extent that for any other member of the team my selection could not have been justified. I wasn't sure I could turn it around. Jonathan Vaughters, the team boss, called me and asked me to tell him what I thought with regard to my Tour de France selection. I remember saying, 'Jonathan, if I'm not good enough I don't want to go.' To which he replied, 'OK, David. Let's speak closer to the time. I will trust you to make the right decision.'

I went on to have a supremely average Tour de Suisse. (We had chosen Suisse instead of the Dauphiné in 2013, deciding it was a safer bet considering my lacklustre form. It's a more predictable race than the Dauphiné, not quite as extreme in its racing or conditions. It's perhaps not fair to say so, but it's the easier option.) Much as I'd done in the past I used the race to overload myself. I was racing hard the first hour then taking every opportunity outside of my team duties to use the race as a training exercise. I finished exhausted but healthy, ready to rest, recover and regenerate. But, unlike this year, I didn't return home to a ransacked house. I felt confident enough to call Jonathan and tell him I would be good enough for the Tour – and that was it, he trusted me. That alone gave me the extra confidence boost I needed.

The Nationals (2013)

Last year I spent five days at home before travelling to Scotland for the National Championships in Glasgow, on the same course that will be used for the 2014 Commonwealth Games. The day of the race everything clicked: for the first time all year I could control the race rather than having the race control me. I was like a motorbike – over the four and a half hours of the race I rode like a man possessed. Alex Dowsett, Andy Fenn, Mark Cavendish and I made an alliance, essentially becoming a team, agreeing to race as such until we got to the final, where we would revert back to individuals to fight out the win. We knew it was the only way we stood a chance against the power of Team Sky, who'd dominated the previous few years due to their strength and numbers. This wasn't out of the ordinary; the Nationals often ended up like this, the continental professionals having to unite their forces in order to stand a chance against complete teams. In the past these were domestically based, but Team Sky changed that – the continental pros now had to compete against their own.

I'd only raced a couple of times in Scotland before. I relished the opportunity to race on home ground – some of my earliest memories are of Glasgow and I've rarely raced anywhere that has such a deep connection to me. Not only are most of my family from there, but the course even passed the university where my parents met. It felt like a home race, and I raced it as such.

Being the Nationals it was anarchic, essentially a war of attrition. The course taking place over a relatively short, hilly circuit made it almost impossible to be controlled – if you weren't riding aggressively at the front you didn't stand a chance. After two of the fourteen laps, 90 per cent of the race were already out of contention. By the final lap there were only three of us left: Mark, Ian Stannard and myself. I knew Mark wouldn't chase me if I attacked – not because of any alliance, but simply because we're such close friends – not that it made a difference because each time I went, Stannard would bring me back. With two kilometres to go I was away and had a moment where I thought I might make it, but once again Stannard slowly but surely clawed his way back up to me, at which point it was a formality for Mark to win. I say 'formality'; the fact that he had even survived the previous 185-kilometre onslaught displayed how much more than a pure sprinter he can be when he is on song.

It was disappointing yet a relief to have finally turned a corner and be able to pay back the trust Jonathan had placed in me. It was also obvious the Commonwealth Games course was perfectly suited to me. Then and there I decided it would be one of my goals, perhaps my biggest, for 2014. Six days later I was fourth in the bunch sprint on Stage 1 of the Tour de France. The next day I was yellow jersey on the road, after the three sprinters who'd been in front of me on general classification had been dropped on the major climb of the day and were now far behind the race.

Ryder came up to me on the descent and said, 'David!' He never calls me Dave, 'You're in yellow. You need anything?' All of a sudden our roles were reversed. He didn't hesitate. I said, 'Sure I'm in yellow? Fuck, I reckon I must be. I'm OK, some bottles when the cars are back would be good.' He gave me both of his, patted me on the back and told me he'd stay near me for anything I needed. I called on the radio that I was in yellow. To this day I don't know why the team didn't react and take control of the race. I think they were so used to me calling the shots that when it came to the moment where I needed them to call the shots on my behalf they didn't know what to do. No order was ever sent on the radio to ride or behave differently. Only Ryder acted as if I was in yellow. It wasn't until ten kilometres to go that I shouted at the team to start riding, at which point Charly, for the first time, ordered everybody to ride. It was too late; a small group had slipped away. We caught all of them, except one. He had one second on the line, meaning he took yellow, leaving me in second place. No big deal: it wasn't that important to me (he writes, while quietly sobbing at the keyboard).

The Nationals (2014)

This year things aren't quite as simple. Being run-down to the point of sickness two weeks before the start of Tour de France was far from ideal. I called the team doctors and told them what was going on – it had all the characteristics of being a classic fatigue-induced cold, with nothing to be done for it but rest. I discussed with team doctors whether I should go to the Nationals or not. I called Charly and told him everything – making sure I was totally transparent as I knew they were making the Tour selection – and I also wanted his opinion on whether I should rest up or go to the Nationals. We both agreed I should go. If nothing else it would give me almost a week in a hotel where I could rest up completely. If, once there, I felt I shouldn't race then I should make that decision nearer the time. The primary objective was for me to recover and get healthy. The next day, Charly told me I was selected for the Tour. I didn't realise how much of a relief this was; clearly that had been another factor that had been weighing heavily on my mind.

The Jersey

All the European National Championships are held the Sunday before the Tour de France starts. I don't know why this is; they just are and that's the way it's always been for as long as I remember. They're important races for all of us, no matter what country you hail from. Every rider dreams of one day winning and wearing their national colours for the following year – it's one of the few opportunities we're given to wear something different from our transient, often ugly, trade team colours.

Joining our first cycling club will have been a seminal moment for many of us. Wearing their jersey for the first time will have affected us in a way we'd never experienced before – every club has its traditions and colours, displayed like a flag on their jersey; and each design has its own history. For me, like many other cyclists, it was the first time I felt like I'd become part of something – for some reason it felt different from any other club or team I'd been part of in the past.

Those of us destined to become professionals are blissfully unaware that from that moment on our lives will be dictated by the cycling jerseys we wear. Before long we'll be moving to a bigger club with better opportunities, then a regional outfit, and on to a sponsored team. From there, the next step is to the national squad. All along the way we dream of one day becoming a professional, of wearing the yellow jersey of the Tour de France, and maybe the rainbow stripes of World Champion.

It doesn't matter what jersey you have as a junior or an amateur – you could even be a multiple World Champion at that level – it still doesn't equate to the pride each of us feels when we pull the zip up on that first professional jersey. It's a powerful flashback to that very first outing with our local club, and that feeling of being part of something.

Then, over the years, it simply becomes team kit. We accept we are paid to be human billboards on bikes; it's the only way we can race. Sometimes we get good kit; sometimes we get bad. We have no say, our houses and garages become swamped with it through the years. The value becomes lost through the accumulation.

It's for this reason the National Championships are important. The winner is awarded the National Championships jersey and is given an individual identity for a year – and, above all, a chance to represent their country and transcend the mercurial world of professionalism. Of course, we're still representing our sponsors – only they become part of us rather than we part of them.

Monmouthshire

The race itself is different from all others we do. We race it for personal reasons; more often than not our team is perfectly happy for us not to do it – after all, if we win we are obliged to wear colours different from those of our sponsors. My team had a policy of not paying for expenses. I don't think they were alone in this, because as far as they were concerned it was a race we did in our own time.

Rod Ellingworth, the Great Britain and Sky coach, began the tradition, a few years back, of using the Nationals as an opportunity to get the GB squad riders together. We'd join up once a year – twice if you were lucky enough to be selected to represent GB at the Worlds.

This was the other reason I chose to go to the Nationals when I still wasn't even sure if I'd race or not: I got to spend time with Team GB, where I knew I'd be looked after well, surrounded by people I trust. Above all, it's invigorating being around Rod and his team. As much as I enjoy spending time with my American team there's something easier and more natural about being back among Brits; there's also the fact I've known some of the staff for close to twenty years.

The day before the time trial, I'm feeling better. The initial classic symptoms of swollen glands and sore throat have disappeared, but riding round the course doing recon with Alex Dowsett I'm still coughing. I know what this means: my whole career I've had the same problem; my lungs have always been my weak point. Instead of joining Alex for a second lap of the course I decide to go back to the hotel where I immediately call Charly, or 'Charles' as I always call him (having done so since we were teen-agers). After the coughing fit in the recon, I ask him if he thinks I should do the time trial. I'm veering towards resting a bit more.

'It puts me in a very difficult position if you don't race, David,' he says, less than chirpily.

I'm not expecting that response from him. I've taken it for granted that he'll understand completely – after all, I am selected for the Tour, and that's the most important thing now. I can feel my anger rising: 'What do you mean? Are you being pressured regards my selection? Fuck, come on. I know I've been shit recently, but I know I'll be good when I need to be good. My weight is bang on, I've done the workload, I just need to rest.' My anger is not directed towards Charly, but at the powers above him that I suspect are forcing Charly to be a dick. I can imagine Jonathan using him like a puppet.

'No, David, there is no pressure,' he replies. 'Jonathan has given me complete control over selection. It's my decision. You have to race, David. It's complicated otherwise.'

Now I am totally confused. I tell him I don't really under-stand, but will try to ride within myself, so as not to do too much damage. I'm trying to grasp why Charly is being like this. Then he signs off with a totally bamboozling remark: 'My advice: if you're going to race, then race.'

'I always race, Charly. You, above all, should know that. OK, I'll call you after.' I'm both fuming and massively disappointed.

I start the time trial then stop after one of the two laps. Trying to race it means I'm coughing even more; it's making things worse rather than better. I phone Charly again. He isn't impressed. In fact, he now says I have to show myself in the road race on Sunday. Things are getting weird. I'm getting properly worried. I now don't trust Charly, just as he clearly doesn't trust me.

After the final race of the week, the road race, I'm heading up to Manchester to stay with my sister for a couple of days, before travelling to join my team in Leeds for the start of the Tour on Saturday. Rod lives near Manchester and has kindly offered to drop me off. So there I am, road-tripping with Rod in a Team Sky Jaguar up the M6 past Birmingham. Direction: Tour de France. We're talking about the day's bike racing, breaking down Pete Kennaugh's victory for Team Sky, and analysing my own performance – I'd ridden a conservative race, trying to make sure I didn't do more damage than I had to. But, being the Nationals, this was nigh-on impossible, as it's at its hardest in the first half, after which it finds its rhythm and turns into a gradual wearing down, the last men standing eventually battling it out for the win. Once I realised the race was over for me, about the time Geraint Thomas decided to head off in pursuit of the breakaway, I retired along with Alex Dowsett. Pete Kennaugh, Ben Swift and Adam Yates had fought out the win, while Luke Rowe and 'G' had played dominant roles in different parts of the race. Rod's boys had done him proud. I was pleased for Rod; Rod and I have always got on well – we both love a bike race, our enthusiasm rubs off on each other – with most people I'd rather not talk about the race, but with Rod it is always a delight.

Just then my phone starts ringing. 'Here we go, it's Charly. "Charles, how's it going?"'

Immediately I can tell something isn't right. He has on his super-serious voice: 'David. Can you speak?'

'Yeah, no problem. What's going on?'

'I'm calling to tell you I've pulled you from the Tour de France team.'

Holy shit. I'm actually speechless. 'What? I'm on my way there now.'

'You're sick, David. I can't take an unhealthy rider to the Tour de France. You didn't finish the time trial or the road race at the Nationals due to illness, and you've been underperforming in the races leading up to those.'

'Charly, you were the one who made me race the Nationals when I told you I was sick. I didn't finish because I want to be healthy for the Tour – you've already selected me. Fuck, are you serious?' I could feel Rod's silence next to me.

'Yes, David. I'm very serious.'

'And that's it? There's no discussion on this?'

'No, David. I've made my decision.'

'I can't believe this is happening, Charly. I'll speak to you later.'

I hang up and sit there staring ahead in my own silence, suddenly becoming very aware I am sitting in a Team Sky car on the M6 near Birmingham, a long way from home and not going to the Tour de France. I try to comprehend what is happening. My hand is in my lap, gripping the phone tightly, in total contrast to the dead weight of my arm. Rod remains silent, clearly understanding exactly what is happening. I think it may have been minutes – I have no idea how long – before I eventually speak: 'Charly has pulled me from the Tour, Rod. I don't understand why he'd do that to me.'

Rod knows how important this is to me: 'I'm sorry, Dave. I don't know what to say.'

I call my sister, Frances, who not only works at Team Sky but was there with Sir Dave Brailsford from the very creation of the team, and who now has the legendary job title 'Head of Winning Behaviours'. She answers with our classic, 'Watcha, mate!'

I try to reply with equal enthusiasm: 'Watcha, mate!'

'Where are you? Is Rod being all slow? Tell him he's allowed to go faster.'

'Somewhere past Birmingham. France, Charly has pulled me from the Tour.'

'What? What do you mean?'

'I'm not doing the Tour.'

'But you're selected?'

'I know.'

'Have you spoken to Doug or JV?'

'I'll try calling them after this. You better get some wine in.'

'Fuck. Why would Charly do that?'

'I don't know. Shit, France, this isn't how I'd imagined it.'

 David Millar
Verified account
@millarmind

For Sale. Been raced, not much. Battery fully charged (I think). Good condition. Reasonable offers please.

The Cairn Hotel

Harvey, Just arrived at this hotel, it 4/7/14
was light though, well, if you could
see light through the clouds, rain, mist
& wind... Welcome to Yorkshire! I flew
into Leeds, then went straight, tried the
Paul Smith shop where I got kitted out
for my three days of TV purgatory. This
will be the first TdF I've watched as
a spectator since 1994. 20yrs! OMG.
Maison Rougegan, we had a lot of fun yesterday
mucking repeating words, TRACTOR, CAR,
DADDY, ... important things in life dearly. Lots of Love, Dad xxxx

HARVEY MILLAR
CAN CRUSIC
PUJALS DE PAGESOS
CORNELLA DEL TERRI
17844
SPAIN

An Evening View of the Cairn Hotel
Ripon Road
Harrogate
N.Yorkshire
Tel: 01423 504005
Fax: 01423 504005
DARLEY Strathmore Hotels Ltd.
www.strathmorehotels.com

Charly

I was devastated not to do the Tour. It was made worse by the
fact that I was back to full health less than forty-eight hours after

the Nationals, and at my ideal race weight of seventy-six kilo-grammes, the lowest it had been since the previous year's Tour de France. Obviously, over a decade of aiming for July has condi-tioned me to perfect timing.

The worst thing about it all was how I now felt about Charly. I didn't want to have anything to do with him from now on. We'd been friends since teenagers, racing together on the national team and sharing our first successes abroad together. I'd even been glassed in a pub in York defending Charly's honour back when we were young professionals.

Charly is from York, near where the Tour de France will start in Leeds. My stepmum, Colette, is York through and through, so when visiting her and my dad while they were over from Hong Kong I arranged to see Charly at the same time. Three birds, one stone and all that (I didn't know about the glass yet). On one occasion we somehow chose the roughest pub in York to meet up – being young pro cyclists at the time we didn't really know how it all worked, especially in England. It was early evening and we were having a jovial time. In France it would have been *l'heure de l'apéritif*. I think that paints a picture of where we were in our lives at that point.

At one point Charly got up to go and spend a penny, normally a reasonably mundane affair. A few minutes later he came back and sat down with one hand holding his face. It turned out he'd been punched by some random bloke when leaving the toilet. Apparently they didn't like the fact he looked at them. I don't know why, but I got up and asked Charly which group of guys it was. He told me to leave it. I couldn't, it was bullshit. I wasn't going to let some idiot hit my friend for no reason.

I got up, and headed over, my sister and dad in close prox-imity, knowing that I was totally out of my depth. The bunch of guys were now sitting at a table. I asked which one of them had hit my friend. The twat got all cocky and said, 'Me.' So I asked him why and he responded with the genius, ''Cause I felt like it.' I nodded and lunged across the table, grabbing him by the neck and pinning him against the wall. Before I could punch him I found myself being picked up by the four other guys, who lifted me and held me against another wall. What happened next I still can't figure out totally. It wasn't their first rodeo, let's put it that way. Next thing I knew, broken glass was showering down from above. I don't know whose they were or where they came from but glasses were thrown at the ceiling above my head. Being an old English pub with low ceilings this was highly effective: the shattered glass rained down on my face and head, gashing it up, one cut in particular being worthy of hospital. They all went and sat back down again like nothing had happened while I stood there bleeding, thinking, 'Well, that went well.' The police were present in about a minute. We learnt afterwards the pub had a big red button under the bar for such moments. It was all very dramatic.

Mine and Charly's careers had taken completely different directions from our initial first footings, his role becoming that of *domestique* while I became a leader. We'd both experienced tumultuous times during our professional careers, for different reasons and due to our different characters and positions within the sport.

But it was a lovely twist of fate that we'd both made it through everything and were now on the same team – a team I'd helped create, build and shape. It seemed right that Charly could now be with us in an environment that offered every chance to young riders, something that Charly and I hadn't had in our day. Charly and I could help fix what we had always felt was wrong. Well, that's how I hoped it would be.

Charly and I are very different: it was clear from when I first got to know him that this was the case. He had an enormous natural talent, he was born to race a bike – tall and skinny, with a crazy endurance ability due primarily to his naturally high red blood cell count. This was so high, in fact, that he was at times over the UCI 50 per cent haematocrit limit and had to get a special dispensation in order to prevent him being stopped from racing. In hindsight this was his disadvantage, because when Charly came into the professional sport his natural advantage was negated by the fact that drugs were being used to mimic it.

Physically, he was amazing, yet he was always so insecure, constantly riddled with self-doubt. I could never fathom how somebody with such obvious natural ability could refuse to believe in it himself. It was like he was constantly self-sabotaging. I, on the other hand, had too much self-belief. I thought anything was possible; I tried to make Charly feel the same.

My career ended up being centred around trying to win races; Charly's became about helping others win races, and he was damned good at it. It's often the way pro sports careers go: our personalities dictate the destiny of our talent.

Garmin

The three of us – Jonathan Vaughters, Doug Ellis and me – had built the team together. Jonathan created the team and its ethical values after retiring from racing, disillusioned by the corrupt professional scene. Doug wanted to create an American Tour de France team and realised that if he wanted to do it in a way that reflected his own values there was only one option: Jonathan Vaughters. I was the third and final element. I had come back into the sport from my ban a reformed man, respected by the people who Jonathan and Doug needed to win over if they wanted to turn their team from a small domestic US outfit into an international Tour de France team.

The first people I had to win over were the riders we needed to recruit. I personally approached and convinced the majority of our initial signings. We were a small American outfit without a title sponsor – Doug guaranteed the initial finance out of his own pocket – so we didn't appear to be the safest bet. We weren't even in the top division, which meant we had no automatic invitations to the biggest bike races – neither the Classics nor the Grand Tours, never mind the others. Generally this would have prevented the majority of good professionals from even considering us, but we offered something no other team could: we wanted to change the sport for the better, we were 100 per cent against doping and had our own internal testing programme that went beyond the official anti-doping controls. We had, before it even existed in the sport, our own biological passport. It was an opportunity for the riders who believed in and loved their sport to do something to change it. I would explain to them how important this was.

That alone couldn't win them over, though; we had to convince them we'd provide the best support possible in order to allow them to perform at their very best. We would base our team in Girona and request that all riders lived there; we'd apply the latest in sports science and only choose suppliers who could guarantee us the best equipment; we had altitude training camps planned throughout the year. We were marginal gaining before anybody else. The final ingredient was the recruitment policy. We made sure we approached riders who had compatible personalities – we generally headed for the mavericks, riders with a higher than average professional cyclist's intelligence. The racers had to understand what we were attempting to do and buy into the fact that we were going to be outspoken about, and proud of, our 100 per cent clean policy. At the time it was a ballsy position to take, and it required a certain type of rider to buy into it. We were going to be transparent – journalists were welcome, to the point I even shared my room with one at the Tour of California while racing for the general classification win.

The last two things I brought were my story and my contacts with the Tour de France. My story helped, as I was the voice for the team. I did interview after interview explaining my belief in what we were doing. I must have done dozens and dozens of feature pieces about my past and our future as a team, and how we wanted to make a difference. Jonathan and Doug placed so much responsibility on me because, being a reformed doper, I was representative of the sport as a whole, not to mention many within our team, who at that time were unrevealed ex-dopers. I became a firewall for them and an honest voice for the team. And my close relationship with the organisers of the Tour de France (and my status in France as a whole) meant that I gave the team access to the race on a personal level, something necessary for a wild card invitation to the race. My involvement was so important that I was made a part-owner of the team. Jonathan, Doug and I were on a mission to do something good for the sport of cycling. Something, now all these years later, I can look back on proudly and say we did.

Unfortunately, as is often the way in professional cycling, the past no longer mattered.

Not the Tour de France

The days following the announcement of my non-selection for the Tour were horrible. I was angry, very sad, and above all so confused. I couldn't understand why the team would do it to me. I had never let the team down at a Tour de France; I had been the linchpin in the team, on and off the bike, since 2007. I had given so much of myself over the years. Yes, I had sucked a bit the previous two months, but my data from training was on an upward curve, my weight was bang on . . . I had proved time and time again that if I announced I was up to the job, then I would be up to the job.

Jonathan Vaughters and the team owner Doug Ellis hadn't answered their phones in the aftermath of the Charly call. A conference call was arranged for the next day between the three of us. I still hoped beyond hope that they would fix it all, yet I knew if they weren't answering their phones to me and wanted to organise a conference call they were treating this in a very clinical, businesslike manner. Something the three of us had never done in the past; we had always had a more personal than working relationship.

As I feared, the call was a waste of time. They treated me like a journeyman professional with whom they had no history or personal relationship. Jonathan and Doug both reiterated the selection policy of the team: that if a rider was deemed unwell he couldn't be selected for the Tour de France, and they couldn't deviate from that. The same selection criteria also stated that no rider who didn't have a contract with the team for the following year could start the Tour de France. Jonathan had even, in one of his rare appearances, gone as far as announcing this to the whole team at the beginning of the year. He felt very strongly about it. The reason being, he didn't want to take a rider to the Tour de France who would use the race as a vehicle to secure a contract for the following year with another team. In other words, you signed on the dotted line of the contract JV was offering before the Tour or you didn't get a start. For some reason that didn't matter this year – the team took four riders to the Tour who were out of contract at the end of the year. So there was obviously some wiggle room – at their discretion, of course.

I have such good memories of my time with the team – we'd been through so much together. Now I could see it was over; I was no longer needed or wanted by them. The past didn't matter; it bore no relevance to their decision-making. I was simply an ageing pro cyclist past his prime, steadily losing his mind, not to be counted on.

That they couldn't see beyond that surprised me. I had expected more from them: my final Tour de France, my most cherished of races, starting in the UK . . . it seemed almost cruel to take that away from me. I could understand their concerns, but history didn't back them up. I had dozens and dozens of messages from people within the sport: fellow pros, other *directeur sportifs*, journalists, race organisers, commentators, even our own sponsors, and, of course, friends. Nobody understood it.

If they had no personal loyalty then I needn't have loyalty beyond the duty and responsibility of my job and friendships. I'd always thought I'd stay involved with the team beyond my contract. That wasn't going to happen now, which was the best thing I was getting out of it all. The cord had been cut for me. Come 1 January I could start afresh, guilt-free. I wasn't there yet, though.

Television's Ned Boulting got in touch the day after it was announced I'd been pulled from the team. After commiserating, he asked if I'd be interesting in working with him and the ITV crew on their coverage of the race in the UK. At first I didn't think so. My sister convinced me otherwise. She was right, as usual; it would be the best thing for me, a sort of halfway house. It would allow me to be there but not there, and prevent me from sinking into a deep hole of self-pity and bitterness, feeling like I'd been banished from my final Tour de France. I returned home for a few days, not feeling like an exile.

Come Wednesday, I knew the teams had arrived at their hotels in Leeds and I accepted I wasn't part of the Tour any more. Any sense of denial evaporated when that reality hit home. I was no longer part of our Tour de France team – it was official; our nine riders were in their rooms, the team cars, the trucks; the buses were all in the car park. Everything and everybody were present and accounted for, preparing to start their adventure. I, on the other hand, was at home. I'd switched mentalities already. I was playing with my boys in the garden. I was no longer the same person. Tour de France! Are you mad?

What I hadn't anticipated were the wider repercussions. I'd never stopped to think that one day I wouldn't be a Tour de France racer. Obviously I knew that was an eventuality, but I'd never actually considered the event crossing the horizon. Since I was a fifteen-year-old in Hong Kong it had been the biggest driving force in my life, a dream turned into reality. Everything had revolved around the Tour de France. I never really noticed how it became such a normal part of my life – I just took it for granted. Now I could see it hadn't been normal – it had been an extraordinary life, something I was so lucky to have lived, even if it had taken me to dark places along the way.

No matter how real it had all become over the years I'd always kept one dream, and that was of racing up and down the Champs-Elysées in my final Tour de France. Ever since my first Tour I could imagine that time coming, and how special it would be: an opportunity to finally bid it farewell and move on with my life. A conclusion to a long and convoluted love letter. I imagined my family and friends present to watch the final curtain close on what had been such a foreign and strange dream for a teenage Hong Kong kid to have had.

Now, looking back, knowing my final Tour de France was behind me, I could see for the first time that it had given me a farewell of its own. One far greater than I could have ever given it.

The Champs-Elysées, 2013

I'd started the final stage of the 2013 Tour de France more worried about my friend Stuart O'Grady. He was the only thing on my mind, really. Our funeral march of a ride through the Versailles gardens on the way to the official start had put me in a bit of a sorry state. I happened to be aching all over from a crash I'd had two days before on a descent. I'd gone down at 60km/h on a wet, sweeping corner – it was slippery enough that I didn't take much skin off, but the impact smashed my upper legs, and I had strained my groin by riding my bike while injured. All in all, I was in a bit of a foul mood.

This didn't stop me telling Stuey we'd get away on the Champs, that he should stick with me, one final hurrah for us to share (I'd told all my teammates at dinner the night before that that was exactly what I was going to do, so I now had to live up to that bravado, and I figured Stuey may as well join in). He didn't seem overly keen on this plan. His head was beyond shot; all he wanted was for it to be over with. After more than twenty years at the very top of the sport it was clear he'd finally let go, he was no longer the same racer he'd once been. I remember thinking, it happens to us all, eventually.

The final stage of the Tour de France is mostly ceremonial: there's a long preamble from the outskirts of Paris and through the suburbs, photos are taken, champagne is passed around; it is a festive and relaxed occasion. Tradition dictates that whoever wears yellow that morning will be wearing it in the evening. While the general classification race is off-limits, the chase for the stage win itself is taken as seriously as any other.

When we hit the banks of the Seine the pace heats up. Not long afterwards we see the Eiffel Tower for the first time. It doesn't matter how many Tours you've done, this remains a spine-tingling moment. It signifies you've made it. The start of the race, three weeks before, seems a lifetime ago, all the suffering is momentarily forgotten and you're left awash with a sense of accomplishment.

The team of the yellow jersey has the honour of leading the peloton past the Eiffel Tower and on to the Champs-Elysées for the first of ten laps. Whatever we felt on that first glimpse of the Eiffel Tower is now eclipsed by what we see, hear and feel on the Champs. There's nothing else like it in cycling, perhaps in any sport.

We turn off the Seine and race under the arches of the Louvre and right through the main square, past the glass pyramid, before turning left on to Rue de Rivoli. The streets have been lined deep with people the whole way through Paris. We've almost become accustomed to the crowds and noise, then, as we enter the circuit, it feels like we hit a wall of sound. It makes everything we've seen up to that point feel like a village fête – this is like entering the most beautiful arena in the world; it feels like a scene from *Ben-Hur*, only bigger.

Rue de Rivoli is more akin to an *autoroute* than a *rue*, the peloton is suddenly dwarfed by its surroundings; the crowds here are the biggest on the circuit and the most vocal. There is an energy in the air that never fails to replenish resources I thought exhausted. As we come to the end of Rivoli we veer left on to the cobbles of Place de la Concorde. After Rivoli, it almost feels quiet here. A few seconds later we turn right, and on to that most famous of boulevards, the Champs-Elysées.

Then we see it for the first time, the Arc de Triomphe. This is what each of us has seen on TV as young fans; the Eiffel Tower is something you only get to know and feel when you become part of the peloton. The Champs and Arc on the other hand are already embedded in our psyche. There is a familiarity to it, though that familiarity doesn't prepare us for the incline, or the cobbles. It all looks so smooth and fast on TV, yet it's far from that; it is a fair old slog on the way up through the finish line to the Arc. All we can hear are the crowds; all that we feel is the heavy, uncomfortable, repetitive shocks of the cobblestones. Then, when we make the turnaround and head down in the opposite direction, it's like somebody has pushed the fast-forward button: everything is accelerated to a higher frequency; the only sensation of air on the way up is our breathing, now, on the way down, it overpowers everything, smothering our ears as the speed increases and the wind rushes in.

The 2013 final stage differed from the 'standard' affair. In honour of it being the 100th edition of the Tour de France we were to do a lap of the Arc de Triomphe instead of the U-turn we normally made before reaching it. This had never been done before. To add a little more *je ne sais quoi* it was held in the evening, so that we were finishing as the sun set. It is hard to imagine it being any more grandiose.

I'd been in a horrible way during the preamble through the Paris suburbs, so much so that I wasn't speaking to anybody, I was too immersed in self-pity. If I did speak it was more Tourette's-like than conversational: 'Oh God, my fucking legs.' I couldn't imagine how I'd fulfil my self-imposed challenge to break away on the Champs. I felt like a fraud.

My first inkling that maybe all wasn't lost came when the speed picked up on sighting the Eiffel Tower. For the first time all day I could take my mind off my 'fucking legs', the increased energy of the peloton forcing me to stop thinking about what was going on inside my head and enabling me instead to begin focusing on what was going on around it. By the time we arrived on Rivoli and entered the circuit I was back in the game, ready to prove to my teammates that I could break away at will on the Champs.

The race follows a fairly predictable format once we're on the circuit: the yellow jersey's team have the honour of leading the peloton in a victory lap. Once that lap is completed the attacks begin. The attacks always take place on the upward incline, as it's almost impossible to escape on the descending side as the speed is so high. The road's so large there is almost no need to fight for position. If you have the strength you can move up the side whenever you please, especially near the turnaround at the top, where everything slows down and bunches up.

Generally the first attacks don't go – too many riders want to be in the move and there are sprinters' teams marking them in a defensive manner; it resembles the very beginning of a race rather than a finale because up to that point the race has effectively been neutralised. Most riders don't appreciate or consider that. I've been in the breakaway a few times in the past on the Champs, I've figured out the best method. It's pretty simple, really: surf the front in the wheels, wait until a move looks to have broken the elastic and is being allowed to go, then counter-attack from the very front on Rivoli before Place de la Concorde, and bridge up to it on the Champs.

Attacking on Rue de Rivoli works because the peloton arrives on to it from a tunnel and through a fast corner. It's normally stretched out in one long line – the snaking passage through Place de la Concorde keeps the peloton strung out – which means it's much more difficult for riders to move from their position, or even notice the counter-attack. By the time the peloton arrives on the Champs and bunches up and notices you've gone it's too late for them to react.

This is basically what I did last year. As soon as I could tell that everybody was tiring themselves out and the attacking verve had diminished I made my first and only move. There was only one rider ahead at this point, but I knew that I could provoke a few others to come with me. That is usually the way: when a strong rider recognised for making it into breakaways attacks, others will follow with full commitment, believing it will work. The advantage of hitting the Champs-Elysées alone or in a small group means you can head straight to the gutter. This is the final little trick that makes the biggest difference. Although the avenue is cobbled it has a smooth gutter next to the curb. It's not wide (maybe a foot maximum), and it's riddled with drains, but riding it is a damned sight faster than the alternative. This is a massive advantage. The chasing peloton won't use it because no team can ride it safely grouped together; the team leaders will prefer their *domestiques* to take the slower but safer option, relying on their strength in numbers to eventually control the race. Hence why getting the gap before hitting the Champs is so important: it means you'll be going faster than the peloton the whole way to the top – if you've got the legs, that is. It's also possible to ride the gutter on the way down the other side, although it gets a bit sketchy at times as you're getting close to 70km/h on a thin strip of concrete next to a big curb, with screaming fans a metre away and a TV motorbike right next to you, ready to capture for posterity the moment you clip your pedal or get stuck in a drain and slap down on the floor. Which is part of the fun, I suppose.

The next hour was a blur. We started as four riders, but two of them were dropped after only one lap off the front – they weren't able to ride the gutter up the Champs. Then there was only me and Juan Antonio Flecha left, the two of us off the front leading the Tour de France on its final stage in its 100th edition, lapping round the Arc de Triomphe, feeling like tiny little insignificant ants in comparison to our surroundings.

I was feeling so strong, I couldn't believe I was actually doing what I said I would do, only a short while after hiding in my little hurt locker, hating the world. I was not asking Flecha for help. Our chances of winning were as close to zero as was perhaps possible, but that wasn't why we were doing it. We were doing it because we both loved cycling; neither of us could help but let the teenage fan out on occasions like this. This was the ultimate occasion.

I know Flecha well; our careers have run parallel. He lives in Catalunya and is a member of my cycling club, Velo Club Rocacorba. We hadn't planned the move in the slightest: it was serendipity more than anything else, we'd barely spoken to each other, we were simply focused on what we had to do. In that sense we were the perfect pairing: friends who trust each other's abilities implicitly. The times I found myself on his wheel in the gutter I never once doubted his ability. I was able to treat it as if it were just a normal stretch of road. Most other riders I'd give a bit of distance, not trusting them to ride it safely. I had no such doubts with Flecha: he's a Flanders Classics specialist, totally at home riding a thin strip of concrete between a curb and cobbles at 70km/h.

I started doing more and more of the work, never asking Flecha for more as I knew he wasn't playing a tactical game, he was clearly just getting tired. Then, as we rounded the Arc for the second time alone, ready to descend, he said, 'David, you go now.'

There was no reason for him to let me go. After all, the hardest bit of the lap was done, but he did anyway. (I spoke to him later, after the stage, and he told me, 'You were so strong, you didn't need me there. I thought you should have it to yourself.')

The next twenty minutes rank as maybe the most incredible I've ever had racing . . .

. . . I'm alone on the Champs-Elysées, leading the 100th edition of the Tour de France on a road I know so well, for numerous reasons. Flecha is right: I have it all to myself, the peloton is at thirty seconds, which would be close in any other circumstances, yet not here. They may as well be on another continent.

Coming around the Arc de Triomphe on my own as the sun sets, hugging the inside near the Arc with acres of road between me and the outer barriers, I feel so small. The size of the Tour de France has never been so apparent. As I exit the Place de Charles de Gaulle that surrounds the Arc I sweep to the right to make sure I'm in the gutter for the high-speed descent down the Champs. Any *trepidation I've previously felt about the risks inherent in riding here are now gone. I have no fear, I'm completely at ease.*

There are gendarmes lined up, standing on the curb between the barriers and the road, preventing any crazy fan from doing anything that might put us or them at risk. Up to this point, when Flecha had been on my wheel, I swerved round each gendarme ever so slightly so as to avoid touching them, not wanting him to be caught out. Now I just hold my line, brushing each of them with my shoulder as I pass. They never move, not in this passage nor the next; there is a mutual trust and confidence between us.

The crowds are so close, but they can't touch me, not that it matters because I can feel their proximity. The occasional voice makes it through the waves of sound, clear as day; the cheering and movement on the other side of the barriers is in complete contrast to me. I'm trying to hold as still a line as possible while going as hard as I can. I have to go fast, I have to stay still.

Coming to the end of the Champs I can see the big screen showing the feed from the TV motorbike shadowing my every move, the same images that maybe some kids in Hong Kong are watching. I give a little salute to the right as I go to the end of the Champs where the VIP section is, hoping that's where Nicole and my mum are, just as I'd done to my family and friends when I was off the front on the Champs on the final stage of my first Tour in 2000.

Coming through Place de la Concorde in this direction offers a moment of respite. There's no gutter and the cobbles are at their bumpiest, making it uncomfortable and slowing everybody down. I know the peloton will be using it as an opportunity to relax – it's the only section of the lap where there is an impression of tranquillity, relative, of course. Coming out of Concorde we rejoin the Seine embankment which is, like everywhere else, rammed with people, but because the cobbles end and the tarmac begins, the rattling and tension disappear from the moving mass that is the peloton. As each of us rolls on to the smoothness of a normal road we exhale relief.

It doesn't last long; just under a kilometre later we turn left into a tunnel that takes us under the Jardin de Tuileries and leads us back on to Rue de Rivoli.

Being on my own through all of this makes it a completely different experience from what I'm used to in the bunch. I can disappear back into my own head, no longer needing to concern myself with what is going on around me, except what I chose to pay attention to, which is the experience rather than the technicalities of manoeuvring within the peloton.

Entering the tunnel is such a contrast to everywhere else; it is like dunking my head under water – it's dark, empty and quiet, except for a group of fireman who cheer, 'Allez, allez, Daveed!' each time I come through. I can't help but give them a little signal of respect: once my bottle is near empty, I jettison it in their direction, making sure it slides to their feet.

As the tunnel comes to an end the noise begins again. It's as if somebody is turning up the volume and brightening the light in perfect unison. Then it happens: as I exit the tunnel into full daylight I hit the wall of sound once more, back into the Ben Hur hippodrome.

It's a ramp back up on to Rivoli. The first corner was commandeered by the Norwegians years ago – they've made it their own to the point of it now being referred to as the 'Norwegian Corner'. They're brilliantly raucous, faces painted, Viking helmets galore; their cheering and chanting clearly amplified by a day of drinking under the Paris sun, they set the tone. Skimming the barriers as I take the apex I'm nearly deafened by the noise; all I glimpse is a sea of red, then it all opens up and I'm faced with the spectacle that is Rue de Rivoli. Thousands and thousands of people are going berserk. Flags of all nationalities are waving, the kilometre-to-go arch is in the distance and there's me in the middle of the road, dwarfed by it all.

I'm way above my limit. There is no point in holding anything back, it is simply a case of trying to stay out in front for as long as possible – it turns into the most spectacular individual time trial of my career. The sprinters' teams controlling the peloton have happily left me out there, using my speed as a reference, yet we all know that I'm going to slow down at some point. There's no way I can hold them off.

After being off the front for nearly forty-five minutes I can feel my strength start to go and my speed to drop. Going round the Arc I can see the peloton closing in on me. I know it will soon be all over. I am relieved; I'm beginning to hurt everywhere again, my mind is no longer able to overcome my body. I give one last big push down the descent, skimming the gendarmes, feeling the crowds. I look at the big screen and can see the powerful peloton approaching, ever closer behind. I want to make it through the tunnel, selfishly wanting Rivoli to myself, just one more time.

I make it to the entrance of the tunnel and glance over my shoulder. Somehow I've held my gap, even increased it a little. I can see I have more than enough to make it not only through Rivoli but back up on to the Champs. Thankfully, and I don't know why, I decide to stop thinking about the effort, and the race, and just start soaking up the moment and the emotions . . .

I'll never forget those final few kilometres. I made sure of it, yet I had no idea it would be the last time I'd ever race there. It was as if the race had said, much like Flecha, 'You can go now, David.'

Letting Go

Being back at the Tour on the other side of the barriers allowed me to see the race through different eyes. For starters it forced me to watch it, which I may not have done if I'd been in Spain wallowing in self-pity. It also stopped me being angry – because, believe me, I was so bloody angry. But it was such a joyous occasion, and being in the UK made it so much more fun than if it had been in France – everybody was so enthusiastic and happy to see the Tour up close and real – it was such a novelty, I couldn't help but join in.

I wished I was racing, of course; there was no escaping that. To have raced on British roads in front of British fans and my family in York would have been such a perfect way to start my last Tour de France. I'd have enjoyed every kilometre, and raced with such pride. I wasn't racing, though, and being there watching from the outside, surrounded by people who didn't really know much about professional cycling and saw it through the eyes of relative newcomers, made me appreciate how many incredible experiences I'd lived over my racing career. So few people had got to do the things I'd done. The Tour de France was behind me now, I'd had a good run, and, in hindsight, the perfect ending. It was time to move on. I had to let it go.

Not the Tour de France (2)

When the Tour left the UK I left with it. While they returned to France, I headed home to Girona. I switched my focus to the Commonwealth Games, less than a month away. Presuming I'd be at the Tour, Nicole had already planned for her and the boys to be in the UK during July. Everything was booked; it made no sense to cancel it. In fact, it worked out better for me as I could go on full-mission mode.

I rented an apartment in the Pyrenees and went about organising a ten-day training camp. I'd had a week off the bike, so needed and wanted to get back into it as quickly as possible. I felt like Bear Grylls. I was my own man now. The team and I had next to no contact, which wasn't all to do with me losing my shit so badly at the non-selection for the Tour but also because all our team's resources were being used at the Tour de France. I'd always taken for granted the fact that at the Tour we had double the number of team staff, more vehicles, bikes, clothing – more everything.

Those of us not doing the Tour were left out in the wilderness to fend for ourselves. This suited me down to the ground. I liked going rogue; I'd built a career on it (for better or worse). My sister, on the other hand, wasn't so keen on it, knowing that, in truth, Bear Grylls and I have nothing more in common than the letter 'a' in our first names. She worried I'd starve myself to death or train myself to destruction, so she kindly offered her services as my resident chef and all-round life coach. So, just like the old days, France and I went on boot camp.

La Molina was our destination of choice. It's only a couple of hours' drive from Girona so logistically was a piece of cake. We bought a juicer, as we reckoned that was a regime-like thing to do, loaded the cars up with bikes and accompanying paraphernalia and set off for the mountains. The next ten days were brilliant.

The first day, I made the grave error of meeting up with José Hermida, one of the world's best mountain bikers, who happened to live near where I was staying. I'd wanted to do an easy three hours to break myself in. I told him this, so he arrived on his mountain bike knowing I was on my road bike. This was a great relief to me as José is a training monster – he was clearly trying to slow himself down in order to cater to my request to take it easy; bringing his mountain bike was the equivalent of bringing a knife to a gunfight. He still killed me. I emailed Christian VdV afterwards to tell him about it. He replied, 'For the love of God. Never. Ever. Train with Hermida.' Needless to say, I took heed of these words of wisdom.

It only took me two or three days to feel good, then I began the block. I knew the roads well – the first time I'd trained up there was in 1999 with Cofidis, the infamous training camp which concluded with me drunkenly jumping off a roof and breaking my foot. Apart from my ban through 2004 and 2005 that was the last time I didn't do the Tour. One day I rode by the very hotel where we'd stayed and whose roof I'd jumped off. It was empty and derelict. It truly did feel like a lifetime ago.

David Millar
@millarmind

July, 1999, Font-Romeu training camp
with Cofidis at this hotel, passed it while
training this morning. Kinda weird.

France and I found our routine quickly: I'd wake up and get dressed into my cycling kit immediately, no procrastinating. France would make juice (spinach, celery, ginger, carrots, apples, berries . . . they got crazier, or, should I say, braver, the longer we were up there) and porridge. We'd have coffee then, between 9:00 and 9:30 I'd set out training.

While I was gone France would do her day job of putting out fires for Team Sky, hoping all the while that nobody noticed she was in the Pyrenees looking after her brother. Then she'd maybe pop down the mountain to the supermarket, and always have some crazy regime lunch ready for me on my return. My weight had not budged since before the Tour. I was still holding seventy-six kilogrammes, which made me angry all over again about not being in France, because it meant my body had clicked exactly when it was supposed to, even if it had left it till the last possible minute to do so.

I loved being up in the mountains. I felt young again – in fact, I was looking younger by the day, it was the weirdest thing. After my bike riding and lunch we'd sit and watch the Tour de France on the computer. It was like afternoons of old when France and I would sit and watch bike racing and I'd explain everything to her – only in the meantime she'd helped create, build and manage one of the biggest cycling teams in the world, one which had produced two British Tour de France winners. She had become one of the most important people in British Cycling, ergo global cycling. Thankfully, I could still teach her things about racing. I still had that.

Once the racing was done we'd go for a sauna. Not because we liked it – we both fucking hated it – but it was part of the regime. We'd begun advocating it on Garmin in 2008, way before anybody else, but like most things we pioneered we let it slip. It was based on the latest sports science at the time, which had actually originated from military testing, preparing soldiers for extreme heat, where they'd noticed unexpected performance increases.

As in the winter, the training we do throughout the year is about overloading the body to a degree that it adapts and recovers to handle the same load a little better next time. The sauna is effectively a training session, it provokes hyperthermic conditioning. The body adapts to handle the heat – increased blood flow, better temperature regulation, higher plasma volume, more red blood cells, etc. All of these are key ingredients in making a better endurance athlete. In theory you are supposed to do this directly after a training session in order to increase the stress on your system, but we couldn't do that as the sauna didn't open till 18:00. The first day I could barely do ten minutes, the last few days I found thirty minutes bearable, something unimaginable only a week earlier.

In the evening we'd have a total regime meal then go to bed soon afterwards. It was one of the best training camps of my career.

PORT DE TOSAS

Harvey, I'm up in La Molina on a boat
Your Auntie Frances & I are going each
basics, it's the only way I start... here
at the Commonwealth Games, juice in the
morning, bike riding in the mountains, distance
& sauna + cold pool every evening. Full
REGIME! We're having a great time. even
though we're not really doing anything...
suppose that's what makes it special,
just brother & sister hanging out, although
be fair we're not normal siblings. I do hope
that you grow up to be as close
as Frances & I are. There is no better friend. Lots of Love, Dad xxx

HARVEY MILLAR
CAN CRUSIC
PUJALS DE PAGESOS
CORNELLA DEL TERRI
17844

I found it easy to motivate myself so soon after my personal
Tour de France non-selection drama because of how much I
wanted to perform in Glasgow. Suddenly my biggest objective

of the year had shifted to winning the Commonwealth Games road race. I was realistic about the time trial: my results over the preceding two years made it clear I was no longer a contender when it came to that discipline, but I still believed that if I worked hard enough and wanted it enough, come the day I could be one of the strongest road racers in the world.

There had been sparks of what I was still capable of in the previous year, but the last real flash had been at the 2012 Tour de France. A Friday the 13th no less. I clearly remember being on the start line in Annecy, talking to my old teacher from Hong Kong, Charlie Riding. He'd made it a tradition to visit the Tour in previous years to see his old student.

Mr Riding had been the only person in Hong Kong who had told me to do it, to chase my dream; that maybe, just maybe, there could be a reality beyond the reverie. I never forgot that, and he clearly hadn't either.

I sat there on my bike, one hand on the barrier, awaiting the neutral start, Mr Riding and his wife and two boys on the other side, among all the spectators. We were chatting away, and in his usual way he said, 'So, you going to give it a go today, Dave?'

I can remember pulling my head back and almost laughing, 'No way, Charlie, I'm wrecked!' I asked him if he'd seen the stage. There were two category one mountains in the first seventy kilometres. And it was the longest of the race. 'No way. Bugger that,' I concluded.

Argh, as soon as I said it I could see the disappointment on his face, never mind those of his two little boys. I tried to recover it: 'I'll see how it goes. You never know, right?' Charlie took this better; the boys clearly weren't that bothered. I don't know why I'd been worrying about them in the first place.

It turned out that I was strongest of the guys who wanted to win the stage that day, which was ironic because I had probably been the least interested in trying. I even let the break of nearly twenty riders form before bridging up to it on my own, so uninterested had I been in fighting it out beforehand. I crossed the two mountains within myself. There were only five of us left at the summit of the second, and I still didn't feel like I'd gone too deep within my reserves. I rode a very clinical stage, winning it in a sprint against Jean-Christophe Péraud.

I punched the air, just as Cyrille Guimard, my old *directeur sportif* at Cofidis, had taught me: 'Only raise your arms after you've crossed the line, David. You'll slow yourself down and open yourself up to those coming up from behind if you sit up before.' I had made exactly the same salute when winning my first Grand Tour stage in the 2001 Vuelta a España.

That day in 2012 I stopped worrying about losing and started caring about winning. In 2001 it had been about me proving to the cycling world that I was more than a time trial-list. Eleven years later it was about proving who I was and what I represented. The deeper I got into the stage, the more I became aware I was going to win (bar broken chains or slipped chains or bad chainrings or no front derailleurs), the more I realised the responsibility I carried. This was the year we'd had the ghastly early crash that had wiped out the majority of the team and all our general classification hopes; as a team we were on our hands and knees with all pre-race objectives eradicated by Stage 6. Due to that loss of hope I was given carte blanche to race for myself.

I hadn't had that opportunity in years. I'd been testing myself in numerous breaks up to that day, and could feel myself getting stronger as each stage passed.

I'd never race for the win unless I considered it to be a realistic chance. I used all my breakaways up to that day as reconnaissance of who was strong, practice at making it into the break, and training my body to handle the specific workload required to win a stage. Considering how much of an emotional racer I generally was, I could at times be incredibly cold and calculated. Friday 13 July 2012 was one of those days I switched off my emotions and read the race like a book. Crossing the line I shouted the exact same thing I'd shouted in 2001: 'FUCK, YES!' Back then I'd got off my bike like cock of the walk, proud to show everybody I was more than a time-trial specialist. Come 2012 all I wanted to do was lie down.

It's become my favourite photo from my career. I can remember lying there on the ground with my eyes wide open looking up at the sky. I was so wired from concentrating for so long that I couldn't close them. The sky was bright blue, mottled with clouds that drifted across with an indifferent serenity. I could have been lying on the deck of a boat. It was the absolute antithesis to my surroundings. For the first time in hours I wasn't thinking about the wheel in front of me, the wind direction, the climb coming up, cadence, what I should eat, how much I needed to drink, other racers in the break, each of their strengths and weaknesses, what I knew about their *palmares*, and how to expect their plays in the final, what was on the radio, the time gap behind, or the fear of losing; am I strong enough to beat them in the sprint? Or should I attack them? All of that was behind me now. Not only could my body relax, but, more importantly, I could switch off my mind. I'd done it. I'd crossed the line first. I wanted to enjoy that moment, I wanted to have it to myself, no matter how brief it was, because ultimately it was just a moment among hundreds and thousands of others – yet I knew straightaway that it was one of the most important of my long and tumultuous career.

I didn't own the day, which is how I would have felt when I was younger. I no longer had that privilege. I'd handed that back years ago – that was my debt for having been given a second chance. I was an ex-doper, and as long as I raced I had to remind people of not only that but, more importantly, that I was now a clean rider. When I win I consider it an obligation to confront my past and the sport's past; to not skirt around it, but to draw attention, not only to where we have been, but where we are now, and the direction we have to go in in the future. I think that's the only way I, and cycling as a whole, can be taken seriously.

As if I needed reminding of this, the cycling universe decided that I should win on the anniversary of Tommy Simpson's death in the 1967 Tour de France. An anniversary I held dear but had given up on anyone else caring about since the 2007 Tour de France when – even though it was the fortieth anniversary, and the year after Floyd Landis' infamous non-victory – nobody had even mentioned it. As recently as then it seemed people would rather forget Tommy Simpson burning up, when to me it seemed more relevant than ever to remember it. That Friday 13 July 2012 was my moment to remind people of something I felt we shouldn't forget, because that's where we come from, and we must make sure we never return.

Lying there on the ground, surrounded by photographers and press, team staff, anti-doping chaperones and race organisation, I was fully aware that the second I raised myself off the ground my moment would be over for ever. I tried to make it last as long as possible, which wasn't long considering I was lying a few metres beyond the finish line, not the safest place for a brief meditation on life. Once I got up I had to become another version of myself – the doper turned anti-doping crusader. I don't remember much of the next hour of interviews, podium protocol, anti-doping control, more interviews – I'd been racing for six hours in thirty-five degrees-plus heat. I'm not sure how I even managed to be so switched on: my hands were cramping in the press conference, I remember that.

One of the first interviews I did was with Ned Boulting. Listening to it again, I'm surprised to hear myself still breathing heavily:

Ned: You've done it. You've waited a good few years to make that kind of statement on the Tour de France again, haven't you?

Me: Yeah, that's why sometimes when bad luck happens it actually turns into good luck, because for the last few years I've been at the disposition of the team. I haven't had the liberty to do things like that. Because we lost our GC hopes I've been allowed to do what I want, so I've taken advantage of it.

Ned: Time after time we've seen you in breaks and it hasn't quite worked out. I think of Barcelona in 2009 and that kind of ilk, but you got it perfectly tactically today, didn't you?

Me: I was determined. I was just saying to Marya [Pongrace] before, as soon as I got in the break, I was just, 'I'm gonna win today,

I'm gonna win today, I'm gonna win today.' In my head I gave myself no options. I was going to do whatever it took.

Ned: Two attacks from Kišerlovski: did they worry you? Or did they play perfectly into your hands, ultimately?

Me: No, I'd already decided I was going to go after every single attack. I knew I could win the sprint, so my tactic was to shut everything down. So that's what I did.

Ned: And on the forty-fifth anniversary of Tom Simpson's death.

Me: Yeah, I mean, that's particularly poignant, I think, especially after what I've been through, as an ex-doper who's now clean and who loves his sport. I'm very proud to have done it today because I think we mustn't forget Tommy's memory and what happened and also what this sport's been through . . . now, we're the cleanest we've ever been, with Brad [Wiggins] leading the Tour, and Chris [Froome] in second, and now four British stage wins. I mean, we're clean riders and we're dominating the Tour de France.

Two years on I still had the power within me if I got everything right. But I had a month without racing while my main competitors were *en tour* around France. Even if they had a bad Tour they would have accumulated a ridiculous level of fitness and strength; rarely in my career have I come out of a Grand Tour weaker than when I started it. Knowing how hard the Glasgow road race course was, this weighed heavily on my mind. I trained as hard as I could in order to give myself every possible chance, and I loved every minute of it. I'd forgotten what a simple pleasure it can be being on training camp. There is nothing to distract, everything is focused on physical wellbeing from dawn till dusk. Only when we're there do we remember how simple life can be. You're stripped of your normal routine. On training camp we find a new routine, created solely to make us faster, lighter, stronger.

The best bit about it is that everybody respects the fact you're on training camp: you're left alone as if you're in deepest India on a yoga retreat. It's a safe haven from the real world. I appreciate this more than ever knowing it's perhaps for the final time. I treat it as a luxury rather than the job I once considered it. After ten days of training, dieting, saunas and, of course, juicing, I left the mountains and returned to Girona. My sister had to return to her real life; the last Sunday of July, as the Tour de France entered Paris and rode along the Seine past the Eiffel Tower and began its last laps of the Champs, I set off for the airport and my plane to Glasgow.

Velo Club Rocacorba

A TGV ride to Paris on the morning of the final day of the 2009 Tour de France. I was sitting chatting away, terribly excited about the day and evening ahead, proud and borderline euphoric about the amazing Tour we'd had. Bradley Wiggins had finished fourth overall (later corrected to third after the Armstrong USADA Reasoned Decision); Christian VdV (after breaking his back at the Giro less than two months before) had finished seventh. Behind them we had ridden as a world-beating team – in total contrast to our first Tour de France the year before where VdV had finished fourth (in my eyes first) on his own. He had nobody with him, we were all hopeless; he'd had to rely on his good relationships with other riders and *directeur sportifs* to help him out when shit got heavy.

The tone of our 2009 Tour de France was set with our mind-blowing team time trial in Montpellier. Two days later I came surprisingly close to winning my home stage, from Girona to Barcelona. Every day we were active. I'd be placing Julian 'Kiwi Guy' Dean and Ty Farrar in perfect position for bunch sprints one day, then dropping Brad and VdV into the foot of their decisive general classification mountain the next – while, of course, being road captain all the time. The rest of the team were always phenomenal: everybody had a job and did it, without fail. The only reason they hadn't been able to help us in the team time trial was because VdV, Wiggo, Zab and myself were just so fucking fast they couldn't ride with us.

It had only been eighteen months before that I'd lined up at the Tour of Qatar next to that weird bloody castle in the desert with the weight of the world on my shoulders. We'd been outsiders back then, we didn't even have a place at the Tour de France at that point, what with being a second division team. To think that I was now sitting on a train to Paris on the final day of the Tour with a British teammate, Bradley Wiggins, who had just become one of the greatest-ever British Tour de France riders, was astonishing. I'd helped persuade Brad to come to our team, and I believed in him completely. We roomed together most of the time, and had formed a close bond. During the race he may as well have been a brother, the same way I felt about VdV, Zab, Ryder, Ty and Kiwi Guy. No question, we were a team. And all of this meant that on that TGV ride up to Paris I was overflowing with pride. More than that, I was happy. We were all on a cloud, even VdV with his broken back and 'what ifs'. He was proud, like me, because at that moment we no longer cared about the 'what ifs' – we'd lived too long with those. Brad was doing it for us, he was better than us, but in us he had the perfect guys around him to guide and protect him.

On this, the last day, Brad seemed to have relaxed for the first time since we'd started, over three weeks before in Monte Carlo. He'd carried not only the professional burden of being our leader for the race, but also his personal ambition and the weight of a nation. The day before had been the general classification judgement day, with a summit finish atop Mont Ventoux. The podium was out of reach, but he had to hold off one of the best climbers of the time, Fränk Schleck, from taking his fourth place. A lesser man would have crumbled. He didn't. He defended his position on that most British of Tour de France mountains, Tommy Simpson's photograph taped to his stem. For that reason the final and twenty-first stage became his own personal holiday which, looking back, is probably why he didn't help us in the lead out that day when he was supposed to. I can understand that now, years later.

In this jubilant mood we rode the train to Paris. We were on top of the world: that's how fourth and seventh can make you feel if you've fought that hard for it. Brad and I started discussing the fact that our quirky little eccentric sport that nobody in the UK had either known or cared about had suddenly become the dog's bollocks. How all of a sudden we kept hearing of these interesting people who were fans of cycling – yet we never really got to meet them, and if we did it was in some super-uncomfortable situation where nothing clicked.

So I said, 'We should start a club, Brad. A cycling and dining club. Invite people we want to be friends with.'

He nodded in agreement: 'Yeah, that's exactly what we need to do. What would we call it?'

I looked at him, shaking my head, 'I don't fucking know! I just came up with the idea ten seconds ago.'

We spent the next hour deciding who we'd invite and what we'd call it. Rocacorba seemed a no-brainer as that was our training and testing mountain in Girona, but should it be Rocacorba CC or Rocacorba Wheelers? Or GS Rocacorba? Or even Velo Club Rocacorba. Yes, Velo Club Rocacorba. VCR. Wait, VCR doesn't work, that's a videotape, VCRC? YES. I'm not even going to go into our list of imaginary members. I remember it vaguely becoming exactly that, imaginary.

Over the years, the club has grown into exactly what I imagined and hoped it could be on that train ride to Paris. Bradley's input didn't go beyond that day – as soon as he left the race he slipped back into his anti-social self – Michael Barry stepped in and together we spent months, nearly a year, in fact, creating it. There are close to forty members now, from all over the world. The one thing we all have in common is a love of cycling, and also the likelihood we'd never have known each other if Velo Club Rocacorba hadn't given us a reason to become friends.

The Style Council

The one thing almost every member of Velo Club Rocacorba has in common, beyond the cycling, is a creative sensibility. Those were the sort of people Michael and I wanted to recruit because they were the types of people we rarely got to meet or know, living ensconced in the professional cycling world as we were.

Four become the VCRC Style Council: Richard Pearce, Max Broby, Kadir Guirey and Douglas Brooks. Richard and Max are from architectural and design backgrounds, and have known each other for years, while Kadir is an actual real-life prince with a near Forest Gump-like ability for being in the right place at the right time over the last forty years. He was the first professional skater in the UK back in the seventies, was in a successful band in the eighties before becoming a producer, has an encyclopaedic knowledge of art and, of course, it goes without saying he knows everybody who is anybody in every London scene. He's just a cool dude, and perhaps the gentlest and kindest person I've ever met. Douglas Brooks is a phenomenal man, a scholar of Eastern religions and languages, who happens also to be one of the world's most respected yoga gurus. He has a brain the size of a planet. All of us have learnt more from Douglas over the years than any teacher has ever taught us.

Richard and I had started working together after I'd had a mad idea with my shoe sponsor, fi'zi:k, to make a different pair of shoes for every race I did in my final season, and then auction them off for charity. I wanted each shoe design to be a mini-story of my history or vision of the race it was representing. Between the five of us we came up with the design for nearly every shoe, as well as the Team Scotland Commonwealth Games cycling kit. What began as a fun little side project became an almost full-time job for Richard, who took it upon himself to make sure every design was up to the standard we all wanted.

Arriving in the Commonwealth Games village and seeing the fruits of our labour in the newspaper cuttings on the wall of the Scottish team common room was a magic moment. Racing for Scotland meant so much to me. I'd now be racing through the streets of Glasgow in front of my countrymen and family and friends dressed in a kit of my own design. It felt like the ultimate honour. Now I just had to hope and believe I'd be good enough on the day to make my country proud.

Glasgow

I felt like a younger version of myself when arriving in Glasgow. I was fit, motivated and refreshingly excited. Getting to the athletes' village brought back all the memories of previous games. There's a school summer camp feel about them – although having never been on a school summer camp I can't be entirely sure if that's the case, but it's how I imagine they'd be.

The 'village' feels like a film set. Everything has been built especially for the occasion, and it looks like it. Everything is new, and, although finished, it doesn't quite feel completed: because it isn't. There are no kitchens in the houses or apartments – every door is a self-closing fire door with its own lock and key, there are connecting passages between buildings. Every wall is painted the same colour, every sofa, bed and wardrobe identical. Nothing there is designed to be permanent except the structure of the buildings and their layout on site. Once the games vacate, the contractors will be back to convert the 'village' into the housing development it is destined to be.

In the middle of it all is the food hall – the biggest canteen you've ever seen. Choosing where you sit, even after all these years, is difficult. It's like your first day of school, but a school where the turnover of athletes is so high and the schedules so random you don't actually know anyone. Even those from Scotland, wearing identical tracksuits, are strangers because within each country there is a multitude of different teams who rarely, if ever, cross paths. Being a professional cyclist I never mix with any other sport. I haven't grown up knowing other athletes; I've been on the road since I was eighteen, of my own volition, and away from national teams and international games. I'd often choose to sit on my own in the food hall, because I never really treated it as a social experience. I treated it as a competition.

All of which is contrary to what the media may have outsiders believe. Certain newspapers regurgitate the same story, every major games, of massive partying and vast sexual promiscuity within the village. This may be the case for some, but they are few and far between – and for professional cyclists it's never the case. We come in, race, party together afterwards, then fly out the next day to race for our pro teams once more. Even though it's such an emotional and rare event for us we can't help but be professionals (our treat being that we don't fly out straight after the race, hence the rare opportunity to party together, but even then we don't mix with other sports).

The food hall reminded me of being a boy again. I'd get self-conscious, even shy: I didn't want to go and sit with people I didn't know. Occasionally I'd try the get-to-know-you conversation that meeting people for the first time involves, and every time it would end up being uncomfortable and forced. I'd have dined with the Scottish cycling guys, but they always ate too early – I was accustomed to Spanish time so that never worked. The only time I didn't eat alone was when the Aussie cycling team were in the food hall at the same time: I had more friends in that team than any other. Their manager/coach, Bradley McGee, is one of my oldest friends and two of their team were my pro teammates;

the other four were friends. They made me feel at home, in my home country, which was confusing.

The Scottish team were fantastic, though. My mechanic, David Sharp, was one of the best I've ever had, and Alastair MacLennan, the Scottish Cycling president, was the same guru he'd always been. The Scottish team felt like home, even if I felt like a stranger in the food hall. The memory of my redemption at the Commonwealth Games in Delhi lived on – possibly this was why I'd even been given the honour of designing the Team Scotland cycling kit for Glasgow. I saw it for the first time in its final form on arriving in the village.

I'd wanted us to have a navy blue kit, like the football or rugby team, and even incorporate a Lion Rampant somewhere. Those things for me are Scotland.

Unfortunately it wasn't possible. We had to adhere to a particular Pantone that had been chosen as the blue for every Scottish kit. Then we weren't allowed to use the Lion Rampant – it being sovereign property. This was all news to me. The Lion Rampant is the royal banner for Scotland, and, although used as a secondary Scottish flag by Scottish sporting fans, apparently it can only be officially used by Great Officers of State who represent the sovereign in Scotland. Which seemed a bit unfair, but these were the things we had to respect. Once we understood these restrictions we decided the only way to represent Scotland in Glasgow was by wearing the flag. The kit was designed as such; Richard Pearce took it upon himself to make it the best possible. He visited the factory, learnt their manufacturing techniques and designed the kit accordingly. For what was ultimately a very simple design there was an enormous amount of work.

The cycling events had already begun the week before my arrival at the velodrome. In fact, by the time I'd got there the majority of them had been completed, their medals already awarded. My two events, road race and time trial, were, as at most of the major games, two of the final events.

The time trial came first. I didn't expect much as I hadn't trained specifically for it, having decided to hedge all my bets on the road race. The weather on the day was beautiful enough to bring more people out to the roadside than any of us could have ever imagined. It felt like a Tour de France stage, only there was blue everywhere instead of yellow, and everybody was cheering my name. As defending champion I was last man off. I felt good right from the beginning, yet even though that was the case I was well off the pace.

Alex Dowsett of England, who had finished second to me in the previous Commonwealth Games, won it convincingly. Personally, I was just glad to get it done – although it was an amazing experience racing in Scotland for Scotland, I couldn't help but feel like I was disappointing everybody by not being in the race for the win. After the time trial I tracked down Nicole and the boys in the area near the finish. It was the first time I'd seen them since they'd left for the UK nearly a month earlier. Somebody captured the moment and kindly sent me the photos. While Alex Dowsett was preparing to receive his gold medal I lay on the grass in the park, blissfully happy.

I was determined to rectify my lacklustre time-trial showing in the road race a few days later. It was to be held on the final day, practically the closing event of the Games. I knew it was a long shot. As is often the way the dedication and self-belief I'd needed to commit fully to the training camp had blinkered me to the harsh reality. Having not competed in over a month meant I'd be at something of a disadvantage compared to the guys who'd been racing – no training camp in the world could replicate the Tour de France – but there was nothing I could do about that. I had to believe it was still possible.

Come the day, the good weather of the previous week has vanished. It is apocalyptic, the rain relentless and the clouds so dark it feels like night. At my best this would have been my dream scenario. With the course being so technical and the peloton made up of such mixed abilities it is in the interest of the big teams to make sure the race is hard from the very beginning, in order to cull the weaker and more dangerous riders.

One of the great things about the Commonwealth Games is that the spectrum of talent is so broad. There are riders who have just finished the Tour de France lining up against guys from small and faraway countries who have never even ridden in a peloton before. As charming as this may sound, it's also quite disconcerting: the professionals don't want to be crashed into and injured by a less skilful, possibly reckless, competitor. Wet city-centre roads and a technical circuit are perhaps the worst combination. For this reason the strongest team in the race, the Australians, go from the gun.

By the end of the first lap, over half the peloton has been dropped, and the shredding doesn't stop there: every lap there are fewer and fewer riders. It's a classic war of attrition. The weather makes it all the harder, as each lap is peppered with crashes, so you have to stay right at the front all the time in order to make sure you are safe, or at least safer. I feel in control for the majority of the race, and still believe it possible that I can be in contention for the finale, but when the real race starts with four laps to go I can't react. The riders who've come from the Tour de France are simply on another level; their condition allows them to handle the load without much difficulty, and the longer and harder the race the easier it becomes for them. I'd feared that would be the case but have refused to let myself think about it, knowing there is nothing to be done. I've trained as hard as I possibly can, and that is all I could've done in lieu of racing.

I watch the race ride away from me, helpless to do anything about it. I hang my head and prepare myself for the long and lonely ride in the rain to the finish. It's heart-wrenching. I've dreamt of being up there racing for the win, giving the Scottish fans a Scot to cheer for at the front of the race. I've been given the perfect opportunity to say thank you and goodbye: it had seemed a dream come true when I'd realised the Commonwealth Games in Glasgow would be one of my last-ever races, and knowing how well the course suited me I had dared to believe it could be a fairy-tale ending. I should have known better.

On the final lap I pull over and stop where my family have been standing, watching the day's racing, leaving the two riders I am with to continue on to the finish. I am still in the top ten at this point. I give my wife a hug and say hello to the boys. It isn't quite how I'd imagined the last lap to be, but in a way it is the perfect ending.

I've done everything I can. I'm not strong enough, is all. I kiss them goodbye and clip back into my pedals then continue to the finish. The rain finally abates and the sun shows itself for the first time all day. I then puncture. Only twelve riders finish. I'm eleventh.

David Millar
@millarmind

Thank you Scotland. That was an amazing day, wish I'd been strong enough to race for the win. Happy G won, he's nice.

View on Twitter

Washed up

My relationship with the team had changed drastically since my Tour de France non-selection and my subsequent public flip-out. I no longer had any input in my race programme. The privileged status I'd previously taken for granted was now gone with the wind. I received a generic email towards the end of July with a revised schedule. There was nothing explaining the thought process or objectives. It was simply a calendar with the races I'd be doing. And there weren't many – two, in fact: Eneco Tour followed by the Vuelta a España.

As far as I was concerned the World Championships were no longer a possibility. I knew the British team would be making its selection mid-August, and I'd been counting on showing myself at the Tour de France and being one of the strongest at the Commonwealth Games off the back of it. In reality, I'd shown nothing to dissuade the selectors from thinking I was a washed-up pro counting down his days to retirement. The Worlds was one more fairy tale I could put to bed.

I'm not a big fan of the Eneco Tour. In fact, I'd be amazed if there are any professional cyclists who are. It's like the Flanders Classics without any of the history or romance, and instead of one day it lasts seven. The fact I've never liked it hasn't stopped me doing well there – I almost won the general classification of two editions and, in truth, it's a good race for the type of rider I am. And, coming two weeks after the Tour de France, I always had a residual super-strength that made it a bit of a no-brainer.

This year I can't see any point in me going there – it will more than likely compromise any preparation for my new principal end-of-season goal, the Vuelta. The team don't care, though. They don't even respond to my very polite (and difficult to write) emails requesting reconsideration. Oh well, the dream is clearly over. I've managed to put myself back to neo-pro status in my final season; I no longer have any influence whatsoever on my race programme. There's nothing for it but to do what I'm told. Charly and Jonathan are getting their revenge for my anger at not being selected for the Tour. I haven't spoken to either of them since before the Tour de France. I sent them a congratulatory message when Ramūnas Navardauskas (my replacement) won a stage. They didn't respond. Ramūnas, on the other hand, thanked me publicly for having spoken to him and wishing him good luck before the Tour (once I found out he was my replacement). I seriously couldn't think of another rider I'd rather have take my place. I asked him to win a stage for me; being Ramūnas he did.

The Honey Badger

Ramūnas and I are rooming together at Eneco. He's the perfect roomie: quiet and respectful, most of the time he resembles a sleeping bear, which couldn't be in greater contrast to his on-the-bike persona. He hadn't been on the team very long before we nicknamed him the Honey Badger.

Ramūnas is Lithuanian. He turned pro with us in 2011, the year of his twenty-third birthday. He'd been so good as an amateur that people thought he was on drugs. If he'd been Australian, American, British or French there wouldn't have been any doubting his pedigree. Unfortunately the Eastern Bloc countries are still tarnished by decades of prejudice and, sadly, some history in this regard. Jonathan Vaughters did his due diligence and checked Ramūnas's blood profile while also putting him through extensive physiological testing. The majority of teams didn't even bother with that, instead basing their decision not to engage him on the vicious rumours they'd heard, or their presumptuous preconceptions of young, fast, Eastern Bloc bike racers.

When he first came to our team his English wasn't so good. His French, Russian, Lithuanian and Spanish were OK, though. Now his English is perfect. Rather than turn on the TV in the room he will read a book. He is generous in his consideration of others to the point of altruism. He sleeps deeply, and wakes up as late as the daily schedule will allow him to. He laughs at every joke, will listen to every story and will always try to stay at the evening dinner table until it is clear that the last there are finished. He much prefers listening to talking. For me, he's more of a gentleman than any Australian, American, British or French rider I know. He is loved by everyone in our team.

Then there's the alter ego, the Honey Badger, so-called because of a YouTube video Dave Zabriskie introduced us to in 2011. Until that moment I'd never heard of the honey badger – a real-life, living creature which, despite its name, bears more of a resemblance to a weasel than a badger. It is ferocious, virtually tireless in battle, and damn near impossible to kill. Fuck knows why it's called the honey badger – there's nothing sweet about it.

But that's Ramūnas in a bike race. We've used him in lead outs in the past, and more often than not I'll be on his wheel as he positions me, Kiwi Guy and Ty. It's in the final ten kilometres of the race – when most people are starting to lose their cool, get aggressive and sometimes push, lean or even head-butt – that I've watched Ramūnas simply weather the storm from all angles, and never once decelerate or change position. While teams all around him are expending three riders to match him, he remains as solid as a rock. Occasionally, I've seen him have no choice but to retaliate to invasions of his personal space, and when he does he always, *always*, wins. It's a beautiful thing to behold, and he *never* loses his cool. After the race he won't even mention it. Most of us will be in the team bus already, regaling everyone with our own stories of the day's events. Ramūnas will come in and quietly sit down in his seat and let out a big sigh and say, 'I'm so tired. You guys were so strong.' We all just stop and look at him, as if to say, 'You have no idea, do you?' Then shake our heads and carry on again. His exploits are legendary. He does things that are simply incomprehensible, not only to us, but to him, too. He just cruises along killing people and races at will.

Nathan

Eneco is going by OK – in the sense that I haven't crashed, which, much as in the Classics, is a win in itself. I've had to shift my

attitude from resentment at being here to a positive mental attitude: I'm using it as training for the Vuelta, with the recognition
that it's the last time I'll race these roads that I've known for so
long.

It's made easier by the team here: my good friend and
Weissbier-drinking partner, Andreas Klier, is our *directeur sportif*.
He knows exactly the mixed emotions I'm experiencing. Then
there's Nathan.

Oddly, the member of the team at Eneco who is having
the most positive influence on me is Nathan Haas. Odd, because
he's only been racing road bikes for four years. Normally it's the
old guard I rely on to inspire me – Andreas, Stuey, VdV, Ryder,
etc. Nathan doesn't know my sport, we haven't grown up together,
we're not the same. Well, that's what I was thinking heading into
this race around the backwaters of Holland and Belgium, mainly
due to the fact that I'd become too old to remember what waking
up in the morning ready to conquer the world felt like. I used to
feel like that, but spending time with Nathan has opened my eyes
to how incredibly annoying the younger me must have been to
the older pros in my team.

I turned up to Eneco pissed off and resentful, still angry with
the team for denying me my final Tour, fucking my Commonwealth
Games in the process, and then, insult to injury, making me do
Eneco. When I got there it was raining, and that didn't make me
any happier. In a nutshell, I was unpleasant to be around.

Nathan and I travelled together from Girona. He spent
hours with me before we even got to the race listening to my
anger at the team. I needed to vent: I'd been keeping it all locked
up the previous weeks. I used Nathan the way I would have one of
my old pro friends. I forgot Nathan looked up to me, though. He
relied upon my leadership; I was his captain.

I didn't realise this until Nathan broke it to me in the hotel
that first evening. We were on our way to join our teammates in
the restaurant when he took me aside and said, 'David, you have
to stop being so negative, you're going to bring everybody down.

We rely on you. I'm just saying, I understand, but you have to remember the influence you have over all of us.'

'Fuck me. He's right,' I thought. I didn't know what to say to him. I don't think I said anything, I was so surprised at how wrong he made me feel. Not many people in my life have done that to me, which is unfortunate, because I've been wrong more often than I've been right.

After that wake-up call I got to know Nathan a lot more. I was curious. Up to that point I'd always treated him as a bright-eyed, eager-to-please, intelligent yet naïve Aussie neo-pro. The things I'd noticed before and let wash over me now became interesting quirks that I wanted to know more about.

I've learnt a lot about him. He took up mountain biking at university in Sydney, where he read philosophy and political studies. He only got into road racing because people told him he should (which was much as it was for me – not the philosophy, the mountain biking). Nathan's grandfather was a Polish emigrant to Australia. He arrived with nothing except injuries from the Second World War. He worked three jobs, had four kids, and passed on a work ethic and joy for life that Nathan displays today; in fact, Nathan credits his blind enthusiasm and his family's eternal optimism to his grandfather.

Nathan's dad was a military officer, and an exceptional athlete in swimming and football. He was Nathan's hero. But, as with me, his parents divorced when he was ten (I was eleven). His father continued to live abroad while he stayed with his mother in Australia. His mother comes from a wealthy Australian farming family, and her passion is ballet: she was good enough to dance with the Australian Ballet for many years. Nathan believes his strength and compassion come from her, qualities he credits to her upbringing on the farm. His ability to endure pain also comes from her – ballet taught her that.

I've learnt all this at Eneco. Nathan fascinates me; the more I get to know him the more I admire him. I don't think I've ever seen him feel sorry for himself, and, unlike most of us, if he sees somebody in a bad way he won't be scared to go and speak to them. He's not the bright-eyed and bushy-tailed naïf I thought he was. Far from it: he's motivated and he's kind – simple as that.

Eneco

All the years I've relied on older pros to guide me – now it's the younger guys who are saving me. Aside from Nathan there's Ramūnas. He also reminds me that, even outside the race, I'm important to them. He's lost his way since the 2014 Tour, only riding his bike once in the two-week interim. He's become more talkative than he's ever been, though; probably aware that this is the last time he'll be able to speak to me in that sacred roomie way.

He's at his wits' end with the state of the Lithuanian cycling federation and their ability to put the dis into organisation. Every night he asks me more questions about what he can do to help change it, that he's worried about young riders coming up and them not being protected, that the women's cycling scene is run by coaches who he fears may be more aligned with the East Germany of the 1970s than the world of 2014. I help him draft a letter. (I don't know if he ever sent it.)

Nathan and I are the only two of the team who are heading to the Vuelta straight after Eneco. This weighs heavily on our minds: we race hard but always with the knowledge that we have only five days between the two races. The demands of Eneco are completely different from those we can expect in Spain. Everything here is explosive, and the peloton is constantly nervous. By the end of each day we are frazzled, more mentally than physically. There are constant battles for position and the narrow roads and wild array of road furniture makes for stop-start racing. We do more braking and accelerating in one day at Eneco than a whole week at the Vuelta. Then there's the fact that it's relatively cool compared to Spain, where we'll be starting in the very south at the height of summer. Seventeen degrees and

50km/h winds off the North Sea isn't exactly the ideal acclimatisation for what will effectively be northern Africa.

Surviving the week without a crash or being too tired is the number one objective. The bottom line is it'll make us better – racing generally does that, whatever and wherever it is. We convince ourselves of this fact, relying on each other for morale, but knowing, deep down, we just need to recover.

The final day is a brutal stage around the Ardennes, finishing on La Redoute, the legendary climb of Liège–Bastogne–Liège. Nathan and I are beat down and now really pissed off that we have to travel to the Vuelta in two days' time to do team time-trial training when what we really need is rest. It makes no sense, and seems more like panic training than anything else. In my opinion the Vuelta team should have been in Girona training for the team time trial instead of doing Eneco. Unfortunately, my opinion no longer matters, so here we are, head-banging around Belgium and the Netherlands instead. Travelling to the airport after the race I realise that I will never have to race my bike up here again. I become suddenly nostalgic, but more than that I am relieved. Farewell, Flanders, it's been emotional.

Archibald! Recycling AGAIN!! I bought extra
when I got these because they're difficult
to find here. I'm writing this at Weeze
airport near Dusseldorf on my way back
from Eneco. I never have to race a bike
in Belgium/Holland again! I've kept
good memories, don't worry (like Tting
along this very waterfront & Knowing
I'm going fast), but there are many hard
memories cold, wet, gutter, crashes, suffering etc.
Still, I wouldn't change .... got to win De Panne.
Podium Eneco, final ... Flanders ... Cancellara with Phil.
Love Dad
xxx

ARCHIBALD MILLAR
CAN CRUSIC
PUJALS DE PAGESOS
CORNELLA DEL TERRI
17844 ESPAGNE

Spain, and the National Characteristics of Racing

I've loved the Vuelta a España since the first time I did it, back
in 2001. Spain as a whole has always been a favourite destination of mine to race; the laid-back culture is absorbed by osmosis
into the cycling. The pressure to win is the same as in any other
big race, yet everybody seems to manage it with a tranquillity
they didn't even know they possessed. Unlike other races riders
will try harder to keep their cool. I feel more at home in Spain in
that regard. Maybe it's the better weather and bigger, faster roads;
probably it's the slow mornings and later starts. All of those are
factors, for sure, but I think the biggest contributor is the simple
fact that it's Spanish.

   In Belgium and the Netherlands the racing is nervous and
aggressive, the riders from those countries have grown up with
that style of racing and so it becomes their default setting – they're
hardcore, one-day racers. Stage racers are a minority among them.

   In Italy there is a culture of both one-day and stage racing.
The races are generally designed with a physically demanding

finale where there will be a series of hills or mountains that will break the race up into pieces. This means that Italian teams and riders have developed into that style of racing. Great Italian bike racers are often tactically savvy climbers who can also sprint. There is very little time trialling, and I don't remember ever having experienced an echelon caused by crosswinds in Italy.

France is fairly chaotic – a state of confusion having probably sprung from hosting all types of racing: from cobbles to Alpine mountains; from the most famous one-day race in Paris–Roubaix to the world's most famous stage race in the Tour de France. Having had a history of excelling in all disciplines the French have, of late, born more resemblance to jacks of all trades . . . and masters of none. Recently, and to their benefit, they've adopted a scientific Anglo-Saxon attitude and are redis-covering success, in stage races at least, although their one-day racing results are still nondescript.

The British, Americans, Australians and Germans have brought a new science to the sport, number-crunching their way to success. The British and Americans have prospered in stage races, where variables are more easily controlled, while the Australians and Germans have found their prowess in the one-day racing world. Each of these countries' triumphs in their preferred area has led to a self-perpetuating cycle of success that is difficult to break free from. Ironically, the Anglo-Saxon coun-tries have proved that even relative newcomers to the sport find themselves sucked into the old world of specialisation.

In every country it's the native riders, in all their forms, who shape the culture. Ex-riders organise, commentate, write, even judge – the current riders just race. Between them they dictate the general characteristics of their races without even knowing it. In Spain it's their friendly, patient, occasionally auto-cratic attitude that rubs off on everybody.

Spain has never really budged from its specialities: climbing and stage racing. Spanish teams are some of the best in the world when it comes to controlling a race. When I turned professional in 1997 it was the year following Miguel Indurain's retirement. His team, Banesto, had spent the previous ten years controlling Grand Tours: they were the masters of it. I can remember we would all breathe a sigh of relief when Banesto had the leader's jersey in any race because we knew they'd control it with clinical precision. They were the experts of economising their effort, and by looking after themselves they looked after the peloton. That, in a nutshell, sums up the Spanish racing style – they are organised and respectful. For a country renowned for having a laidback 'hasta mañana' attitude they are a paragon of highly disciplined and very effective teamwork. For years at the World Championships the Spanish team were considered to be the best outfit. Where the Italians, the Belgians or the French would always have some sort of polemic going on, you could rely on the Spanish to do what they had to do, and do it damned well, and, most importantly, without drama.

Some years they had a hit squad of riders, yet there was never a concern there'd be a clash of egos; they were always able to work as one. The Italians in the meantime would be arguing among themselves while buying-up competitors, as well as each other.

The Vuelta embodies the Spanish style of racing. I've always said that I've felt it to be the bike racer's bike race. We can go there and race our bikes without any of the peripheral stress that often comes with being a professional. It's probably always felt like that to me because I've come to it from the recently finished Tour de France, where pressure and stress are inherent and where it's easy to feel like a tiny cog in a colossal machine. I was one of the very few Tour de France riders who really wanted to go to the Vuelta. It was always my race. I could go there and race without expectation or pressure to perform. More often than not whatever team I was on was just happy to have one of their big riders putting their hand up to go. It's helped that the majority of times I've raced there I've won a stage or come close.

The Final Grand Tour

Arriving at a Grand Tour is different from every other race. For starters we arrive days in advance rather than the standard day before that we allow for most other races. This is mainly due to the fact that we have a blood test two days before the start. This is a UCI quarterly test, rather than a random control, and is a remnant of the first-ever blood controls (referred to as 'health checks' at the time) that were brought into our sport (well, any sport actually) back in 1997, my first year as a professional.

At the time there was no test for EPO (an injected hormone that replicates the effects of altitude training) so, in an attempt to curb the blatant abuse of EPO, a limit was put on the effect it had: the 50 per cent haematocrit limit means you aren't allowed to have more than 50 per cent of your blood cells made up of the oxygen-carrying red type. A higher percentage of oxygen-carrying red cells is considered dangerous, likely to result in blood thickening. That thickening, *in extremis*, can cause heart failure. It's worth mentioning here that Bjarne Riis won his Tour de France in 1996 with a haematocrit of over 60 per cent. He was taking vast quantities of EPO at the time.

Those initial quarterly tests helped educate the authorities as to the effects of EPO and other drugs. They began to realise that in the long term the only way to stay ahead of the doping curve was to bio-mark athletes – in other words to monitor them with regular blood tests that would eventually give them sufficient data to create a biological passport for each rider. They didn't need to build this passport for ever, they simply needed to do it for long enough to see natural trends that identified their biological make-up – then they could randomly blood test to monitor for anomalies. If any were spotted they could then begin random anti-doping blood and urine controls, in and out of competition. These would target whatever drug or drugs the UCI perceived to be creating the anomalous result they spotted in the passport data.

The pre-Grand Tour test is done on the Thursday morning before the race starts on the Saturday. So the latest we will arrive is the Wednesday evening. When there's a team time trial on the first stage, as is often the case these days at the Giro d'Italia and Vuelta a España (but not so the Tour de France), we will arrive even earlier to allow us an extra day or two to recon the course and do some final training exercises to be sure the team is well drilled and everybody is on the same page regarding their role within the team. Hence, when we arrive on the Tuesday, Nathan and I hardly feel like we've stopped since Eneco, which is never the ideal way to arrive at the start of a Grand Tour – we were hardly fresh as daisies after tapering the previous week. But we just had to suck it up and try to ignore how tired we were.

The buzz of arriving at a Grand Tour is always the same. They're the only races where each team will bring a full arsenal of staff and vehicles. For Garmin this meant twenty-six people and nine vehicles at the 2014 Vuelta:

9 x riders
2 x *directeur sportifs*
1 x sports scientist
1 x doctor
1 x chiropractor
4 x mechanics
5 x *soigneurs*
1 x bus driver
2 x chefs
1 x bus
5 x cars
1 x truck
1 x van
1 x kitchen truck

At the Tour de France there'd be even more support, as we'd have extra hands on deck to handle media and sponsors. This is one of the reasons the Tour de France can become so hectic:

beyond the fans, media and the race itself each team is operating at a level that it doesn't come close to at any other time of the year, which makes for a slightly strained working environment when things aren't going so well.

Whereas at the Vuelta, when things don't go to plan nobody really gives a shit. For a team like ours, with its American owners and sponsors, the Tour de France is the be-all and end-all. A close second is the Tour of Colorado (where our team is from), which takes place three weeks after the Tour, and which means that the Vuelta begins just as the pressure is released, with the completion of the race in Colorado. We are left to our own devices, almost operating like a splinter group. To use an American expression, it's awesome.

It's always possible to judge how the atmosphere for the next month will be from the first evening meal at the hotel. It's the only time in the day when the riders really get to sit down and spend time together. Breakfasts are fairly freestyle in that we're given a deadline to be there, but it's up to us what time we eat (as long as it's not after the deadline). I'm always up so early it's possible for me to go through an entire Grand Tour without ever sharing the breakfast table.

Dinner in the evening, however, is where we relax; the day is done. The Vuelta being the Vuelta means that everybody is fairly chilled in the days leading up to the start. The fact that it's my twenty-fourth Grand Tour means I'm particularly relaxed, the trepidation of younger years a distant memory. Immediately I can see everybody has a similar disposition. From that first meal we are all on the same page: we are in hysterics, riffing on random subjects, taking the piss out of each other – the usual banter of a happy team. This doesn't mean we are carefree – we have serious ambitions for the race: Ryder and Dan Martin are riding for the general classification, while I want to win a stage; Talansky is here to redeem his poor showing at the Tour de France, while Cardoso, Nathan, Koldo and Vansummeren are present to work for the team and seize any opportunities that arise. We have one Grand Tour virgin in the young American Nate Brown – and even he seems pretty blasé about the whole thing. That said, there is an elephant in the room.

The team time trial on the first stage has us concerned, largely because of the fact that, out of the four previous Grand Tour team time trials Garmin have undertaken, we've crashed in three of them. In fact, five of our team starting the Vuelta had been involved in the 'car bombing' of the Giro earlier this year.

The team time-trial course in Jerez does nothing to alleviate the nerves. It is highly technical, with roundabouts galore on a road that looks like it has been polished to within an inch of its life. A glass of water spilled on a corner could take out a whole team – well, that's how most of our team are talking. It's not that they are worried: they are shit-scared. That much fear breeds humour; we can't help but find it funny, me especially considering in my eighteen years of racing I've never once been involved in a team time-trial crash. On the bright side it somewhat lowers expectations: our primary goal is not to crash. My final team time-trial, and that's what we were aiming for: to stay upright. Oh, how the mighty fall.

Team Time Trial (2)

I've never been one for team talks – that's the job of the *directeur sportif*. As riders we don't really have a moment to rally together where we huddle and high-five like in the movies. Ultimately, our loner personalities aren't designed for such flagrant displays of solidarity. The only time there is the opportunity for such a call to arms is before a team time trial. We arrive at the ramp ten minutes before our start time and sit around uncomfortably, waiting to be called up. It has crossed my mind many times in the past to speak to the guys during that moment, but we used to win team time trials without such cinematic behaviour so I've always thought better of it. This time I didn't. We were all sitting there, nervous, but not in a healthy way, so I thought, 'Fuck it. It's my last team time-trial anyway. I may as well go all American.'

'Guys, let's have a chat.' I gestured for them to pull their chairs closer, and we found ourselves in a sort of circle, sitting there with our baby blue Alien helmets, all bent over as it was so hard to hear with all the noise. 'I know everybody is nervous, but there's no point, it's not gonna change anything,' I continued. 'We're not here to race for the win, so already that makes our life easier. We only have one objective, and that's to make sure Ryder and Dan lose as little time as possible.' I nodded to the two of them; they and everybody else nodded back. 'Everybody does their job and does it to the best of their ability. You can't do any more and you shouldn't think about having to do any more. We ride as a team, and we look after each other. It doesn't matter what our result is when we cross the finish line as long we all know we gave everything and we did the best we could – as a TEAM. Honestly, that's all that matters. OK?' They all nodded their heads, some of them repeated 'OK'.

I finished off with 'All right! Well, this is the last team time-trial I'll ever do. I'm proud to be doing it with you guys.' I then smiled, 'Please, let's try not to fucking crash.'

We didn't crash. As sad and sorry a goal as that may have been it still felt good to fulfil it. We finished in eighteenth place, forty-one seconds down. We crossed the line pleased.

JEREZ DE LA FRONTERA

Handwritten postcard text:

PPS. Famous for horses & sherry here.   23/8/14

Archibald, So I've begun what I think will be my last pro bike race, la Vuelta, one of my favourites. It's my 24th Grand Tour which seems ridiculous now that I think about, I used to just turn up to these things fearless & itching to go, convinced anything was possible, I must have been mad. Getting older has made me saner, slightly. or maybe it's simply the accumulated experience of knowledge, sometimes it's not so good to know what awaits! It's super hot down here, we did a 12km TTT through the roundabouts of Jerez today. We were not the fastest.

PS. My last TTT & the first time I gave a token talk... short of heroes. Dad xx

ARCHIBALD MILLAR
CAN CRUSIC
PUJALS DE PAGESOS
CORNELLA DEL TERRI
17844

JEREZ DE LA FRONTERA
Catedral y plaza de la Encarnación

JRP-EU4429 © EDICIONES A.M. Tel: 91 637 02 46
Fotografía: José Banús

Day 2

Started out from Algeciras. A classic Grand Tour sprint day. Break went, teams rode, break caught, sprint contested. It's so hot that racing has become secondary to drinking. I'm drinking 3 x 700ml bottles an hour, a total of twelve litres over the duration of the race, and still I lose weight from dehydration. Nathan Haas saves the day for us by winning the one and only mountains classification point up for grabs, so at least people are aware we're in the race after our invisible team time-trial result.

Day 3

Cadiz. Fucking hot. We start on an aircraft carrier today. Ryder gets a selfie of us while I'm filming a video for Archibald and Harvey. That is the highlight of the day.

Dan is second to Michael Matthews in the uphill sprint to the finish line. The run-in to it is sketchy as hell, so much so that it splits the bunch up, causing minor gaps. My job has been to position Ryder and Dan before the sketchy section. I do this, then roll in at my own pace, treating it as my warm-down.

Day 4

On the way to sign-on today I see Dave Brailsford. I see him at a lot of races, but we haven't actually spoken in what feels like years now. We used to be damn-near best friends. It all went a bit pear-shaped when I publicly spoke out against Team Sky's zero-tolerance policy. I didn't think it was realistic or ethical in a sport with a history like ours. Unfortunately, I was proved right on more than one occasion as Sky kept falling foul of its own policy by recruiting people who would soon after be found out to have had a doping history.

It was inevitable. Dave and Sky came into the sport with the best intentions but without a true understanding of the history of professional cycling. They've since learnt, yet, oddly, zero tolerance remains. I've let it go somewhat of late, understanding that we both want the same for the sport, only we have different ways of doing it. Our relationship was damaged significantly because of it, though.

Dave had been one of the first to get in touch with me when I wasn't selected for the Tour, expressing his sympathies as well as his incomprehension. The rekindling of the friendship has been one of the best things to have come out of that situation. Although we've been in touch we haven't actually spoken face to face. For this reason when I see him I stop and call out. He hears me immediately and comes over, spilling his coffee on the way: 'Ah, shit, that burns! Dave, how are you?' I can tell he's a bit nervous, as am I – we've been at loggerheads for a long time. I tell him I'm good – and that his boys are looking good.

'Yeah, Froomie's injury was worse than we'd thought. He gives everything, though. It's great for the younger guys to see him try so hard. What about you? Near the end, huh?'

I say that, yeah, this is it, the last race with Garmin anyway. 'I'd love to do the Worlds, though. We'll have to see how I come out of this.' I shrug.

Dave replies nonchalantly, 'You want to do the Worlds? Well, you should do the Worlds. I'll speak to Rod and Shane. They've asked me to manage the team. Leave it with me.'

I was shocked. 'Seriously?'

'Yeah, I'll speak to them. You just stay healthy. I see no reason why you won't be there.' He smiled knowingly.

That was that then. Dave and I were back!

We finish in Córdoba, one of the legendary Vuelta a España stages. It's a classic finale, a bit like Milan–San Remo in that it's flat most of the day before hitting the final climb that precedes the finish. I flew up there in 2003 to win solo. I don't fly today. I'm overheating so badly that my eyeballs feel like they're on fire. Never before have I experienced that. The whole day we are in survival mode till we get to the final forty kilometres and start racing for real. It's hard to switch from 'off' to 'on' in those conditions.

Unlike 2003 we aren't finished when we cross the finish line; we have a circuit to do which takes us back up the other side of the climb we've just completed. I decide to shut it down. My whole mission in the first week is to do my job helping Ryder and Dan and then pull the pin the moment I can't help them any more. This should conserve as much energy and prevent as much damage as possible in order to allow me to be at my best for the last week. It's a method I've often used in Grand Tours – race hard then sit up and roll in when my job is done. I've never understood battling in, continuing to push myself, if it isn't serving a clearly defined purpose.

Day 5

What a shit day. The heat is still oppressive, cauldron-like, and the peloton slips into a full state of lethargy. We bear more resemblance to wandering Bedouin than a peloton of racing cyclists. Two riders slip away early on, normally the perfect scenario as we could allow them to take a big advantage before slowly reeling them in. Unfortunately one of the two is Tony Martin, World Time Trial Champion, meaning there is no chance the peloton will allow the pair to get much time as Martin is too strong to be allowed anything but the smallest of margins. It doesn't matter how long he's been out there, he can't be expected to weaken. He'd broken all the rules twice in the previous year. The Vuelta 2013 had seen Tony break away solo at the beginning of a stage, then spend the whole day out there on his own. The teams chasing him were confident in their ability to reel him in. After all, a solo rider is no threat to a full team when they decide to chase him down. The maximum gap Tony got that day was seven minutes; the sprinters' teams then took control, and with twenty kilometres to go his gap was down to one minute. There's a rule of thumb that exists when it comes to hunting down a small, stage-long break – once the concerted chase to bring the rider back begins he'll lose approximately one minute every ten kilometres. The gap decreases exponentially the closer it gets to the finish, as the breakaway rider(s) tire and slow and fresh teams increase the speed behind.

When, twenty kilometres from the finish of Stage 6 of the 2013 Vuelta a España, the peloton had reduced Tony Martin's advantage to one minute it seemed like a foregone conclusion. A typically unfair game of cat and mouse. It was impossible for one rider, no matter how strong, to hold off a charging peloton after a day-long solo breakaway. According to the laws of pro bike racing anyway.

What happened next was one of the greatest perfor-mances I've ever seen, in any sport. I was in Canada with Ryder. We weren't watching bike racing at the time, but VdV called and told us to turn on the TV. With ten kilometres to go Tony's gap was down to ten seconds, the peloton were as near as dammit on top of him. Then he did something nobody should be able to do, or has ever done in modern cycling before or since: he went faster. It was possible to see the panic at the front of the bunch; whole teams started doing peel-offs. They were throwing every-thing they had into the chase and still they couldn't get closer. He increased the gap to eighteen seconds. What had been an organ-ised team pursuit at the front of the peloton turned into a bunch of solo kamikaze efforts as each team exhausted their resources and found themselves forced to engage their protected riders in the chase.

By this point I'd slid off the sofa on to the floor in front of the TV in Ryder's living room, hands on my head in disbelief. With two kilometres to go Tony had nine seconds, but the teams behind were spent. It looked like he was going to get it; with one kilometre to go he had six seconds. By now I was on my knees, fists clenched, willing him on. Then the final lead outs began, much earlier than any of the sprinters would have wanted, but they had no choice: it was either lose their lead-out man before the sprint and risk the mayhem or save him and sprint for second place.

They caught Tony in the final 100 metres – only six riders got by him. It was jaw-droppingly impressive. I've been in that situation; I know how fast you have to go and how strong you have to be in both body and mind. I lay down on my back on Ryder's floor, hands over my eyes, exhausted. Ryder filled the silence, 'What. A. Fucking. Freak.'

Martin did something similar in this year's Tour de France, only even more impressive – but that's another story. For that reason we don't let Tony get very far up the road. Tony's too strong to be trusted. Normal rules don't apply to Tony.

So we slip into a fairly benign state on this hot bastard of a Stage 5. Tony is being controlled, so much so that he ends up throwing in the towel out of frustration with the peloton's policing of him, leaving his breakaway companion to continue solo. When Tony comes back and there is just the one rider left up the road, we become complacent, the stage seems a dead cert to be a bunch sprint. The route itself isn't complicated: there's a long gradual climb about thirty kilometres from the finish, but it's on a big road, so shouldn't pose any threat. About forty-five kilometres to go and our *directeur sportif*, Bingen Fernández, comes on the radio and tells us there's a village approaching that we are about to climb up and through, which has a narrow street that we should be near the front for. Doesn't seem such a big deal. We can see the small hill-top village coming. There isn't the slightest bit of stress in the bunch. Of course, those are the moments when the most damage can be done.

We ride up into the village on a big, gentle, rising road, the pace lifting a little as we do so, which is normal. It certainly doesn't feel like the beginning of something bad. As we enter the village everything slows down, the width of the modern road disappearing as we pass narrowly between the centuries-old buildings on either side of the main street that takes us through the village. Then the road turns an abrupt right-angle and begins to climb rather than rise, and with it the tarmac turns to cobblestones. In that moment the peloton loses all semblance it previously had of a wandering desert caravan and all of a sudden becomes a stretched and breaking piece of string.

I catch a glimpse of the front of the bunch. It's yellow, and they are moving with conviction. It's Alberto Contador's team. What the fuck are they doing racing on a sprinters' stage? Oh shit. They know something we don't.

I think I manage to reach my radio microphone to shout, 'MOVE UP! MOVE UP! SAXO ARE GOING!', then move out of the line and sprint as hard as I can up the outside, trying to move up as many places as I can before we get to the exit of the village, because Saxo will only be doing this if they know there's something awaiting us on the exit.

There's only one thing it can be: crosswind.

And that means trouble. Crosswinds rip the peloton to pieces, of forming scattered echelons of riders. If you're not in an echelon, you're in the gutter, because instead of the slipstream being directly behind the racer, it is slightly to the side. If the wind is coming from the right, you'll find the slipstream to the left of the racer you're following, and vice versa. You'll position your front wheel next to their back wheel, instead of directly in line behind as you would in normal conditions. This means that the number of riders in each echelon is dictated by the width of the road. A road can only accommodate so many riders racing in this diagonal formation until it reaches the gutter, then unless you manage to make it back into the rotating formation you will be spat out the back where there is no protection from the wind. Very rarely can one rider match the speed of an echelon, so once spat out into the no man's land between echelons you simply bide your time and wait to jump into the rotation of the echelon that is inevitably chasing behind. If you can, that is. I've never let Christian Vande Velde forget his own Day of Shame in one particular Paris–Nice where he got spat through three echelons. All of us have experienced it in one form or another at some point in our careers. Stuck out there in no man's land watching your previous group disappear up the road into the distance before switching your attention to what's coming up from behind; repeatedly looking over your shoulder at the rapidly approaching group; getting psyched up while trying to recover from your very recent explosion; then giving another glance over the shoulder in order to perfectly time your sprint up to their speed only to realise you're actually going a lot slower than you thought you were and they're already right there on top of you and it's too late to scrap your way in. You're bashed about the road as that group shouts and dodges or pushes you out of their way and then, all of a sudden, the stampede is over and you're left out there in the windy, lonely badlands watching that group disappear up the road ahead into the distance, and you begin the whole process again. That was Christian. Three times on one Paris–Nice stage.

So, at moments like this, you can't think, you just have to go. It doesn't matter that I'm looking after our general classification leaders – they have to be acting in exactly the same way as I am, because if any of us hesitates now, when we are clearly too far back and scattered, then we don't stand a chance. The first few minutes of entry into crosswinds are about self-preservation: you have to try and make it . . . have-to-have-to-have-to. The more experienced we are the more we recognise the action required and the decimation that's coming, all the time hoping beyond hope that when it does happen it happens behind us.

The beginning of it is brutal. It's a flat-out effort that continues until you blow up, unless you make it into the echelon; the closer you are to the front the shorter the effort because it will take you less time to find yourself in the sanctuary of slipstreams. The team, or riders, that have created the echelon will be turning like machines on the front of the peloton, protecting each other in their echelon. Behind, it's chaos: nobody helps anybody until they have to. Which is normally provoked by the realisation that they can't do it on their own.

If you're strong and you've been caught out you find yourself dodging the riders in front of you who can't hold the wheel and so let the gap open. There's no point in teaming up with them because they've blown up and are slowing down, so you give everything you have to try to make it to the wheel they just got dropped from. It's double or nothing, full commitment to make it, deep into the red, in the knowledge that if you don't make it you're going to have destroyed yourself in the process. If that happens you'll have no choice but to slow down to give yourself time to recover, by which time you'll be in a group of similarly exploded guys who didn't make it, with the front of the race disappearing over the horizon.

This all starts to happen as we leave the village. Saxo have had the intelligence and confidence to surprise the peloton; they've strung us out before we've even left the village, meaning that when we hit the crosswinds (that we don't even know about) we are like lambs to the slaughter. Almost nobody in the peloton has considered crosswinds affecting the race. Contador's team must have had an intelligent ex-racer (Andreas Klier-style) in a recon car in front of the race. They must have seen that village and the conditions on the exit and realised that if done with full commitment they could, on this calmest of days, create a storm.

I watch it all unfold. We exit the village strung out into a long, straight, descending road, the speed constantly increasing to the point where I enter the Suck, only focusing on the wheel in front of me, everything else blurring. I sense the wheel I'm concentrating on losing speed. I glance up and see they are losing the wheel in front of them. FUCK. Thankfully the rider knows to move over to give me a chance to try to close it myself – that move in itself is what every pro should do. It gives me a chance, and it totally ends his chances, because as soon as he does it he knows he will be getting pushed and shoved and refused entry back into the rapidly disintegrating line out. He is no longer moving forwards, only backwards.

Eventually groups start to form, the gaps between riders being too big to close individually, and that's when the echelons form. It goes back to game theory: you have to make friends, lose alone or stand a chance together. It's at this moment that I start to figure out where I am, and, more importantly, where Ryder and Dan are.

The only teammate I have near me is Talansky. He asks me what we should do. I say, 'Where are they?' He knows who I mean and replies, 'I think Dan's here.'

I get on the radio, 'Dan, are you here? Can you see me?' I'm near the front so can see all the riders ahead of me in the group. He isn't there, so it is up to him to spot me because I can't keep looking behind as it's too dangerous amid the chaos and stress; everybody is so cross-eyed from the effort that their spatial awareness can't be trusted. Everything is strung out and in pieces; even if I did trust the battered riders around me, looking behind won't help because it's impossible to see who is where, everybody has their head down trying to hide from the wind, tucked as closely to the wheel in front of them as they can be.

There's no answer. Ryder comes on the radio: 'FUCK! Where are you?' Oh shit.

'Ryder, we're in the second group. Where are you?' I fear the worse.

'I'm behind you guys. Where are you?' I don't respond directly. Instead I try to confirm that Dan is here. Dan has to be here. He's Stephen Roche's nephew; he's not called Crosswinds Dan for nothing, for fuck's sake. (The name has stuck since Dan's first race with Garmin the previous year, battling through the mistral in Provence where Dan, fresh on the team and improbably team leader, had announced to Whitey – Matt White, the *directeur sportif* – with all the nonchalance in the world, that no one need worry about him, he was 'one of the best in crosswinds', something of a specialist in fact. Sure enough, within the first hour of racing, Dan was out the back in the first crosswind section, face covered in spit and snot, with his saddle halfway up his arse and his nose on the handlebars. The peloton up the road ahead was oblivious to the fact that the Garmin team leader had already been dropped. Whitey pulled up next to him, rolled down the window and shouted in his cheery Aussie manner, 'Crosswinds Dan! How ya doin', mate?') Anyhow, now I'm losing my cool at his lack of response, especially as Ryder is clear as day on the radio, and he isn't even in our group. 'DAN, JUST TELL ME YOU'RE FUCKING HERE.' I can't understand why he isn't answering.

Then the *directeur sportif* comes on the radio: 'David! Dan is with you, Ryder is behind.' Thank God, now I know we have no choice.

I find Talansky, 'Gotta close the gap. I'll get it as close as I can. When we hit the hill you go with Dan.' I know from the profile that we have a ten-kilometre gradual climb coming up – what had been an insignificant element to the profile now becomes the saviour of our race. There is no point in both of us riding as we have limited resources, and other teams are in the same mess. I was one of the fastest bike riders in the world on the flat: I figure I may as well give everything I have on my terrain. I'm not alone: Trek are in the same boat, their general classification rider is in our group and he only has one teammate with him. Fortunately he is a weapon, Fabian Cancellara.

So, unlike in the past when we always raced against each other, Fabian and I find ourselves in a two-up time trial chasing down the front group, urging each other on, pushing each other when we have to. We go so deep. Others start to join us, but not for long. In one of the respites I look behind and still can't see Dan and still haven't heard anything from him on the radio. I lose my shit, and drop back looking for him. He has to be sitting up near the front to be ready to counter with Talansky when we get close.

I have to go so far back to find him, everything is so strung out, and when I do find him I shout, 'Fuck sake, Dan! You have to be at the front. Come on, let's go.' I battle my way back up to the front with him on my wheel. When we get there I tell him, 'Stay with Talansky, you two go on the climb.' I then go back to chasing. At the same time Ryder comes on the radio again: 'Guys, I need help back here!'

I hate having to tell him over the radio, 'Ryder, we can't wait.' He is one of my best friends and I am the one having to tell him we aren't going to help him. What is bad for Ryder is good for Dan, because I know at that moment we have no choice but to fix it. I can't get to the finish, having sacrificed Ryder for a failed attempt to save Dan. I ride out of my skin the next kilometres; everybody starts giving up, and before long I am on my own on the front slowly bringing the group back. I am so far over my limit I know I only have a few minutes left till I nuke and will be incapable of helping myself let alone anybody else, but the gap is closing and I know that if I get it to within a handful of seconds when we hit the climb Talansky and Dan can do the rest on their own.

I peel off when we hit the climb, the group in front within reaching distance. As I peel off, Talansky and Dan set off in pursuit, Talansky giving everything he has, ultimately exploding himself, just as I've done, but only when he's got Dan back to where he has to be.

Ryder never makes it back. He passes me (an empty shell by then) not long after I've peeled off and come to a near stand-still. I'm incapable of giving him the slightest bit of help. Talansky, on the other hand, has recovered enough from his effort helping Dan that when Ryder gets up to him he is able to help him to the finish. It is a seminal moment for Andrew; he shows what he is capable of as a loyal teammate when the chips are down. That is something we haven't been sure of until now. He gains more respect from us this day than any victory could bring.

Day 6

Today we took control of the race. There are two reasons: 1) we believe Dan stands a chance of winning as the finish suits his abilities; 2) we want to prove to ourselves we are better than yesterday.

There are easier ways of doing it than this, though. We foolishly play bluff with other teams, in the process allowing a two-man break to take fourteen minutes after forty-five kilometres. I should know better, but, given the near complete disaster of yesterday, I allow us to commit to chasing a gap we should never have let get so big. We have 120 kilometres to close the fourteen minutes (that represents an almost ten-kilometre advance on us) – doable, but with the heat and terrain it stretches us to our max. It stretches Dan as well. He isn't able to race for the win having gone so deep sitting at the front of the peloton, behind his team in a position he isn't accustomed to. On the bright side we've made everybody else in the race suffer. On the bus afterwards we take that as consolation. The fact I am too tired to shower is neither here nor there.

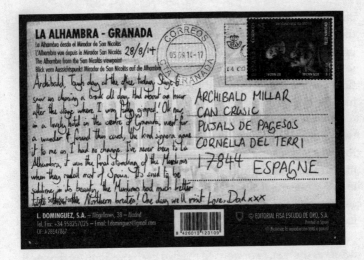

Archibald, Tough day at the office today, Stage 6
saw us chasing a break all day. Had about an hour
after the stage where I was fully gimped! Ok now
in a lovely hotel in the centre of Granada, went for
a wander & found this card, the kind señora gave
it to me as I had no change. I've never been to La
Alhambra, it was the final stronghold of the Muslims
when they routed out of Spain. It's said to be
sublime in its beauty, the Muslims had much better
taste some for the Northern brutes! One day we'll visit. Love, Dad xxx

ARCHIBALD MILLAR
CAN CRUSIC
PUJALS DE PAGESOS
CORNELLA DEL TERRI
17844   ESPAGNE

Day 7

Ryder goes on the rampage today. He's been pretty down after the Stage 5 crosswind débâcle, which is understandable. He's worked hard to be in shape to race general classification – now any chance of doing well here is gone, it means there is only one thing to do: go for stage wins. We cover all the attacks at the beginning; I'm feeling particularly good, forcing moves and bridging across to others. I've told Andrew and Ryder to hold back until we hit the first big climb after thirty kilometres. If the break hasn't gone by then it's sure to go there. So Nathan and I cover the majority of the moves leading into it. I'm in a break that's caught at the bottom of the climb, which isn't ideal as I'm super-deep in the red. The climb is nine kilometres long, steep the first half before levelling off the second. Ryder moves from the bottom, which is the last I see of him till the team bus after the race. He goes full berserker, the race is in pieces by the top, everybody scattered as far as the eye can see, each of us having to find our own maximal sustainable rhythm just to survive it and stay in the race. Ryder is already minutes up the road by the time the peloton regroups twenty kilometres later. It's mind-blowing. Three other racers eventually make it up to him. The four of them together are uncatchable, even when teams became fully committed to bringing them back. I am convinced Ryder has it wrapped up.

He would have done if he hadn't crashed on a fast corner twenty-five kilometres from the finish – proper bad luck, as Ryder is one of the best bike handlers in the world. The roads in Andalusia are weirdly slippery; the fact it almost never rains means dust, grease and dirt accumulate on the polished smooth surface, and you never know what the next corner has in store. Ryder got caught out big time.

All of us are gutted for him – he finishes second but he deserves the win. I am worried the two big blows in three days will leave his head shot to pieces (no question that would've happened to the younger Ryder, but he is more resilient these days). I'm in full roomie-psych mode, keeping his morale up and trying to make light of it all. We're at the Vuelta, after all – even if it's going badly it's still good.

We are having fun, even during our less than stellar first week. All of it has been made slightly more comical by the fact the air-conditioner broke on the bus on the first day. It's been like a goddamned sauna since. We are putting ourselves under the most extreme conditions possible, and as much as I know that saunas can be beneficial in training I'm not so sure about putting our bodies under more stress. There's only one thing for it: shandy.

The race is sponsored by Amstel, and they are pushing their new 'panaché' beer called Radler. Ryder and I have ensured our bus is stocked up at all times. Instead of jumping in the air-conditioned cars to race back to the hotel we commit to the leisurely cruise home on the hotbox bus, Radlers in hand, music jacked up, sorting the world out, living the dream. Shandy will never taste as good again.

Day 8

Another classic Vuelta stage: 207 kilometres on the same road, travelling in one direction, with ten kilometres neutralised before we even get to the official start. Like the other day, nobody is really in the mood to race, the outcome seems inevitable, being flat and so simple it's a given it will be a bunch sprint. Once again, that's when bad things can happen, especially on the Spanish plains.

We had a suspicion there'd be crosswinds in the finale, but it was hard to believe as we'd be travelling in the same direction all day on the same road – it seemed a little far-fetched that things could change so much all of a sudden at a certain point. Even though that's the case I'm not going to take any risks. With forty kilometres to go I tell Dan to stay glued to my wheel, and sure enough everybody has the same information and the race starts to speed up as every team tries to position themselves at the front.

I've studied the map this morning and have a good idea of where it will happen. We've had a tailwind all day, and the wind is forecast to shift slightly from westerly to southerly in the final, with the road also turning slightly more to the east – all this has made the possibility of crosswinds real. Most teams are drag-racing each other at the front. Dan and I stay out of the way slightly behind them. I reckon we are best to punch through at the last minute when I start to feel us going into the gutter.

Dan and I trust each other implicitly. I know he won't lose my wheel. Like Tyler Farrar he knows me well enough to predict what I'm going to do. He has a similar style to me when it comes to riding in the bunch – we're both relaxed, able to float among the wheels. He keeps a cool head just like me. We lose the rest of our team doing just that, so when it starts to happen there are just the two of us left against all the other teams that are still drag-racing up front.

I take him up the moment I start to feel the race breaking up, holding him in position next to Saxo for as long as I can before I blow up, by which point all the damage is done behind. I leave him near Contador as I explode. Job done. I ride in relieved we didn't fuck it up this time.

Dan Martin
@DanMartin86

Aug 30

Im really gonna miss @millarmind next year

Day 9

First proper summit finish today, which also means a big old breakaway day. The whole team ride brilliantly, covering everything at the beginning. Ryder is our man for the break and makes it in there again, along with Summie; the rest of us look after Dan. He is on a stormer, attacking the Contador group, proving he has the legs for the mountains and is a genuine general classification racer. It rains towards the end, which is pure bliss compared to the heat we've endured so far.

The highlight of the day is the 250-kilometre bus transfer to Zaragoza. Ryder and I decide to up the game and get some real beers instead of our faithful Radlers. We are drunk by the time we get off the bus. Long pre-rest day bus transfers are my favourite thing about Grand Tours. The bus turns into a mobile disco, only we're too tired to dance.

Rest Day

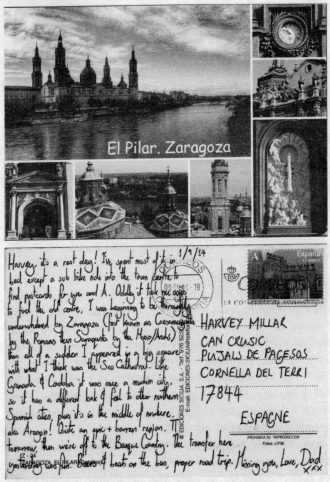

El Pilar. Zaragoza

Harvey, it's a rest day! I've spent most of it in
bed except a solo bike ride into the town centre to
find postcards for you and A. Oddly it took me ages
to find the old centre, I was beginning to be thoroughly
underwhelmed by Zaragoza (first known as Caesaraugusta
by the Romans then Saraqusta by the Moors/Arabs)
then all of a sudden I appeared in a big square
with what I think was the Seo Cathedral. Like
Granada & Cordoba it was once a muslim city,
so it has a different look & feel to other northern
Spanish cities, plus it's in the middle of nowhere,
aka Aragon! Quite an epic + barren region.
tomorrow, then we're off to the Basque Country. The transfer here
yesterday was fun. Beers & beats on the bus, proper road trip. Missing you, Love, Dad
xxx

HARVEY MILLAR
CAN CRUSIC
PUJALS DE PAGESOS
CORNELLA DEL TERRI
17844

ESPAGNE

I think Ryder and I drank too much last night, although it doesn't
matter because it's a rest day. It's a pure joy not having to go
anywhere. Although we've become so institutionalised by now
that we're almost lost as to what to do. The only thing we have to
do each day is race. Everything else is done for us, so being left to
our own devices for a day is like throwing a spanner in the works.

Every day has a schedule that is decided for us, and we rely on this competely. It used to be a sheet of paper we'd receive at the dinner table in the evening that listed the timings for the following day; now it's all done by email, and we're forever checking our phones to confirm departure times, none of us ever know for sure, so we're always asking each other, 'What time are suitcases?' 'When are we leaving?' 'What time are we eating?' 'How far is the hotel from the finish?' 'Is it far to the start?' It never stops, all day, every day.

The bus is our constant; it ferrys us everywhere. It picks us up at the airport then takes us to our hotel, then to the race, then to the hotel, then to the race . . . Our hotel rooms are allocated before we arrive. We don't even go via reception: our room keys are handed to us as we step off the bus on arrival at the hotel and we wander in like zombies, straight to wherever our rooms may be.

Our suitcase is already there. A lot of the time we won't even open it immediately, preferring to collapse on the bed, awaiting the knock on the door that will beckon us to massage. We'll have a forty-five-minute massage then, on the way back to our room, look on the room list that's stuck to a door for where the 'food room' is, pay a visit there, have a bowl of cereal, or a yoghurt, some biscuits or maybe some fruit, then wander back to our room. By which point we might have the energy to open the suitcase. Although there's not much reason to – the only thing we need from it is our toiletry bag. We just open it a lot of the time in a poor attempt at nesting. We lie on the bed again and wait for dinnertime. If our roomie is there we chat a bit, or stay in silence. It depends on the dynamic. Then one of us will say, 'Shall we go down? It's nine, that's when we're eating, right?' Then we go down to the restaurant where Sean and Olga, our team chefs, will have whatever incredible meal they have prepared for us ready. They're amazing. We can have a whole Grand Tour where we never eat the same thing twice. Every meal has a different twist to it; it's like fine dining for athletes. It's perhaps the best part of the day, when we all relax and pretend we're not at a bike race. Then, once we're done, we all slowly get up and head back to our rooms to lie on our beds, talk to our wives or girlfriends, and wait for when we're tired enough to sleep. Which can be harder than people would think, as a lot of the time the more fatigued we become the more difficult it is to sleep.

In the morning we wake up and head straight to breakfast. Or, rather, I do, before everyone else. Even when others are around, there's not much laughter at the breakfast table. We then collect our washing bag containing our previous day's kit, which we'd left on the bus after our post-race shower the day before. It's been picked up and cleaned and left in a basket near our breakfast table to be collected. We then head back up to our room, put our toiletry bag back in the suitcase, decide if there's actually anything we need from it – probably not, so close it and leave it outside our hotel room door to be collected and whisked away to the next hotel. We empty our laundry bag, and pack everything into our backpack for the bus, then lie on the bed again and call our wives or girlfriends, and wait for the departure time, which usually comes around way too fast. Then it all begins again. That's the bike-racing life. Almost every race follows the same routine.

Day 10

Day 11

It's always the way in a Grand Tour: a couple of days easy then everybody is game on. It is possible to feel the enthusiasm at the start today – the polar opposite to how the bunch had been feeling at the start of Stage 9, when everybody still had everything to lose. Now, with the first mountain-top finish done and the time trial completed, the general classification has taken shape. For the guys still at the top of the classification the stress remains, but they are now a minority. For many teams their general classification hopes have evaporated, which means their priorities have now switched to stage wins, just the way Ryder's race plan has shifted.

We still have Dan, however, and although he's racing general classification he doesn't require a full team to look after him, so we are split between looking after him and helping set Ryder up for breakaways. Although one rest day and a thirty-seven-kilometre time trial isn't enough time to offer recovery to the body, it is plenty for the mind. This, with the altered tactics of many teams, means the first hour of racing is manic. We average 51km/h, and it isn't exactly flat. I feel better than I have done the whole race, covering numerous moves, not with the ambition of being in the break – because the summit finish won't suit me even if I do make the move – but more to check out the movers and shakers for when I really want to go for a stage win in the final week. It also means things are covered and we are always represented, allowing the team to remain relaxed behind.

In the end a small group breaks free, but is not big enough to make it to the finish, so the race in the peloton becomes general classification- and stage win-orientated. We drop Dan off at the foot of the final climb, and he ends up being one of the strongest – maybe too strong as he attacks so many times he becomes marked out, allowing other riders to counter him. Coming up the mountain far behind but still in radio contact means we can hear all the info and encouragement from the *directeur sportif* to Dan. It feels like we've gone from being a part of the race to a spectator, albeit without seeing anything. I can hear Bingen, *the directeur sportif*, 'COME ON, DAN! You've got ten seconds. Froome's in trouble.' In every *gruppetto* you'll see loyal teammates with their fingers in their ears trying to hear what's going on up ahead with their leader. There's a pride in knowing the work you've done is paying dividends up front. At the same time it always seems incredible that they're capable of attacking each other while racing up the same mountain we're struggling to ride up.

PAMPLONA · IRUÑA

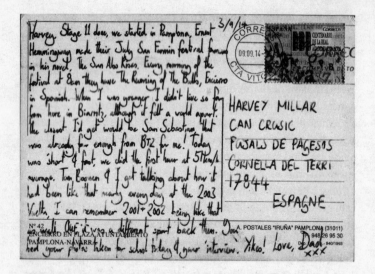

Day 12

Logrono. The bus is going to the garage after the start to repair the air-con.

So that means there'll be no bus at the finish, and we'll have to do it old Belgian-style: jump in the car and direct to the hotel.

What a boring bloody day: eight laps, pan-flat, around Logrono. Everybody is bored and saying so, which goes to show how stupid we all are as it was, in many ways, a wonderful active recovery day and generous of the organisers to think of it. We should be loving it. The only way I can alleviate the boredom and make something of it is to give myself a challenge, and that is to keep my pedalling cadence above an average of ninety. This sounds quite simple, but we are going so easy, easier than I ride in training, that it turns into a real challenge, and an uncomfortable one at that. I decide it will be good training, to keep the muscles firing without actually putting any stress on them.

About halfway through the stage I regret massively having set myself this goal, but I can't give in as that would be showing weakness.

I am thankful, then, with two laps to go, when the speed increases and with it the power required to pedal. I feel incredible, I've effectively been making my life supremely uncomfortable the previous 120 kilometres, so that when the race does get uncomfortable I weirdly find comfort in it. I look after Dan and make sure he is safely at the front in the final, out the way of any potential crashes. I am supremely strong.

The internet went bonkers today accusing Ryder of having a motor in his bike, the reasoning being that his rear wheel kept turning after his crash on Stage 7. We think it's pretty funny. Well, we did until other professionals started accusing him, too. I went apeshit defending Ryder's honour at least twice in the peloton today. I keep telling him that it's a compliment. Let's face it, there aren't too many professional cyclists who can ride fast enough to be accused of having an engine. I was going so fast in the final today I guess I could have been accused of this. Nobody said anything, though, and I'm a bit disappointed by that.

They couldn't fix the bus air-con. We're quite relieved, really. That would have killed the post-race, shirtless, Radler-drinking vibe.

Day 13

I totally messed up today. Rule number one: if the race starts on a narrow uphill road do not stop for a piss. I know this. I still did it. I subsequently found myself right at the back of the peloton as we crossed the official start line, watching from a distance as the first attacks went and the break almost instantly formed. What a dickhead.

CABÁRCENO
PARQUE DE LA NATURALEZA / CANTABRIA

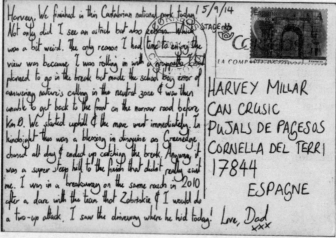

Harvey. We finished in this Cantabrian national park today 15/9/14
Not only did I see an ostrich but also zebras. Which
was a bit weird. The only reason I had time to enjoy the
view was because I was rolling in with a gruppetto. I'd
planned to go in the break but made the school boy error of
answering nature's calling in the neutral zone & was then
unable to get back to the front on the narrow road before
Km 0. We started uphill & the race went immediately. In
hindsight this was a blessing in disguise as Greenedge
chased all day & ended up catching the break. Anyway, it
was a super steep hill to the finish that didn't really suit
me. I was in a breakaway on the same road in 2010
after a dare with the team that Zabriskie & I would do
a two-up attack. I saw the driveway where he hid today! Love, Dad
xxx

HARVEY MILLAR
CAN CRUSIC
PUJALS DE PAGESOS
CORNELLA DEL TERRI
17844
ESPAGNE

Day 14

We start in Santander today. It's the first of three big mountain days. In the pre-race team meeting I recommend we race conservatively while knowing for a fact that Ryder is itching to

254

go. I calculate this is the best method – this way he can make the decision all on his own without any pressure. Ryder's at his best when he has no responsibilities and something to prove – he can then just race for the sake of racing; he's a purebred in that respect. He's at his best when he makes up his own mind. The bottom line is that the stage is so hard there's little we can do to help him anyhow.

Once the team meeting is done I go out looking for post-cards for the boys. I find myself in full kit, race-ready, standing in some bucket-and-spade beachfront shop with folk looking at me like I'm some super-dork fan. The race numbers really confuse them, though. After dropping the cards off at the bus I make my way to the start. I pass the Sky bus, aka the Deathstar, and see Dave B standing outside talking to fans. I pull over and join in. It's just like the old days: we stand there joking around, making conversation with some Brits who've come to watch the bike race. Dave is on fine form, taking the piss out of himself as much as me. After a few minutes we shuffle aside to have some privacy.

Dave says, 'OK, you're in for the Worlds. It's not official yet, but I've spoken to Rod and some of the guys and we all agree you should be there.'

I can't believe how relieved I am; I realise how paranoid I've become since the Tour de France last-minute non-selection. I tilt my head back and groan, 'Ah, fucking hell. Thank you.' I don't know what to say beyond that. It takes me a moment to continue: 'I'll be good, Dave. I've been careful to take the first two weeks here relatively easy; next week I'm going to start racing for real. I'm getting better and better as the race goes on.'

Dave nods. 'We know, we can see it, so can the guys in the peloton. It'll be good to have you at the Worlds, for the whole team. It's how you should finish.'

I well up ever so slightly behind my glasses, repeating my previous sentiment, 'Ah, fucking hell.' I can't help but be myself with Dave, and just tell him how I feel: 'I didn't realise how much this meant to me. Stupid bike racing.' The siren goes off for the neutral start. I shake my head and groan. The bloody emotion. Dave pats me on the back as I turn away. As I roll off he shouts after me, 'Dave! Just stay upright, will you?'

I laugh, and look back, 'Oh, you bloody know it!'

Sure enough, Ryder makes the break of the day, although the fact that he isn't stressed about it probably helps, as it takes nearly an hour and a half of racing for it to form; these are the days when if you try too hard you're guaranteed not to make it. He then single-handedly rips it to pieces, using his classic self-counter-attacking technique. This involves him attacking, waiting for everybody to get to him, then attacking again. Once they reach him again, he rides as hard as he can until they start getting dropped, before attacking them again. He's like a four-man team.

The finish is atop a three-kilometre climb – not just any climb, one of the steepest climbs we've ever done, in any race. It has an average of 15 per cent, peaking out at 24 per cent in places. What we like to call a total form-fucker. We have on the smallest gears possible, 36x30 for me. Ryder has whittled the break down from twenty-three to fourteen by the bottom of the final climb to the finish. He knows he is strong but there is one rider in particular he is worried about: the Swiss rider Oliver Zaugg of Saxo.

Being a member of race leader Alberto Contador's team means that Zaugg has the tactical right not to work in the break. Saxo are behind, leading the peloton. Zaugg's job is simply to be up there marking the move. This means he is sitting, sucking wheels while Ryder is counter-attacking himself on his one-man demolition derby. From the early slopes of the climb, it's possible to see Ryder drop almost everybody apart from Zaugg, who then forges ahead, leaving Ryder in his slow-motion wake.

Ryder recounts the stage to me, blow by blow, over a Radler on the bus ride back to our hotel. He'd had it under control all day till that point. When Zaugg went he was convinced the win was slipping through his fingers, to the point that he looked behind, realised nobody else was getting near him, and thought, 'Ah, second isn't so bad', before resigning himself to respectable defeat.

It's hard to explain to people how incredibly steep the climb was. Everything was happening in slow motion, everything except heart rate and breathing, which were operating at maximum capacity. So, although Ryder gave up, he had enough time to recalibrate, disengage his preconceptions of it being only two kilometres from the finish, and how close that would normally be, before realising they still had over ten minutes left till the line. That's when he said to himself, 'Don't be lame.' And engaged 'BEASTMODE'. He timed his effort to perfection, passing and leaving Zaugg for dead in the final 200 metres.

I was in a *gruppetto* twenty minutes behind when I found out. Word spread around the group and somebody told me – we were too far behind to be in radio contact with the front. It made my three-kilometre creeper of a climb up to the finish totally bearable. I crossed the line at the exact moment Ryder was going from the podium to the anti-doping control, a crowd of people surrounding him. I called out to him, he saw me immediately and broke into a massive smile and changed the trajectory of his entourage towards me. When he reached me we hugged and he took me by the shoulders, looked at me, and said, 'That was for us, man.' We hugged again and then he went off to continue the winner's protocol, while I looked for somebody from my team to give me a bottle and tell me where the bus was.

The post-win bus ride to the hotel is one of those times I hope I never forget. Normally when we get to the bus it's the end to our day; we just want to be left alone and taken home (hotel). When we arrive at the bus we park our bike against the side, twist our Garmin off and try to avoid eye contact with anybody so we can get inside as quickly as possible. Once inside we make a bee-line for our seat, because each of us will have his own for the duration of the race, his own little safe haven. Nobody fucking touches it. Ryder and I inhabit the front two seats, mine on the left side, his on the right. We sit there, remove our glasses, take off our helmets, pull out the earpieces, lean back and relax. Not for long, though, because if we stop for too long we can't get moving again. So, after a few beats we start taking our kit off. Then we head back and have a shower.

Once out of the shower, wrapped in a towel, we'll pick up a recovery drink that's sitting on the sideboard and help ourselves to a bowl of rice or pasta or whatever 'real' food has been prepared for us. Then we go back and sit down and relax again. Most of us can't eat straightaway as our bodies are too messed up, so we drink our recovery drinks, check our phones and allow ourselves a few moments. Then we get dressed into our team tracksuits, because if we don't do it quickly we'll be too tired to be bothered.

Then we start putting our pile of race kit that's on the floor into our personal washbag. All pretty simple, apart from the fact that we have to unpin our numbers, which is such a pain in the arse, especially as we know we'll have to repin it in the morning. I'm OCD with my numbers: I have to cut them down to size to fit the pockets of the jersey that I'll be pinning them to just perfectly. I probably resemble the little boy I once was, crunched up over a table, tongue out, gripping his pencil like it's a matter of life or death, while attempting to draw a straight line. Then the pinning is equally traumatic: all the pins have to be exactly the same size and colour; there's one for each corner and then another for each central point between the corners (except the bottom horizontal, where I don't consider a pin to be required). That's seven pins per number. I have to start all over again if I finish and they're not perfectly symmetrical. Most days this is a therapeutic exercise, almost meditative; unfortunately there are other days when it feels like I'm trying to thread a needle while driving.

Our bus is so ridiculously hot that we're just wearing our team-issue board shorts. We sit there and sweat more than we did in the race – well, it's probably about the same, only now there's no air to evaporate it. The next thing we do is get pissed off at the guys who are taking their time, because all we want to do is get on the road and begin the transfer. There's nothing worse than being the last bus in the team car park; it feels like we're off the back, even when not racing.

Which isn't the case when we've won, of course, because that's what it feels like when a teammate wins: we share the joy. There's no longer any rush. We'll happily sit there in the teams' car park, long after all the other team buses have gone, waiting for our triumphant teammate, who is now having to go through the podium, anti-doping controls and media commitments. We can be so delayed – blocked at the finish area by spectators leaving, the organisation packing up – that we are *way* off the back. None of us care, because we all feel like we're winners. As a team we've always acted like that, and I think most teams do, unless they win every single week; then I can imagine you have to start being a little less joyous, which is ironic.

I have a Radler waiting for Ryder when he gets back. The transfer to the hotel is a good long one, so we have plenty of time to share the moment. We all start talking about previous exploits and wins and similarly good stuff. Getting closer to our hotel I see a town name I remember: Torrelavega. Bingen Fernández, our *directeur sportif*, is on the bus. Bingen and I had been teammates years before on Cofidis. He was one of the most loyal teammates I had. We always rode similar programmes – he was one of the best *domestiques* I've ever known. I ask him, 'Bingen! Torrelavega? Is that where I won the stage in 2001?'

He replies in a totally matter-of-fact fashion, 'Yes, Stage 6. You and [Santiago] Botero.'

I then recount the events of that stage in the 2001 Vuelta a España, the vivid memories of my first Grand Tour road-stage win, the same one where I punched the air as I'd done in my final-ever Grand Tour stage win in the 2012 Tour. As I conclude the story we drive by the track where the horribly long two-up sprint had taken place, where thirteen years earlier I'd refused to celebrate because I wanted to win so much. It is the weirdest thing.

When we get to the hotel I ask them if they have postcards. They have tons, years old, all the same: a picture of the hotel. The old man at reception says if I give him a euro I can have all of them. I give him a euro and take two; the day has been enough of a success, I needn't take the piss.

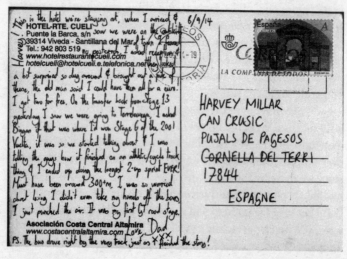

Day 15

Highs and lows – I've built a career on them. What is it my old friend the Major said? 'If the road isn't bumpy, then where's the fun?' Something like that, anyway.

I feel so good today. I feel like I can decide what the race will do if I so please. I'm near the back when we pass the official start, just outside Oviedo. I have no difficulty moving up to the front while everybody is going balls out – once there, I simply surf around the pressure wave the front of the peloton creates. I can see everything, I'm hyper-aware; I'm finding it strange that guys will attack and not be able to prolong their effort. It's not as if the peloton will speed up to chase them, it's more like they'll break free and soon realise they aren't strong enough to continue. Then before they know it they are being sucked back in like dust into a vacuum cleaner. That's classic third-week form; guys forget how tired they are.

I have the lucidity only facility can bring. I hadn't even been interested in the stage, I had no plans for it, but now I'm out here on one of my magic days I realise that I have no choice but to make the most of it. I know the road becomes hilly at thirty kilometres, only ten kilometres away, and from what I am witnessing at the front it will be relatively easy for me to rip the race to pieces when we get there, so I continue to surf, watching everything that is going on, making sure nothing unexpected happens.

Then it does. We sweep off the 'normal' road on to a motorway, the bunch spreads across and starts to snake from one side to the other as rider after rider tries to break the elastic holding them back, only to be followed closely by the chasing bunch. As one rider is caught on the right, another will attack on the left; this isn't strange behaviour, it is totally normal, if totally futile, as nobody is going to get away on such a large, flat piece of road when everybody is still so 'fresh'.

Which is exactly what I'm thinking as one more time we sweep across to the right-hand side of the road. Then, BANG. I'm on the floor.

I don't remember much, it all happens so fast. I've been in dozens and dozens of crashes in my life – all sorts of crashes, not just cycling. Yet I've never experienced anything like this.

I had the tiniest fraction of time to react, there was next to no warning. As we swept across the road we took ourselves into the path of the bollards that separated a slip road from the main carriageway. I was far enough toward the front to be one of the first to sweep through them. I guess a couple of guys further ahead managed to dodge them but didn't have enough time to give a signal to those behind. The guy in front of me smashed straight into one. It was like he exploded in front of me: one second I was on his wheel, the next he was in the air. I remember instinctively dodging, yet before I knew it I hit something. I don't remember being airbound, as the impact had been so big that it was still resonating through my body when I hit the ground.

(I found out on the bus after the race from Nathan Haas, who wasn't very far behind me when it happened, that he was sure I was Game Over. He heard the crash noise and suddenly saw my red shoes way up in the air above the peloton in front of him, then saw me sliding along the floor as he passed me.)

But now, in the space of five seconds, I've gone from total control at 60km/h to motionless and shell-shocked on the ground. I know I've gone down hard – my back and shoulder are burning like a bastard – but it doesn't take me long to realise I haven't broken anything obvious. The guy who's gone down in front of me is foetal on the ground, in full groaning mode. I stand up as quickly as I can so that they know I'm OK and they can focus on him. As soon as I do I start to hobble. I've smashed my knee really badly. I look down at it: it's deep enough to be white rather than bloody. Ah fuck, that's not good.

I go and sit down on the grass next to the road. Oh shit, this really hurts. Everything starts to burn. It is impossible to pinpoint anything. Alex, my mechanic, comes running up with wheels. 'Oh, dude, no! Fuck, Dave. You OK?'

Alex is my man, more than my mechanic, a friend. 'I dunno. Hurts a lot already. I think I need my spare bike,' I say. He's running back to the car before I've even finished. I can hear him shouting, 'GET THE FUCK OUT MY FUCKING WAY!'

I've been like Harry Houdini most of my career, born with a sixth sense to make it through crashes that I've no right to escape from. Which probably isn't fair, as I often put myself in the stupidest situations where crashing is likely. Of course, lady luck hasn't always been on my side – this bollard incident is a prime example of that.

The first stage of the Giro the year before had been another.

Our second son, Harvey, was born the day before the Giro started. So I didn't miss the birth, I was given special dispensation to arrive at the last minute. As can be imagined, I was a little tired when I got to Italy. Any sane person would have taken it easy the first stage. Obviously, I didn't. I wanted to help with the lead out for Ty Farrar, so was right up at the front in the mix with two kilometres to go. We came flying round one of the final corners, and I was taken out by some halfwit who came in way too fast on the inside and lost control and smashed right into me. He may as well have been aiming for me. I hit the ground so hard I snapped my bike without my feet leaving the pedals. The muscles in my right leg were smashed to smithereens. I got back up and limped my way to the finish and the bus. When I got back on the bus afterwards, I collapsed in my seat, monumentally pissed off. I said to anybody who was nearby, 'What the fuck? I mean, why was I up there? First fucking stage and I've ruined my leg.' Ryder, who was walking back to his seat carrying a bowl of rice, chipped in, all matter-of-fact, 'You can't help it, man, you're a racer. That's what racers do.'

But now I'm sitting in the grass, nodding at the sagacity of Ryder's remarks while Alex, the mechanic, sprints off to get my spare bike from the team car, when the team doctor arrives. Lorenz is German, young, and one of the best in the business at his job. We almost always have a doctor in the following car – all our team doctors are trained in trauma care, most of them having worked, or are still working, in the emergency rooms of hospitals.

This has been a policy for us since the team's creation – as good as race doctors can be, we prefer to have our own doctor first on the scene of a crash, one we know and trust and who knows the medical history of our riders. They also know our personalities, how each one of us handles crashes differently, some needing to be told to get up, others needing to be told to stay down. I'm definitely in the latter category.

Lorenz tells me not to move. He doesn't even ask me how I am because he knows I won't be able to give him the answers he needs, my body is still in shock. I don't really know what's just happened, let alone what I've done to my body. My left knee looks fucked. Lorenz starts by checking my collarbones, then moving my arms. He has a quick look at my ripped-up back and glances over my helmet. He looks me in the eyes and asks me if I know where I am, who he is, etc. I tell him my head is fine. He then asks me if I can stand up. He gives me his hand and helps pull me up. I can't help but wince and try to avoid putting too much weight on my left knee. I tell him I'm OK, just really banged up. He knows I'm getting back on my bike and back into the race. I go and check my crashed bike on the floor. I hate it when I break my bikes; even now, after all these years, the kid in me still sulks seeing my bike all broken up.

It's strange how alone I feel at this moment. All I can hear are the last words Dave B said to me, the day before, 'Just stay upright, will you?' He knows me too well.

The look of concern on the faces of those asking me if I'm OK doesn't fill me with confidence. Once Alex gets back with my spare bike I get going again, immediately. The race is ripping along, only twenty kilometres into the stage, with no breakaway yet formed and hills coming up. It's the point in the day where the peloton is going fastest; I can't faff about feeling sorry for myself.

But my jersey is ripped up and there is blood everywhere; it's pretty obvious I'm fucked. Everybody wants to help an injured rider, other teams' cars don't hesitate to offer me their slipstream. When my team car makes it back up to me they pull up alongside.

I hold on to the roof rack and let them pull me back up to speed while Lorenz leans out and starts looking closer at all the damage. I stop pedalling, knowing that I need to use the team car as much as possible while I can. The commissaires will turn a blind eye to this – it's one of those times where they know I need every advantage I can get, as I'm not doing it for any other reason than to survive the day.

I can't pedal anyway. I have to stay as still as I can while hanging on to the side of the car at close to 70km/h so that Lorenz can start cleaning the wounds and bandaging them. My back and shoulder are in a state, as are my left arm and knee. At first I hold on with my left hand, but it's proving too difficult for Lorenz to do my left shoulder and back as they're almost up against the car. So I swap sides and hold on to the other side, that way Lorenz can lean across me and get to them more easily. As soon as I switch sides and start holding on my right hand starts to hurt, but that makes no sense as all the damage is on the left. There's not even a graze on the right side of my body, yet my right hand begins to ache, then throb, then plain hurt. I must be holding on to the roof rack too tightly and straining it. But I can't exactly loosen my grip; this is the only thing keeping me in the race.

Once everything is cleaned and dressed I have to let go of the car and make my own way. The commissaires can no longer turn a blind eye once the doctor has finished his work on me. The race is still in full flight up ahead. Only a few kilometres before I was at the front in total control, now I'm off the back in full survival mode. The strength I had hasn't gone, but where it was sharp before, now it's blunted and not much use. But it's still there. I get myself to within five cars of the back of the bunch as we hit the first of the climbs. I'm moving up past riders who are getting dropped, which is a relief but also frustrating because I know I would have been attacking off the front at this very moment if I hadn't hit the stupid bollard. Before the top of the climb I'm on the back of the bunch. Ryder and Nate are there. Nate's in a world of suffering, Ryder is just being Ryder, chillin'.

As we come over the top the race calms down a little and begins to bunch up a bit. I pull up alongside Ryder. He looks at me and says, 'I thought you were gone, man. You OK?' I reply as nonchalantly as possible, 'I'm fine, just banged up.' He then says to me, concerned, but also a little pissed off, 'Are you fine? Or are you just saying you're fine?' I can't help but smile, 'My hand hurts.' And I show him the one piece of my body that isn't ripped up. He just shakes his head and smiles, 'You're sick.'

I go back to my road captain role, knowing it is an important day for Dan as we have a big summit finish. All I have to do is keep the team organised and place Dan safely at the front for the foot of the penultimate climb, then I can sit up and crawl in to the finish. And that's exactly what happens. Ryder pulls off with me, engaging the 'buddy system' his priorities lying with helping me to the finish rather than racing up the front. We shut it down as soon as the *gruppetto* forms, all of us finding a gentle rhythm that will take us to the finish inside the time delay.

For the first time since the crash I relax. My hand is hurting more than anything else now, which I still can't understand, but I know I have to finish the Vuelta. It will be a tough last week, and not exactly the fun racing I had in mind, but if I make it through I'll still be good for the Worlds. Any chances of winning a stage are gone, I know that, but I have to be thankful I'm still in the race considering the scale of the crash.

We start to chat and joke a bit, making light of it all, then, only minutes later, we come around a corner on the climb and see five of our teammates down a little ravine. They look like the Keystone Cops, a human chain: Dan in the middle, being lifted from below and pulled from above. Ryder and I look at each other: 'What. The. Fuck. Is. Going. On?'

It turns out that Dan had been squeezed up against a barrier on the inside of a switchback and had flipped over it, falling down into the ravine – not far, but far enough that he couldn't get out by himself. His bike was still on the road, jammed up against the barrier. Dan had somehow jettisoned himself off it, which added to the Keystone Cops scene. This all happened going uphill. Summie, Nathan, Koldo and Cardoso had stopped to help get him out. The team cars were still too far behind, so they had to fix it themselves.

I can't believe it. I've never seen anything like it. If Dan is OK we have a monumental chase on our hands. Ryder and I stop, Dan gets out of the ravine. The first thing he does is try to get on Summie's bike, which doesn't bode well, as Summie's bike is about a foot too big for Dan. One of the guys hands Dan his bike, then we set off. At first it appears Dan is badly injured, as he won't accelerate and it looks like he's giving up. This is good in a way as it allows the guys who've helped him get back on to the road to catch up with us and regroup. There are now six of us together. I lead, slowly winding the speed up. Dan starts to get his head back in the game; we are now behind the *gruppetto* which was blocking the narrow mountain road, travelling at the speed Ryder and I had previously been enjoying.

I am being calm, just shouting, 'SERVICE! SERVICE!', the peloton command to let you pass by if you have a job to do. Some riders aren't aware of our situation and are taking longer to get out of the way. This is all happening at *gruppetto* speed; being trapped here means we are losing more and more time to those at the front, who are racing at speed ahead of us. Nathan, who's behind me, starts losing his mind, shouting, 'WILL YOU FUCKHEADS GET OUT THE FUCKING WAY! FUCK! COME ON!' Obviously this doesn't help, as everybody starts shouting back at Nathan, 'OOOOO, FUCKHEAD, WHAT'S THE MATTER? YOU CAN'T GET BY?' So Nathan shouts back, 'OH, FUCK YOU. WE'VE GOT A JOB TO DO. GET OUT THE FUCKING WAY.' I have to tell Nathan to calm down while simultaneously trying to part the *gruppetto* sea to let us pass. It's a true comedy of errors.

Eventually we break free from the *gruppetto* and begin our pursuit. I do the first few kilometres knowing that's all I have and that I only trust myself to pace it right – it's too easy in that situation to let the adrenalin of panic put us all in the red. The other guys then take over. By the top of that climb there is only

Ryder and Cardoso left with Dan. Cardoso then crashes on the descent. So it's down to Ryder to take Dan back to the front of the race. Somehow he does it, Dan eventually finishing seventh on the stage atop Lagos de Covadonga, actually taking time out of some of his main general classification rivals.

Definitely one of the more random days I've had on a bike.

David Millar ✔
@millarmind

This is what happened to my jersey. The old cycling High-Level Skin Protection System.

View on Twitter

Day 16

I decide not to go to the hospital for X-rays, as whatever they tell me won't change the fact that I'm going to carry on, and, anyway, tomorrow is the rest day, so I can get myself properly checked out then. The day after a big crash is always bad: the body inflames and seizes up, and it's usually hard to sleep because of all the wounds. Things are not made any easier today by knowing it's the queen stage of the race: the biggest mountain day. Not ideal.

My hand hurts more than anything else now; it has swollen up like a balloon during the night. My other injuries don't bother me much in comparison. I wake up early as usual. For some reason I decide to shave – I suppose it makes me feel like I'm not giving up – but just holding the razor hurts so much. I watch myself ever so delicately put the razor against my cheek: it's like I'm shaving for the first time, my hand doesn't feel like mine, and it certainly doesn't look like mine. Suddenly it crosses my mind: if I can barely shave, how can I race? I stand there in front of the mirror. I put the razor down, and look at myself. I'm not going to cry, don't cry. I hold it back, my eyes just tearing up a little. This can't be my last day racing.

I go and sit on the end of my bed and regroup. It doesn't take long. I stand back up. I can do this. I go and shave in an almost ritualistic manner.

I go down to breakfast. Koldo is there, which is rare. Sean, our chef, has made us pancakes, among other things. We stand at the breakfast table, where everything is laid out. I have my plate in my left hand and try to use the tongs with my right. I can't do it. Koldo gently takes them off me without saying anything, puts his plate down and takes mine, then asks what I'd like for breakfast. We sit down at the table. He can see I'm not good. He hasn't asked me how I am, or commented on the hand. He just looks at me and says, 'It's difficult, isn't it?' I can't speak for fear I'm going to lose it, so I just look down and nod. Koldo's words feel like the most empathetic thing anybody has ever said to me.

I make it through the day, painkiller-free, as per our new team policy. It's difficult.

Rest Day

Go to the hospital. I have two broken fingers and a fractured rib. Now wearing splints for my fingers.

Day 17

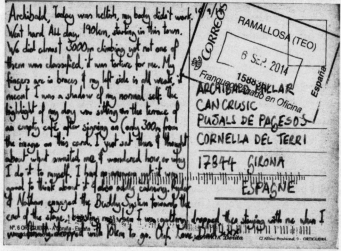

Day 18

Oddly my handwriting hasn't been neater since I was a little boy. I am forced to hold my pen so lightly and move it so slowly, with such small movements, that it can't help but be controlled. So that's a good thing. I should probably learn something about life from that.

Day 19

I still do my job. But I've made it more difficult for myself by not having my head in the game. I'm stuck near the back, wallowing in self-pity. I can see Dan in front of me, and even there he is way too far back. I manage to get my head out of my arse at the last possible moment and go and get him, telling him not to lose my wheel. I end up drag-racing Sky on my own with Dan on my wheel. I drop him off with the very front guys into the switchback that takes us into the final climb. I peel off and very nearly unclip. I'm that fucked.

PLAYA DE SAMIL

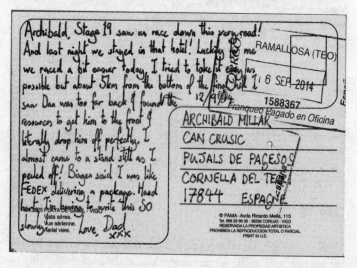

Archibald, Stage 19 saw us race down this very road! And last night we stayed in that hotel! Luckily for me we raced a bit easier today. I tried to take it easy as possible but about 5km from the bottom of the final climb I saw Dan was too far back & found the resources to get him to the front & literally drop him off perfectly. I almost came to a stand still as I peeled off! Bingen said I was like FEDEX delivering a package. Hand hard Tibi.... I wrote this so slowly. Love, Dad xxx

RAMALLOSA (TEO)
1 6 SEP 2014
12/9/94
1588367
Franqueo Pagado en Oficina

ARCHIBALD MILLAR
CAN CRUSIC
PUJALS DE PAGESOS
CORNELLA DEL TE...
17844 ESPAGNE

© FAMA -Avda Ricardo Mella, 113
Tel. 986 29 88 35 - 36330 CORUJO - VIGO
RESERVADA LA PROPIEDAD ARTISTICA
PROHIBIDA LA REPRODUCCION TOTAL O PARCIAL
PRINT IN U.E.

PLAYA DE SAMIL - VIGO
Vista aérea.
Vue aérienne.
Aerial view.

Day 20

I see Dave B at the start. I tell him the truth, that my hand is bad, but that everything else is healing and that I'll update him a few days after the Vuelta finishes. He doesn't seem overly worried; he expects me to be road captain, as much before the race as during it. His confidence makes a refreshing change to that of Charly, Jonathan and Doug. I know the British team are looking after me. There's no real reason for them to take me in my current state, apart from out of respect and, possibly, affection. It makes me want to be better. It reminds me of where I come from.

The stage is still a struggle, though. I'm OK at the beginning, keeping myself right at the front when everything is going crazy. Then, as the race progresses, the closer I get to the finish, the harder it becomes. I can feel myself letting go: the more certain I am of finishing, the easier it feels to give up. It's as if I'm holding on to a rope, being pulled up a cliff face – the nearer I get to safety, the more my grip loosens. On the final mountain, up to the summit finish, I'm barely able to stay in the *gruppetto*. I'm so incredibly tired. I end up riding up on my own, not even sure if I'll make it inside the time limit. I'm that beat down.

Coming inside the last kilometre, realising I'm almost finished, I experience a sense of relief I've never felt before. As I come around the final corner, with only 300 metres to go, there's Graham Watson (*the* cycling photographer, who has been taking pictures of me since my first-ever professional bike race in 1997) taking my photo, and shouting out, 'Go on, David! It's over.'

This is it. I've done it. I've finished. I still have tomorrow's time trial and the Worlds, but I'll never have to go as deep again. Graham has seen me over the previous eighteen years turn myself inside out, race after race, day after day, week after week, month after month, year after year. He is right, it's over. I don't have to hurt myself any more.

Day 21 – The End of the Road

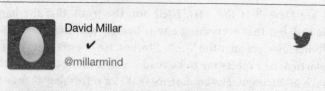

David Millar ✔
@millarmind

I think today, for the first time in my life,
I'm not going to make myself hurt in a TT.

My last race with the team, and the finish line is on El Final del Camino in Santiago de Compostela, the end of the pilgrims' trail. I couldn't have made that up.

This is shaping up to be the worst time trial of my life. I'm in pain, everything hurts, I'm exhausted. I'm so beat down I don't even warm up. I just sit on a cool box outside the bus in my speedsuit awaiting my start time. I don't even recon it. I glance at the race book, that's it. Bingen comes up to me as I sit behind the start ramp and gives me a hug. He has tears in his eyes. I'm totally fine. As far as I'm concerned I may as well be sitting in a café, about to set off and ride home. I think in a way this has made him more sad – he's only ever known me as the most focused, edgy, occasionally crazy person. He's only ever known me as David Millar, the racer. I've spent over twenty years doing time trials, the majority of them I've wanted to win. Everybody will be expecting me to try.

For this, the final one, I don't even try. I just do what I have to do to make sure I finish inside the time limit. Yet, weirdly, I don't think I've ever suffered so much in a time trial. I can't even hold the handlebars the final kilometre as it's on cobblestones, the vibration through the bars making it too painful for me to grip with my mangled hand.

I cross the line and find Luca, one of our *soigneurs*. I stop next to him and remove my helmet. He takes it and puts it on the floor and, ever so gently, gives me the biggest of hugs. He's crying for me.

It's for this reason that, moments later, when I'm interviewed by Matt Rendall for ITV, I can't help but be emotional. None of my team would have asked me the same questions Matt does. It's his job to spell out to the viewer what's going on, to ask me what's going through my head. Koldo, Bingen, Luca, Ryder, all of them, they know what I'm going through, and none of us want to talk about it.

Nathan finishes his time trial soon after me. I've agreed to wait for him. When he gets here we hug and then I suggest a drink. We find the nearest café and order a bottle of Cava and spend the next hour talking about the world and all its weirdness. We're half cut when we leave to ride back to the start, to where the team bus is parked. It's a fun ride back to the hotel. We're happy. I'm not sad any more. I managed to puncture again about two kilometres from the bus. Which seemed perfect.

This evening the team has organised a small farewell dinner for me. It's strange facing the realisation that I'll never again be one of them. It still feels like my team, the one I'd helped to build back in 2007. I've put my heart and being into it for years. That evening I received neither a message nor a call from Jonathan Vaughters. Nor have I since.

Among the speeches at the meal Nathan chose to read a poem. It was a good choice: although not cold and dead, I was now gone. The team would carry on without me.

'O Captain! My Captain!'
Walt Whitman

O Captain! my Captain! our fearful trip is done,
The ship has weather'd every rack, the prize we sought is won,
The port is near, the bells I hear, the people all exulting,
While follow eyes the steady keel, the vessel grim and daring;

> But O heart! heart! heart!
> O the bleeding drops of red,

> Where on the deck my Captain lies,
> Fallen cold and dead.

O Captain! my Captain! rise up and hear the bells;
Rise up – for you the flag is flung – for you the bugle trills,
For you bouquets and ribbon'd wreaths – for you the shores a-crowding,
For you they call, the swaying mass, their eager faces turning;
> Here Captain! dear father!
> This arm beneath your head!
> It is some dream that on the deck,
> You've fallen cold and dead.

My Captain does not answer, his lips are pale and still,
My father does not feel my arm, he has no pulse nor will,
The ship is anchor'd safe and sound, its voyage closed and done,
From fearful trip the victor ship comes in with object won;
> Exult O shores, and ring O bells!
> But I with mournful tread,
> Walk the deck my Captain lies,
> Fallen cold and dead.

Epilogue

The Worlds

As Team GB we'd been through a lot. I'd had the honour to captain the team in our two greatest-ever performances: the Copenhagen World Championships, where Mark Cavendish had won, and the London Olympics Road Race, where we didn't win but rode with a commitment rarely seen by any team in any sport.

It's not easy coming out of a Grand Tour at the best of times – not only are we physically exhausted but also psychologically wasted. It almost feels like mild depression, which I think it probably is. Added to that, my hand and rib meant that I couldn't even pick up the boys or play with them when I got home to Girona, which put me in an even deeper hole. But after discussions between my doctor in Girona and the GB team we decided I'd be good enough to race. That was the only thing that mattered now.

The bottom line was that I was the most experienced bike racer that Great Britain had, and Dave and Rod wanted me in Ponferrada, more than anything to be the role model – to take the mantle of leader off the bike as much as on it, something I had assumed over the years. It was official: my last pro race would be in a Great Britain jersey at the World Championships.

Asking me to captain the GB team in my final race was the ultimate gesture of reconciliation from Dave Brailsford. More than that, it felt like I was coming home, finishing where I'd begun with the people who cared the most about me. The greatest thing about it for me was the fact that Dave was doing something based more on emotion than rationality. Dave, Rod, Shane (Sutton) – even the riders who had backed the decision for me to race – were all taking a punt on me. I had a broken hand, after all. It was the opposite of how my professional team had acted when it came to the Tour de France. They had probably read *The Chimp Paradox* and believed they were doing what Dave Brailsford and Steve Peters would do – that is, make a decision based on facts and policies, purely rational in its construction. The irony was, the people who had created that way of thinking were showing that it didn't always apply: sometimes a decision could be made using both emotion and logic.

Any disdain I'd felt towards the professional cycling world was eradicated by Team GB's gesture. They didn't adhere to the age-old, cynical, 'there are no gifts' belief system. It was not as if they were treating me as a charity case: they knew I was an asset to the team, they'd seen how I was able to do my job as road captain in the final week of the Vuelta when properly buckled. I could only be better than that with time to recover before the Worlds.

The Worlds is one of my favourite races. It has an energy about it like no other. Outside of the Olympics or the Commonwealth Games it's the only time in the year we get to race for our country, which means different riders, different staff, different team kit. It all feels new, which is something of a tonic by September, after a season of racing, travelling through airports and constant hotel hopping. We're exhausted; we just want it to be over – and so, for many of us, the Worlds will be our final race of the year, which gives it a last-day-of-school buzz. The fact we're reunited with old friends and have been chosen to represent our home nation makes it all the more meaningful.

The pro Worlds have held a special place in my heart since the very first time I raced them in Spain in 1997. The national team felt small and amateur back then – it had limited resources, most of the staff were part-timers, some were volunteers, and we barely had enough kit to go round. I'd spent all year in France with my French pro team, learning the hard, unforgiving ropes of professional cycling. It wasn't a pleasant environment back then – looking back, I'd go as far as to say it was a criminal world: black money galore, drugs, illegal doctors, dealers, trafficking; cheating was part of the culture. Spending a few days with the British team was wonderful, by contrast. For starters, I could speak English instead of French (not that I didn't like French, but at that time it remained a foreign language and culture to me). Being with the British felt homely and, more importantly, I felt safe. Pro cycling didn't feel safe to me. I didn't care that the GB team was a small, insignificant set-up back then; it was preferable to the big, harsh, professional teams, where everything and everybody seemed expendable.

It only took a few years for me to feel more at home in the pro scene than the GB team, though. By 2001 I bore little resemblance to the innocent twenty-year-old pro who turned up to the 1997 Worlds. Then, in 2002, Dave Brailsford took over the national team and created a new version of cycling. The national team began to operate on a higher level than almost any professional team, and without any of the criminality the pro scene had embedded within it. He managed to keep all the ethics and team spirit associated with the older, smaller GB team, yet added a level of excellence it had never known.

This new version of cycling gave me belief in the sport again, something I'd lost with my conversion to hardened, cynical pro. Dave Brailsford and the GB team began the process of fixing me long before anyone or anything else. Dave may have been ignorant of the doping problem, but that didn't make him stupid. In less than a decade he proved himself to be not only one of the smartest people in cycling, but in any sport.

Although held in a different country every year, the Worlds always follows the same format. The race is the same distance as a Monument, anywhere from 250 to 275 kilometres, and it's always held on a circuit of approximately fifteen kilometres. That's a lot of laps. Some years the circuit is on rolling roads, others hilly, and occasionally it's flat. This way all types of rider will, at some point in their career, find a Worlds that suits them. It's one of the few one-day races where specialisation is not of such importance; all types of racer battle it out for the win.

The circuit in Ponferrada, north-west Spain, was, as usual, not particularly challenging. But this didn't mean the race wasn't.

I knew some teams would want to make it difficult in order to thin the peloton down – and, sure enough, they did, which is when myself and Geraint Thomas were distanced (he, like me, had injured his hand a few weeks before, in a training crash). Like every Worlds, the speed increased with each and every lap in the second half of the race, whittling down the peloton in the process. As is usually the way, everybody awaited the final lap. This has become a monotonous annual display, and although the spectators may not particularly like this patience game it is, in fact, the surest way to stand any chance of success. Almost without exception those who move earlier than the last lap will fail. The whole race has become a competition in economy and efficiency, much like Milan–San Remo – he who does this best stands the most chance of being able to make the difference on the last lap, when it matters.

I wasn't able to offer much in the race – the only thing I brought to the team was the ability to predict other teams' tactics and the general organisation and motivation of our team on the road. With absolute precision I called exactly which lap the Italians would launch an offensive, the guys paid heed to this and were at the front ready when it happened. I would have loved to have been able to race in the final and help Ben Swift, Pete Kennaugh and Luke Rowe, who all rode superbly, but I wasn't able.

Luke Rowe, whom I'd first met at the Worlds in Australia in 2010, had grown into a natural road captain himself. It was clear he would be taking over my role in the future, so much so that he stuck by me and paid attention to everything I said and did, sponging as much as he could, knowing it would be the last time. We even went together and bought pizzas and beers for the team after the race. Thinking about it, that was perhaps the pivotal moment: without him knowing it I handed over my captaincy to him there and then. Over the pizzas and beers in the hotel foyer, while Froomie was next door buying kebabs and a bottle of vodka, Dave B gave me a present: three race numbers, 9, 64, and 11 – 9 was for the number of Worlds time trials I'd done for GB; 64 was my final race number from that day (and also happens to be the postcode for Biarritz, where Dave and I had lived some of the darkest hours of my life); and 11 was for the number of Worlds Road Races I'd raced for GB. They were signed by the team, and Dave had written a personal note on them. Those three *dossards* will be framed to become one of the few pieces of cycling memorabilia I'll have on display at home. They mean more than any jersey.

We then had a four-hour bus ride to Madrid, where we were staying the night before flying out, going our separate ways. We got hammered. It was over. Just as with Christian Vande Velde almost exactly a year earlier, this was the end.

Luke Rowe
@LukeRowe1990

The #vengabus is in full flow on route to Madrid. Worlds done, season over. Where's good for a rave in Madrid?

Retweeted by @millarmind

Only it wasn't quite the end. I still had one more race to do.

Circle Completed

We shall not cease from exploration.
And the end of all our exploring will be to arrive
Where we started and know the place for the first time.

'Little Gidding', T. S. Eliot

Towards the end of the first part of my career, before I was banned, I had my own personal *soigneur*. I made sure it was in my contract (I also had two *domestiques*, a mechanic and a *directeur sportif*). I did it because that was what hitters did. In the latter part of my career I didn't need or want any of those things. I trusted all the staff and never wanted to be shown preferential treatment. More importantly, I didn't want to act like an egomaniac; I wanted to lead by example, and that meant not acting like a spoilt brat. I never asked for anybody in particular: the head *soigneur* and head mechanic would allocate who worked on my legs or my bike. My mechanic became Alex Banyay, my *soigneurs* either John Murray or Garry Beckett.

There were reasons for this: Alex was the mechanic Geoff Brown trusted the most, and he knew that we'd get on well, on and off the bike. And John and Garry are English – I think that's the only reason they were allocated to me in the first place. John's a physiotherapist; football had been his life's work, cycling had been his life's passion. A few years ago he decided to make the leap to cycling – at the time a move more than likely considered mad by those who knew him, but which can since be looked upon as prescient.

Garry – I call him Gazza – has been my primary *soigneur* the last few years. I know he'd do anything for me if I asked, but I never ask. He's a Londoner; he fucking hates the place, as only a true Londoner can. To say he's had an interesting life would be doing it an injustice. Much like Ryder, he's a grinder. He's been a trainee Jaguar engineer, a coffee blender, a dentist's assistant, a

282

barman, a mechanic, a signwriter, a Harrod's technical engineer, a panel beater and sprayer, a Forex broker, a mini-cab driver, a builder, a life assurance and pensions sales executive . . . and that's just to name a few of his jobs over the years.

At the Vuelta this year Gazza was in charge of rubbing my legs (technical term for massage). I knew a lot about Gazza – it's difficult not to, he loves telling a life story, and most of the time I love listening to them. Although there were times when I was so tired I just switched off, letting his voice become a relaxing background noise, while also hoping beyond hope that the story wouldn't become so animated that he'd have to stop the 'rub' and engage his hands into the body language required to *really* tell the story.

One of the few things that's been a constant in Gazza's life is the Bec CC, his cycling club in London. His parents had been founding members, but the club moniker had nothing to do with the family name, Beckett, and everything to do with south London's Tooting Bec.

It was Gazza's mum and dad who, while out on a tandem bike ride, discovered the road that is used to this day for their annual end-of-season time trial. 'The Bec' has become a stalwart of that particularly quirky British racing scene, the Hill Climb time trial, always held in October. They're short, explosive efforts, where aerodynamics come a lowly second to weight, and specialists will go as far as removing their bar tape – which seems a little excessive but is part of the tradition; bikes are stripped down to their bare minimum. After all, the effort is only a handful of minutes long.

Gazza has been organising the Bec Hill Climb for twenty-eight years, a role he assumed from his father. He's done it out of duty, he's lost money, hair (he has no hair), and God knows how much time, making sure that every year it takes place. It's a labour of love in the truest sense. He'd always talked to me about it; I'd even been the guest of honour at the Bec CC annual prize-giving a couple of years before, so I knew the club and what they were about.

They're a classic British cycling club, of which there are many. Some go back over a hundred years; sadly, most of them have been in decline over the past fifty. It's been these clubs that have kept the spirit of cycling alive in the UK through thick and thin, and many of their value systems and eccentric behaviours date back to Victorian or Edwardian times.

The recent cycling boom in the UK makes everything seem fresh and modern, and because of that it's easy to look upon these traditional clubs as old-fashioned stick-in-the-muds, out of date and behind the times. Everybody's using technology to monitor their bike rides these days – how far/fast/high did I go? What's my ranking? Did I hit my target TSS? They judge their bike ride by looking at a screen, they go riding with virtual partners, they get kudos from people they've never met and probably never will. There's nothing wrong with all that, just as there's nothing wrong with meeting at seven o'clock on a Tuesday evening to do a time trial, then going to a village hall for tea and cake to chat and mingle when it's done, meet for a chain-gang ride another evening, do a weekend reliability trial, or organise a crazy little hill climb – or even have the annual prize-giving lunch. The difference between the old and new is that with the old you're doing it with real people; the social network is a handshake away rather than a screen and a keyboard.

I have a lot of time for this peculiarly British scene. I owe much of my life in cycling to my local cycling club, High Wycombe CC – it was with them that it all started for me. I was a clueless kid from Hong Kong; all I knew was the Tour de France through videos or magazines and books. I'd never done a time trial until they told me to come along to one of theirs. I had no idea what I was doing, but I never felt daunted or insecure – they made me feel welcome; I was immediately taken under their wing.

For this reason, when Gazza asked me if I'd do the Bec as my final race – I was on the massage table at the time, during the first week of the Vuelta – I agreed. Everything was still going swimmingly at that point; I had no idea that somewhere, hundreds of kilometres away, a bollard was quietly awaiting my arrival.

The week following the Worlds I felt like an old man. I didn't touch my bike once, and I went and got my hand looked at again and found out it needed to be operated on, I'd done so much damage to it. I delayed the operation until after the Bec, but any ideas I'd had of finishing on a mini-high were gone.

Everybody knew it would be the last time I'd ever race. For this reason, and unlike my other 'final' races, this was the only time I had the people close to me come and watch: my family and friends were all planning to be there. Better than that, being a club event meant that Nicole and members of the VCRC could even take part.

There was something so perfect about it being a club event. There were no barriers or buses, no helicopters or motor-bikes, zero professional teams and barely any media. It felt like I'd turned back the clock. I was back where I'd started all those years ago.

An hour before my start I went and got changed, pinning on a race number for the very last time, going through the process I'd performed 1,087 times for professional races. I wasn't in the slightest bit emotional about it. It was hard to be when I was so relieved by the knowledge I'd never have to do it again. When I was kitted up I went and watched some of the riders finishing. It didn't look like much fun – it only lasted a little over two minutes for the fastest, but because of that it was sick-inducingly intense. Short, sharp and steep, designed to hurt. I repeated what I'd kept telling myself all year: 'One last time.'

I gave my goodbyes, got my good lucks and headed off to warm up. It wasn't my greatest warm-up – it was hard, what with it being on public roads that I'd never ridden on before. I couldn't even remember the last time I'd done a warm-up on an actual road instead of a static trainer.

I got to the start a few minutes before my time. I felt like shit, my hand hurt and my legs felt like lead. I cheerfully said 'Hi' to the guys around me then started to take my leg warmers off. As I was pulling the first one off I heard a familiar voice: 'David, how are you?'

I looked up. The man who'd spoken was taking his jacket off to reveal an old High Wycombe CC jersey. I looked at him for a moment. 'Scott? What are you doing here?' It was Scott Paterson who, twenty-two years earlier, had held me up on the start line in a lay-by near Thame for my very first time trial. Back then, just before he started that first of many count-downs I'd go on to hear, he'd told me, 'Now, David, remember: pace yourself, and don't think about anybody else. It's just you against the clock.' I remember nervously nodding, unable to speak.

I couldn't believe Scott was here now. I'd seen him only a couple of times in the previous decade. He came over and shook my hand. 'When I read you were doing this I thought I had to come.' He smiled, 'You know, I was there for the first, I wanted to be here for the last.'

I couldn't help but smile. I forgot about everything hurting, about feeling old. If I hadn't known before I knew then that I'd made the right choice for my last race. Scott introduced me to his son, who was about the same age as me: 'David, this is James.' I shook his hand and saw he had a camera ready. 'James, could you get a photo of us please?'

We chatted briefly. I told the people nearby about Scott having held me up for my first-ever time trial. My start time rapidly approached. I shook Scott's hand and said, 'Thank you.' He patted me on the back, and as I rolled away I heard him say, 'One last time, David.'

Acknowledgements

I'd like to thank a few people from my publishers Yellow Jersey Press. In particular my editor Matt Phillips helped shape my ideas at the very beginning, when I had no words, and then at the very end, when I had too many words. His was a voice of enthusiasm and cutting excellence. Matt, I thank you for being such a wonderful not-so-invisible-hand.

He wasn't alone at Yellow Jersey Press, there was also the designer James Jones, who has always shown patience with my uneducated yet picky eye. His sister is Bethan Jones, who also works for YJP. Rarely in all my career have I met somebody as professional and visionary as Bethan when it comes to the machinations of publicity. Phil Brown, whose unseen work in producing this book will remain, well, unseen. Thank you for never making me feel stupid when it came to my more outlandish ideas. Finally there's Richard Collins, the copy-editor – you made this into a proper book, thank you.

Nadav Kander – probably the only true artist I've known in my life – thank you for giving me the confidence to do things differently. I can't mention Nadav without mentioning Kadir Guirey, my dear friend who introduced us, you are a Prince among men.

I'd like to thank the VCRC Style Council, Richard Pearce, Kadir (again), Max Broby, and the magical Douglas Brooks. The four of them were nothing but an inspiration to me in my final year as a professional cyclist. They opened my eyes to a world beyond racing bikes and gave me the confidence to attempt to enter it. Nicolò Ildos of Fi'zi:k, who provided the reason to create the Style Council with our madcap plan to design a pair of shoes for every race of my final season while at dinner together after the 2014 Worlds in Florence, where this book begins.

Then there's Graham Watson – who will always call me 'Junior' – thank you for giving us your photos for free. It's been a trip, old boy. You've seen me do shit I can't even remember. Thank you for being there to capture what I'd have otherwise forgotten. Francois Marie of FMB tyres – you are the last great artisan. If heaven exists and bikes are ridden there, for sure they'll all be equipped with FMBs.

Ryder Hesjedal – who'd have thought we'd become the greatest of friends? Yet we have, and that alone is reason enough to love bike racing, because without it we'd never have even met.

Stephen Frears, Tracey Seaward, Alan Macdonald, and everybody else I met working on *The Program*. You made my world seem totally sane and normal in comparison to yours. Thank you for that reality check. It was such a wonderful experience, which helped me break free from what I was convinced was my totally insane and extraordinary environment.

David Luxton, aka Der Kaiser, my literary agent, without whom I would have never even thought it possible I could write a book, let alone two. You have never doubted me, which has been terribly important as I have spent most of my time doubting myself. Ian Preece, my first and hopefully last editor, you know my voice better than anybody and you let me swear. You're a fucking legend, albeit a quiet one. I love you for it, Priest.

My parents, both my mum and dad, helped me believe I could write this when I genuinely thought I couldn't, thank you, both of you, for never having let me think something was impossible. My sister, France, who has been there to pick me up everytime I've fallen down, I love you very much. Finally, my wife, Nicole. You watched me retire from racing, thankful to have me home, only to see me disappear back into it once again, this time inside my head, all on my own. It's done now. Thank you for putting up with it all.

List of Illustrations